Pio Gama Pinto, Kenya

1927 - 1965

Edited by

Shiraz Durrani

Nairobi

Published in 2018.
Vita Books
P.O. Box 62501-00200
Nairobi. Kenya
http://vitabooks.co.uk
info.vitabkske@gmail.com; info@vitabooks.co.uk

Distributed Worldwide by:
African Books Collective
P.O. Box 721
Oxford, OX1 9EN
orders@africanbookscollective.com
www.africanbookscollective.com

ISBN 978-9966-1890-0-4 (Paper)
ISBN 978-9966-1890-4-2 (eBook)

Design and layout by
Vincent Uba
Cell: +254724 592 309
www.vumacoolgraphics.com

Printed in Kenya 2018
By CLC Christian Booklink Kenya LTD
P.O Box 26665-00100 Nairobi

Message from Emma Gama Pinto

Dear friends and readers of this tribute book about Pio

I am grateful to you for keeping Pio's work and ideals alive. It is hard to believe that it has been 53 years since Pio's assassination in 1965. I am now 90, my own memory is failing and my girls, who were so young at the time, have little recollection of their father.

When Pio proposed marriage to me, he informed me that his calling was the freedom and dignity of the Kenyan people. So, it is fitting that Kenya and Kenyans keep his memory, what he worked for and what he gave his life for, ever present.

People have used words like "communist" and "socialist" to describe Pio. I feel at his core he was a humanist. It truly grieved him to see people suffer. He understood that every person's dignity deserved respect. He also believed that ignorance was just as much an insult to human dignity as poverty. Many of you know the story of how he walked out of Manda barefoot, because he had given his shoes to another detainee; how he taught other detainees to read using my letters. It is also true that I never knew how much money he earned, because he gave much of it away to support the widows of the freedom fighters.

Pio truly lived his values of equality and brotherhood. It is unfortunate that his example was not allowed to light the way for a few more years. Who knows what more he might have achieved for Kenya and its people!

I will conclude with the lines that are etched on Pio's gravestone:

"If I have been extinguished, yet there rise

A thousand beacons from the spark I bore."

Thank you, friend and readers, for helping to spread the spark.

Emma Gama-Pinto

September 2018

Contents

List of Illustrations

1. *Pio Gama Pinto Road, Nairobi*

Photo by Nicholas Mwangi (02-07-2018)

Dedication

PIO GAMA PINTO

BORN 31-3-1927

ASSASSINATED 24-2-1965

SOCIALIST and FREEDOM FIGHTER

POLITICAL DETAINEE 1954-1959

MEMBER OF PARLIAMENT 1963 -1965

"If He Has Been Extinguished Yet There Arise A Thousand Beacons From The Spark He Bore."

This book is dedicated to Pio Gama Pinto and all those who lost their lives in the battles against colonialism and imperialism.

Acknowledgements

The publisher would like to acknowledge the contribution of many institutions and individuals. They include the following:

- *Awaaz* Magazine for photos and material from the Magazine.
- Churchill Archives Centre, Churchill College. Cambridge for research support and permission to reproduce material from Fenner Brockway papers.
- Donovan, Alan for permission to reproduce material on Pio Gama Pinto
- Emma Gama-Pinto for photos and material on her husband Pio Pinto, and for her courageous support of Pio during his selfless struggle for the Kenyan people; Pio and Emma's three children, Linda Gama-Pinto, Malusha Marie Charles, and Tereshka Gama-Pinto for their insights on their father.
- Joseph Murumbi Archives for providing material on Pio Gama Pinto.
- Kenya National Archives for material on Pinto
- Malcolm MacDonald Archives, Durham University Library for permission to reproduce material on Pinto.
- Njogu, Kimani for proofreading the book
- Noronha, Frederick for permission to reproduce interview with Emma Gama Pinto.
- PALIAct Ukombozi Library, Nairobi for research support.
- Panafr Press for material for their proposed book on Pinto for the Panaf Great Lives Series.
- Patel, Zarina for permission to reproduce material from her book, Unquiet, the Life & Times of Makhan Singh. 2006. Nairobi: Zand Graphics.
- Pereira, Benegal for support and providing access to video recordings of conversation with Emma Gama Pinto.
- Pinto, Audrey Da Gama for her father's article "Pio, My Brother", photos and insight on events and facts.
- SOAS Library, Archives & Special Collections for research support.
- The Murumbi Archives for permission to reproduce material on Pinto.
- The Murumbi Trust for permission to reproduce material on Pinto.
- The National Archives of the United Kingdom for research support.
- The Standard Media Group, Nairobi for permission to reproduce material.
- Waweru, Kimani for research support.
- Zed Books for supplying material from Panaf Press.

Without their support, this book would not have been written. We are immensely thankful.

Preface - No Easy Journey to Publishing Pinto

2. Vita Books announces book on Pinto (1987)

Material on or by Pio Gama Pinto is difficult to acquire, for reasons explained in this book. This book was first announced in 1987 but work on it had been started in early 1980s. It finally comes out in 2018 but with many changes from the original plans. The unfavourable political situation in Kenya after independence has ensured delays and cancellations of any work on Pinto. This is not the first attempt to publish a book on Pinto. There have been a number of earlier attempts to publish his biography.

One such attempt was in 1972 when Panaf Books in London planned to commission a book on Pinto in the Panaf Great Lives series which had earlier published biographies of Frantz Fanon, Patrice Lumumba, Nelson Mandela, Kwame Nkrumah, Sekou Toure, among others. This indicates the status of Pinto as one of the great revolutionary leaders of Africa - regarded with great respect by revolutionaries around the world yet ignored by his

Pio Gama Pinto, Kenya's Unsung Martyr

own country. While June Milne of Panaf Books collected some material as early as 1972 from a number of Pinto's contemporaries and from Emma Gama Pinto, the book remained unwritten for various reasons. A number of key potential authors were not able to write because of pressure of work or other reasons. The material collected by June Milne was passed on to Zed Books who had previously published *InDependent Kenya*. Zed Books passed on this material to Vita Books in 1987 for its proposed book on Pinto. Vita Books is grateful to June Milne and to Zed Books for this material which has been used in this book. Some letters between June Milne and Emma Gama Pinto, J. D. Kali and Joseph Murumbi are reproduced in the following pages as they are of historical importance. This correspondence, with other material, was included in the file that June Milne passed on to Zed Press which then gave it to Vita Books. June Milne explains the scope of the proposed Panaf book to Joseph Murumbi in a letter dated 09-06-1972 (Panaf files):

> I intend to reprint the pamphlet which was published soon after the death of Pio Pinto, but want, if possible, to add more about the man himself and his role in the African Revolution. I would like to be able to include the text of some of his more important speeches and letters.

Emma Gama Pinto in her letter to June Milne (21-07-1972) poses a huge challenge to those seeking to "tell the truth about Africa" (Panaf files):

> So few people have the generosity of looking at the African Revolution from an African point of view that quite often the "inside Africa" opinions are not always as the indigenous people see it. I hope and pray that your Publishing House does not 'lift' newspaper articles to tell the truth about Africa, but rather from locals themselves - and not necessarily by any means from those at the helm now. The work was done by unsung heroes who still toil in the background and often trampled by limelight seekers.

June Milne responds to the challenge in an admirable way in her reply to Emma Gama Pinto dated 04-07-1972 (Panaf Books files):

We are still at the stage of collecting material for the book in our Panaf Great Lives Series in which Pinto is to appear as having made a very significant contribution to the African Revolution. There will be no author doing the section on Pio Pinto. We intend to reprint in full the pamphlet *Independent Kenya's First Martyr*, and to add the tribute you have written, and also material I am awaiting from Mr. Murumbi.

No author names are appearing on any of the titles in the Series. This is partly to protect the authors, all of whom are actively engaged in the revolutionary struggle, and partly because we do not want in any way to distract the reader from the subject matters of the books. There is too much author-emphasis in books published by bourgeois publishing houses. The Panaf Books imprint is now well known and has an established reputation among progressive circles throughout the world and is sufficient guarantee of authenticity.

Here is a challenge to Vita Books, and indeed to all African publishers. As far as meeting the criteria mentioned by Emma Gama Pinto and June Milne, it has not been possible for this book to meet them all. Milne's search for "more about the man himself and his role in the African Revolution" has been met only partially. Material on and by Pinto is still not easily available. Even in 1972, Joseph Murumbi was not able to dig out the material that Milne had asked him for. Nor were we able to track his response, if any, to specific questions sent to him by June Milne. The letter, dated June 9, 1972 seeks specific information on Pinto from Murumbi which if supplied would have enabled us to get a clearer picture of Pinto and the struggles he was involved in. Specifically, Milne asked for the following information:

...I intend to reprint the pamphlet which was published soon after the death of Pio Pinto, but want if possible to add more about the man himself and his role in the African Revolution. I would like to be able to add text of some of his more important speeches and letters...If you would be able to find time to write, however briefly, in answer to the following questions it would be most helpful:

1. How do you assess Pinto's contribution to the African Revolution?

Pio Gama Pinto, Kenya's Unsung Martyr

2. What do you consider his outstanding qualities as a man, and as a great patriot and revolutionary?
3. Are there any particular experiences in the course of his political struggles which you remember as being of special significance? Can you remember any of his actual words?

If you can give a brief description of his character and personality, and his qualities as a friend of long standing, it would help to make him live, for the reader. Any photographs you are able to supply would be very welcome.

The Panaf files do not contain any response to this letter, nor has it been possible to trace a response from the Murumbi Archives. Had Panaf been able to publish this book on Pinto, it would have become a treasured item on Pinto. It is significant that as Milne was seeking material on Pinto, a new title on Patrice Lumumba in the Panaf Great Lives was scheduled to be published in September 1972, as June Milne mentioned in her above letter to Joseph Murumbi. Pinto would have joined this august assembly of Great Lives series, but it was not to be.

As for information on Pinto's role in the African Revolution, it is very likely that material exists in various national and personal archives in the world. While the Editor and Vita Books did not command resources to look for and include such material in this book, the way is very much open for others in the future to do so.

There have been a number of other attempts to publish Pinto's biography. Pinto's brother, Rosario Da Gama Pinto, was "in the process of revising the booklet on my late brother, Pio, which I hope I shall be able to publish next year to commemorate his 10th death anniversary" as he wrote to June Milne on November 28, 1974. As far as we know, this was not published.

The approach taken in this book is to provide information on Pinto from different sources: some from Pinto's writing, some original material, others taken from published and archival material. The key document on Pinto remains the book initiated and published by Ambu Patel - *Pio Gama Pinto,*

Independent Kenya's First Martyr: Socialist and Freedom Fighter. It is included in this book as is an excellent history of Kenya written by Pinto in 1963. It was not possible to include Pheroze Nowrojee excellent booklet published in 2007: *Pio Gama Pinto: Patriot for Socialist Justice.* (Nairobi: Sasa Sema) but remains an important resource for the general reader as well as for scholars. Other archives that need to be explored are papers of Oginga Odinga, Achieng Oneko, and Fitz de Souza.

Yet another attempt to write Pinto's biography is mentioned by Zarina Patel (2006). Ambu Patel, who set up the New Kenya Publisher and was also active supporter of Kenya's war of independence also planned to write one. He collected photos and material on Mau Mau fighters with a view to publishing a book on them. Patel, Z (2006) mentions that "in early 1966, Ambu Patel was in the process of publishing a booklet on Gama Pinto… Ambu Patel died in December 1977 and the book was never published." It is not clear whether the booklet Zarina Patel (2006) mentions is the one he did edit and publish, *Pio Gama Pinto, Independent Kenya's First Martyr: Socialist and Freedom Fighter* which was published in 1966 by Pan African Press established by Pinto. Ambu Patel was the editor of the booklet, as his letter to Joseph Murumbi (reproduced in this book) indicates, although his editorship is not mentioned in the booklet. It is highly likely, however, that Ambu Patel was planning to write a larger book on Pinto, as he had collected a large amount of material on Mau Mau activists, on Kimathi, Pinto and other leaders. According to Nazmi Durrani, Nazmi (communications with the Editor in early 1980s), Ambu Patel faced threats from the Kenyatta government as part of its attacks on all progressive leaders associated with Mau Mau or who had material on Mau Mau. However, he managed to rescue his archives from the government agents and took it all to India for safekeeping. Unfortunately, it has not been not possible to recover the material and it is believed to have been destroyed or lost. As with Pinto's material, yet another resource has been lost in the face of the hostility of the Kenyatta government.

There have also been a number of academicians who had also planned to write Pinto's biography and some of them had managed to collect much material on him. Yet none has been published as far as is known.

This book does not aim or claim to be a comprehensive record on Pio Gama Pinto. It is only a beginning of a long journey necessary to record the history of Kenya from an anti-imperialist perspective. It introduces readers to voices of many people who have written about Pinto to build up as clear a picture of Pinto as possible. In that spirit, it seeks to make history available to those whose story it is - people of Kenya, Africa and progressive people around the world.

Shiraz Durrani
June 20, 2018

3. *Panaf Great Lives planned Pinto's biography (1972)*

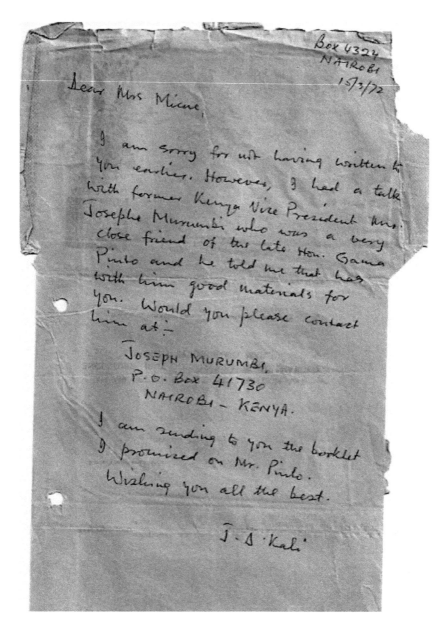

Box 4324
NAIROBI
15/3/72

Dear Mrs Milne,

I am sorry for not having written to you earlier. However, I had a talk with former Kenya Vice President Mr. Joseph Murumbi who was a very close friend of the late Hon. Gama Pinto and he told me that has with him good materials for you. Would you please contact him at:-

JOSEPH MURUMBI,
P.O. Box 41730
NAIROBI - KENYA.

I am sending to you the booklet I promised on Mr. Pinto.
Wishing you all the best.

J. D. Kali

4. *J. D. Kali to June Milne of Panaf Books (15-03-1972)*

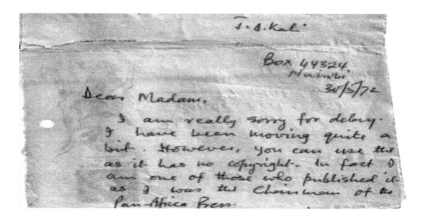

5. J.D.Kali to June June Milne on copyright to Pinto's anniversary publication (30-05-1972)

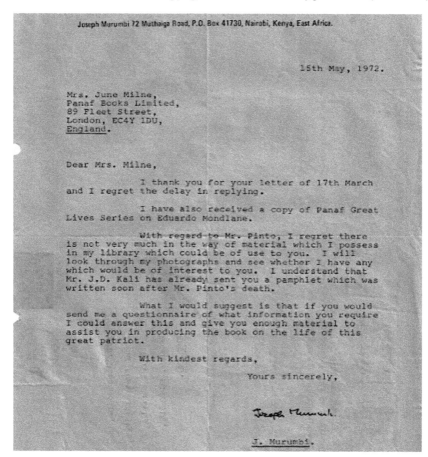

Joseph Murumbi 72 Muthaiga Road, P.O. Box 41730, Nairobi, Kenya, East Africa.

15th May, 1972.

Mrs. June Milne,
Panaf Books Limited,
89 Fleet Street,
London, EC4Y 1DU,
England.

Dear Mrs. Milne,

I thank you for your letter of 17th March and I regret the delay in replying.

I have also received a copy of Panaf Great Lives Series on Eduardo Mondlane.

With regard to Mr. Pinto, I regret there is not very much in the way of material which I possess in my library which could be of use to you. I will look through my photographs and see whether I have any which would be of interest to you. I understand that Mr. J.D. Kali has already sent you a pamphlet which was written soon after Mr. Pinto's death.

What I would suggest is that if you would send me a questionnaire of what information you require I could answer this and give you enough material to assist you in producing the book on the life of this great patriot.

With kindest regards,

Yours sincerely,

J. Murumbi.

6. Joseph Murumbi to June Milne (15-05-1972)

Pio Gama Pinto, Kenya's Unsung Martyr

ZED BOOKS

57 Caledonian Road · London N1 9BU · Tel: 01-837 4014/0384

1 December 1987

Shiraz Durrani
 and Wanjiru Kihoro
Vita Books
PO Box 168
Wembley
Middx. HAO 4BQ

Dear Shiraz and Wanjiru

Enclosed is some valuable material - photographic and textural
about Pio Pinto. It has been made available to me by June Milne,
who used to run Panaf Books, which she has recently asked us to
take responsibility for. At one stage, she was thinking of getting
a short biography of Pio Pinto written, and that is why she had
this correspondence and collected this material. I mentioned to
her that you were considering doing the same thing through Vita
Books and we agreed that it wuld be sensible for you to have this
material. Obviously, I hope that you will take the greatest care
of it, and that it will be useful to you for the biography.

I really am unclear about the THUNDER FROM THE MOUNTAIN situation.
I think it is necessary for you to give me a ring, and for us to
set up a meeting with my colleague, Paul Westlake, so that the
whole thing can be sorted out finally.

My warm regards.

Yours sincerely,

Robert Molteno
Editor

PS letter done before we met on Netuble!

ZED BOOKS LIMITED Reg. No. 1760273   VAT No. 382 9976 73

7. *Zed Books to Vita Books re Panaf book on Pinto (01-12-1987)*

Pio Gama Pinto, Kenya's Unsung Martyr

INTRODUCTION

Pheroze Nowrojee[1]: A Threefold Cord to Independence

A Threefold Cord to Independence: Senior Chief Koinange, H.E. Apa Pant and Pio Gama Pinto

As an introduction to this book I deal with two of the major influences on Pio Gama Pinto: the first was Senior Chief Koinange; the second was the Indian Independence Movement. Pinto, of course, had other major ideological convictions and drew on other influences too. This introduction however is restricted to the above two aspects. The following highlights how these influences came together to change Kenya's political path from an indefinite status as colony onto the irreversible road to independence - Pheroze Nowrojee.

Senior Chief Koinange[2]

Senior Chief Koinange is one of Kenya's most important heroes. *This is the Koinange of Koinange Street in Nairobi.* It is not his son, Mbiyu Koinange. Most of us would now think that the street is named after the latter, a Minister in the first Cabinet in 1963. It is because we do not know enough about Senior Chief (SC) Koinange. He is one of our great Kenyans. He is a hero for whom we need a separate day too. And a hero whose achievements we must ensure are known widely. He is a critical figure in our history and in the Independence struggle.

1　Pheroze Nowrojee is a Senior Counsel, prize-winning human rights lawyer, poet, columnist and writer. He is the author of *Pio Gama Pinto: Patriot for Social Justice* (Nairobi, Longhorn Sasa Sema Books, 2007), *A Kenyan Journey* (Nairobi, Transafrica, 2014), and *Dukawalla and Other Stories* (Nairobi, Manqa Books, 2017).

2　*Marshall S.* Clough Koinange was Mbiyu: Mediator and Patriot in *B.E.Kipkorir* (Ed.) Imperialism & Collaboration in Colonial Kenya (Nairobi, Kenya Literature Bureau, 1980) 57; *Jeff Koinange* (Senior Chief's Grandson) *Koinange-wa-Mbiyu Mau Mau's Misunderstood Leader* (Lewes, The Book Guild, 2000); *Pheroze Nowrojee* The Paradox That Was Senior Chief Koinange *The STAR* 13 January 2010, 14.

Senior Chief Koinange was born around 1870. About 1905, the British Colonial Government appointed him a Headman for Kiambu District[3]. In 1938 he was promoted to Senior Chief. He retained this title till his death in 1960. He was a far-sighted leader. He perceived that certain issues were central throughout the colonial occupation and were key to ending it. Therefore, his focus was t on these issues throughout: land deprivation, education, economic opportunity for all and, firmly, the rejection of colonial rule. He kept these continuously in the forefront of Kenyan politics. His clear-sightedness, his consistency, his understanding of reality in politics, his patience, his judgment of when to move and when to retreat, were the marks of true leadership. They remain the model our politicians have to follow.

He baffled the British. At all times, publicly and in closed council chambers with the British administration, he raised the injustice of land deprivation. In 1931 he went as part of the government delegation with other chiefs to Britain. Canon Harry Leakey went with him as interpreter, as Chief Koinange maintained that he did not speak English. Neither this, nor his position as a serving chief, inhibited him when he gave evidence before the Parliamentary Joint Committee on Closer Union of the East African Territories in the British Parliament. This was a thinly disguised push towards White Settler self-rule in Kenya, and East African federation with the Rhodesias and South Africa. "He spoke out strongly for the restoration of the alienated lands, for greater investment in African education, and for the inclusion of Africans in the Legislative Council. Koinange also attacked the Hut Tax, the Registration Ordinance and the expropriation of land in the Reserves." [4]

Education was a major pursuit of SC Koinange. He saw in education not only that the British had brought something of value to Kenya, but also that it was this very education that would be the tool for the removal of the British. He campaigned for a government high school in Kiambu District. When the Government reneged on its promise to set it up, Koinange

---

3   *Carl Rosberg & John Nottingham* The Myth of Mau Mau (New York, Meridian/New American Library, 1966), 84.

4   Jeff Koinange Koinange-wa-Mbyui Mau Mau's Misunderstood Leader (Lewes, The Book Guild, 2000) 53.

became a key figure in setting up of the Kikuyu Independent Schools. These schools enrolled students from all over the country. In 1926, he sent his eldest son Mbiyu overseas for studies. Mbiyu studied at Hampton University, a historically Black college and at Lincoln University in the United States, and then at London University and Cambridge University in the UK.[5] When Mbiyu returned in 1938 after 12 years abroad, the Senior Chief led again by the setting up of the Kenya Teachers Training College at Githunguri, with Mbiyu, and later Jomo Kenyatta, as its Principal. Kenyatta also became a son-in-law of the Senior Chief, when he married the latter's daughter Grace Mitundu. Again, we can see in the field of education, the constancy in Koinange's goals and political leadership.

In the agriculture arena, the colonial government had passed laws making it illegal for African farmers to grow coffee. Koinange saw this as blocking economic advancement for the majority of the people. In challenge to this law, Koinange planted coffee on 500 acres of his land. Criminal charges were brought against him, resulting in a conviction. In appeal, the High Court held the Governor's prohibition invalid and upheld Koinange's right to farm coffee.[6] Koinange's lawyer in the case was Chanan Singh (1900-1977), another freedom fighter, later an MP and Assistant Minister (1963-1964) to the Prime Minister Jomo Kenyatta, and then a High Court Judge (1964-1977).

Demands for freedom were being ignored and suppressed by the British, and it was apparent to Koinange that they had little intention of leaving. The British too saw that Koinange was a major political leader *against* British rule in Kenya even while he was serving them as a Senior Chief. Even though he handled his duties as a colonial chief with great ability, he was paradoxically leading his people out of colonial rule. The British decided to remove him. But by 1941, he had held office for so long and his influence and popularity with the people was so high that the British thought it more politic only to strip him of his duties in Kiambu District but to leave him still holding the post of Senior Chief.

---

5   *Mbiyu Koinange* The People of Kenya Speak For Themselves (Detroit, Kenya Publication Fund, 1955).

6   *Koinange v Rex* (1951) 24 Kenya Law Reports (2) KLR 130.

After the War ended in 1945, the further land settlement schemes only for white soldiers and no political gains in African representation but with the blocking of trade unions, only confirmed the decision of the Senior Chief to take tangible steps towards a challenge to British rule in Kenya; a conclusion he had already come to earlier. In furtherance of this aim, Koinange kept a close eye on the political developments in the country. An example of this was the events of May 1950. Makhan Singh, the founder, with Fred Kubai, of the trade union movement in Kenya, was summoned to the High Court at Nyeri to face detention proceedings. Chanan Singh was also Makhan Singh's advocate. Chanan Singh recalled:

> On arrival at the Law Courts at Nyeri, I found a large crowd of people waiting outside. Among them was the old Senior Chief Koinange [then 80]. He told me he thought the Government was accusing Makhan Singh of making public statements to the effect that the City Council of Nairobi was contemplating taking African land just outside the boundaries of the City. If so, he was prepared to give evidence in support of Makhan Singh. We thanked the old Chief for taking the trouble to travel so far, but told him his assistance would not be needed because the issue before the Court was not whether the City Council had in the past taken over African land – an issue on which he could speak from personal knowledge – but whether the Council intended to take more land now. [7]

The Senior Chief had considered Makhan Singh and his work important enough to have openly shown his support by travelling from Kiambaa to Nyeri, and saying all this personally, both to Chanan Singh and, effectively, to the large crowd.

The Chief was of course more than probably aware of all the issues, but he had nevertheless come in person to Nyeri, and made clear that he was prepared to give evidence on behalf of Makhan Singh. The Senior Chief's presence alone, was making a statement to his own people: that he approved of Makhan Singh, of the latter's trade union and political work which was

---

7   *Chanan Singh* Makhan Singh Cases, (1976) cited in *Zarina Patel* Unquiet: The Life and Times of Makhan Singh (Nairobi, Zand Graphics, 2006) at page 258. See also Endnote 5, Chapter Six, page 504.

bringing freedom closer, and of Makhan Singh's speeches, among which was the clear statement to the colonial government and to all East Africans: *"The only solution is the complete independence of the East African Territories."*

In the years after 1945, Koinange began to organize an army of resistance. Money and arms were collected. Oaths were administered. This was done at his homestead at Kiambaa and at other places. Mau Mau's army came into being. The attacks on colonial targets in 1950 and 1951 resulted eventually in the declaration of the State of Emergency on 20th October 1952 by the British, and the open war for independence.

In 1953, Koinange was arrested and sent into detention at Marsabit. In August 1959, he was moved to Kabarnet under restriction orders. But by then the Senior Chief was dying. He was then released to return to Kiambaa. He died soon after, in December 1960.

If we are to retrieve a national direction we must know its historical architects and know its design. In a changing Kenya, and over many decades, Senior Chief Koinange kept a focus, clarity and consistency. These are particularly relevant today to meaningful change and its management. There is no absence of ideology in our history. There is only its suppression and attempted erasure.

He is one of our history's paradoxical figures – a British-appointed Senior Chief who was the architect of our armed struggle against the same British. At every stage, the British were puzzled by this strategic thinker. He contained their power in ways they did not anticipate. Patient and many-sided, they could not fault his work as a chief. But also, they could not fault the logic, or his facts, in his opposition to them on selected issues, particularly land and education. Their rhetoric and pretenses of racial superiority never wore him down. He saw through them and their oppression, and he never allowed his mind to give up that ability, that power, over them.

At the age of 80 in 1950, in bringing Mau Mau into operation, he was determined to endanger himself and his family to free Kenya. At 84, in

1953 he and most of his family members, were put into detention by the British. It was because his presence as a free man empowered others to be free. He was flown to Marsabit. He spent six years there till August 1959 when he was moved to Kabarnet. There he found Pio Gama Pinto also serving out his detention.[8]

The two old friends were together again; forthey had been working together very closely in the years immediately before the Emergency. Pio persuaded the authorities to allow him, in Kabarnet, to visit the Senior Chief, because persons in restriction could not otherwise meet or speak to each other. He immediately began to do all he could for Koinange and the members of his family who were accompanying him. There is a poignant photo of Pio Gama Pinto with the infirm and very aged Senior Chief and the latter's family members at Kabarnet.[9] Together Koinange and Gama Pinto had achieved much.

But it was clear that the Senior Chief, now 90, was dying. So the British, unwilling to have the death of a martyr while in their custody, released him from detention in Kabarnet and returned him under escort to his home at Kiambaa in Kiambu County, where he died soon after in December 1960. "His funeral was attended by perhaps the biggest crowds ever assembled in Kenya for such an occasion."[10] His mausoleum is at the Koinange Homestead at Kiambaa, Kiambu County.

This was Pinto's master in our freedom struggle.

---

8   Both Pinto and Senior Chief Koinange were first detained under Detention Orders and then put under Restriction Orders. Pinto's detention was from June 1954 to February 1958 at Takwa Special Detention Camp on Manda Island, Lamu. From there he was placed under restriction at Kabarnet, from February 1958 to December 1959. Senior Chief Koinange's detention was from 1953 to August 1959 at Marsabit. From there he was placed under restriction at Kabarnet, from August 1959 to December 1959. Here I have used the terms 'detention' and 'detained' to refer to both the forms of imprisonment – detention and restriction.

9   *Ambu Patel (Ed.)* Pio Gama Pinto: Independent Kenya's First Political Martyr (Nairobi, 1966) 7.

10   *Carl Rosberg & John Nottingham* The Myth of Mau Mau (New York, Meridian/New American Library, 1966), 84.

Indian Independence Movement

The second influence on Pinto was the Indian Independence movement. It is important to understand that the Indian Independence Movement was not a phenomenon that was restricted to that country. India was the largest colonized unit anywhere in the world, with the largest colonized population, and its struggle was against the most powerful empire then in existence. Therefore, its struggle became the example and aspiration to all the colonies worldwide, especially in Asia and Africa. Its example was everywhere: Ireland, in the Caribbean, the Black people in the United States (Marcus Garvey, before the Civil Rights surge of the 1950s and 1960s), Ghana, (India was the first overseas country visited by Kwame Nkrumah in 1957), Indonesia, (the Dutch East Indies). Its example was also of the organization of a freedom struggle. The Indian National Congress had been formed in 1885 and was in existence for decades by the time Pinto was in India from 1938-1949. It was a veteran of many modes of challenge to British rule in India, including *satyagraha,* mass mobilization within India and a British lobby in Britain for freedom for India.

India's struggle was in effect the struggle for the decolonization of the whole world. It led in the dismantling of colonial empire. The leaders of India's struggle were therefore global leaders in total decolonization. It was freedom of both land, and mind, for the latter too, like the captured colonized land, were captured colonized minds.

Pinto spent the years from 1938 to 1949 in India studying and, briefly, working. He was present in India in the final decade to 1947 (when India won Independence), and saw the systematic and determined dismantling of colonialism in India, by its leaders, Mahatma Gandhi, Nehru, Vallabhai Patel and others. Gandhi and Nehru were the principal architects of the dismantling of colonialism globally. Pio was clear that just as it had been established that the British had no right to rule in India, so too they had no right to rule in Kenya. Pio was determined that what had been done in India had to be done in Kenya. By 1949, when Pinto returned to Kenya, the land of his birth, Gandhi had died, assassinated in January of that year, and Nehru was the Prime Minister of India.

The preceding year, 1948, was critical for Kenya. Because it was the year in which Nehru established the Indian embassy, the Indian High Commission[11] in Nairobi, and appointed the first Indian High Commissioner here. His name was Apa Pant. An Oxford trained lawyer, son of the Chief Minister of a Princely State, from a family total in its following of Gandhi and freedom. He had been specially selected by Nehru for this post and for his task. His stated task was to move Kenya to freedom and do all that he and India could do to that end.

By 1950, Pinto and Apa Pant were working closely together. It was in the greatest secrecy and caution. For Pant's office and residence, though protected by diplomatic immunity, were nevertheless raided by Special Branch more than once, in vain searches for incriminating documents, arms, or wanted persons. British protests over years against Pant and against the suspected activity were ignored by Nehru.

But finally, Pinto was arrested and detained in June 1954. Among the Grounds for his Detention Order were "1) that he had knowledge of illegal arms traffic; that he had assisted Mau Mau in drafting documents and arranged for the printing of membership cards of the 'African Liberation Army'; and 3) that he had given assistance to the non –militant wing of the Mau Mau in planning its subversive campaign."[12]

The Indian High Commission was the only diplomatic embassy then in Kenya which was in support of Kenyan freedom. There were only two countries that provided those arms: India and Ethiopia (through Emperor Haile Selassie). An academic and Warden of Northcote Hall at Makerere University in the 1950s, and then civil servant, S.J. Coleman wrote later:

---

11   At that time, it was termed the Indian Commission, and the ambassador was the Indian Commissioner, as Kenya was still a colony and not independent.

12   *Pio Gama Pinto* Glimpses of Kenya's Nationalist Struggle (1963; Reprint, Nairobi, Asian African Heritage Trust, 2014), 24.

Mau Mau had proved themselves most ingenious at building homemade guns, and adept at smuggling weapons in from Ethiopia.[13]

On the declaration of the Stae of Emergency in October 1952 and the arrests of Jomo Kenyatta, Bildad Kaggia, Paul Ngei, Kung'u Karumba, Ochieng Oneko and Fred Kubai, Nehru sent another carefully chosen person, with the same aims. It was the Dewan Chaman Lal, lawyer, diplomat, trade union leader, ambassador and Member of Parliament. He was sent to represent Kenyatta in the trial at Kapenguria, which he did with D.N. Pritt and A.R. Kapila and others. The British continued complaining against Pant, till finally in 1954, Pant was recalled, by which time the Mau Mau war had been launched and was at its highest pitch.

In the same year, 1954, Pinto was arrested on 19th June 1954, served with Detention Orders and sent off to Takwa Special Detention Camp on Manda Island, Lamu. He was to remain there till February 1958. He was then moved to Kabranet and in the final months was together with Senior Chief Koinange.

A Threefold Cord

But before Senior Chief Koinange was detained, before Pant was recalled, before Pinto was arrested, there was an event of significance to us. There was a ceremony. Pant was brought out of Nairobi to Kiambaa, late at night in great secrecy. With Senior Chief Koinange presiding, and in the presence of twelve other Elders, with full traditional ceremony, Pant was made an Elder of the Kikuyu community.[14] The person who brought him there from Nairobi, and who took him back, in secrecy and safety, was Pio Gama Pinto.[15] "And [as] a threefold cord is not quickly broken,"[16] their work together, though thereafter defeated militarily in the field, won in the end, by the bringing about of irreversible political change and Independence.

---

13   *S. J. Colman* East Africa in the Fifties: A View of Late Imperial Life (London, Radcliffe Press, 1998) 118.

14   *Apa Pant* Undiplomatic Incidents (Hyderabad, Sangam Books,1987), 26-28.

15   Ibid. See also *Sana Aiyar* Indians in Kenya: The Politics of Diaspora (Cambridge, Harvard University Press, 2015) 184.

16   Ecclesiastes 4:12.

The Unsung Martyr

Shiraz Durrani: Pio Gama Pinto Lived and Died for Revolutionary Change

Contents

List of Illustrations

Pinto, the Hand Behind the Curtain

Pio Gama Pinto was born in Nairobi on March 31, 1927. When he was eight, his father sent him to India for his education. He spent the next nine years there. He studied Arts for 2 years before joining the Indian Air Force in 1944 as a clerk for a short time. He then took a job with the Post and Telegraphs Company in Bombay. Here he got early experience in working-class struggles. He enthusiastically took part in a general strike and got his first glimpse of mass action and organisation. He was a founder member of the Goa National Congress whose aim was to liberate Goa from colonial rule. This experience was to prove invaluable in later life in Kenya where he was active in almost every aspect of the liberation struggle: radical trade union movement, setting up progressive political and learning institutes, publishing and popularising socialist policies and politics. When it became obvious that an organised, armed struggle was needed for liberation, Pinto became active in Mau: supplying arms, cash, medical and other support to activists and their families while helping to strengthen resistance organisations. He was active on many fronts - ideological, political, organisational and social - and was becoming popular for advocating the return of stolen land, fighting for justice and equality and for the aims of Kenya's war of independence - land and freedom. Pinto was assassinated February 24, 1965. [17]

Nowrojee (2014) provides a succinct overview of his political contribution to the Kenyan struggle:

> Working as a journalist, trade unionist and political worker, by 1952 he was the Editor of the Daily Chronicle, the Deputy Secretary-General of the Kenya Indian Congress, and a founder member of the Kenya African Study Union, a think-tank for the Kenya African Union (K.A.U.). Pio worked with K.A.U., and also very closely with the Mau Mau Central Committee, particularly with Bildad Kaggia and Senior Chief Koinange.

Pio Gama Pinto's life, his actions, the principles he stood for and the reasons for his assassination can all be understood in his political stand which he

---

17   Further background material on Pio Gama Pinto has been provided in a number of articles included in this book. This article therefore avoids duplication of facts on his life.

explained at the time of Kenya's independence (Pinto, 1963c:39) in the following words:

> Kenya's Uhuru must not be transformed into freedom to exploit, or freedom to be hungry, and live in ignorance. Uhuru must be Uhuru for the masses — Uhuru from exploitation, from ignorance, disease and poverty. The sacrifices of the hundreds of thousands of Kenya's freedom fighters must be honoured by the effective implementation of KANU's policy —a democratic, African, socialist state in which the people have the rights, in the words of the KANU election manifesto, "to be free from economic exploitation and social inequality".

Pinto worked tirelessly all his life to make that dream a reality. While his stand, as shown above, was popular with the working people of Kenya, those who had engineered an independent Kenya which was not "free from economic exploitation and social inequality" were not happy with his stand, or the fact that he proclaimed it loudly and, more importantly, that he was ready to act to turn that dream into reality. It was they who were ultimately responsible for his assassination. The colonial governments in Goa and in Kenya had earlier sought to silence him before independence. But they had done so by detaining him; the engineers of the neo-colonial Kenya feared him even more than the colonial authorities did, and they had him assassinated.

In life, as in death, Pinto exposed the class nature of the Kenyan society. He exposed colonialism, imperialism and capitalism as the evils that the working people of Kenya needed to defeat. When it was time to write political and legal cases for people's rights, Pinto was there. When it was time to form strong political parties, Pinto was there. When it was time to develop working class and anti-imperialist ideologies, Pinto was there. When it was time to face the enemy with guns, Pinto was there. When it was time to support victims of colonial and neo-colonialism terrorism, Pinto was there. When it was time to take a political stand after independence, Pinto was there. When people in other countries - in Africa and elsewhere - needed support to fight colonial and capitalist exploitation and oppression,

Pinto was there. When it was time to make personal and family sacrifices for a greater cause, Pinto was there. And when the end came, when it was time to stand for his principles and to die for his country, Pinto was there.

It is rare to find all these qualities in one person. But to fully understand him, it is necessary to understand the historical context in which Pinto lived and died. All his actions are linked to the history of colonialism, imperialism, capitalism and resistance to them in Kenya, Africa and India as well as elsewhere. In order to understand Pinto, it is necessary to understand the struggles of the people of Kenya against colonialism and imperialism. Pinto symbolises that resistance in a way few others do.

Kenya Resists; Repression Intensifies

Initial drafts of this article were published in the University of Nairobi student paper, Sauti Ya Kamukunji and in the University of Nairobi Library Magazine. It was when a revised version was published in the national daily, The Standard, in September 1984 that the article and the author came to the notice of the Kenya Government and its notorious Special Branch. Subsequent events led to the author's exile to Britain. The article was part of a study of publishing in Kenya which was later published as Never Be Silent, Publishing and Imperialism in Kenya, 1984-1963 (Vita Books, 2006).

People of Kenya resisted Portuguese and then British colonialism for over 500 years. Their resistance was to the system of exploitation and oppression that were part of capitalism brought to Kenya by colonialism and by imperialism after independence. Their resistance against the system did not end with independence, whatever form this system took in a different historical periods. Resistance continued after independence, but this time against the successors of the homeguards - the comprador regime put in power by the departing colonialists and sustained by neo-colonialism.

In essence, the struggle has been a two-line struggle, or "Two Paths Ahead" as Barnett (1972: 5) put it: either for capitalism with a rich elite growing

Pio Gama Pinto, Kenya's Unsung Martyr

richer while the majority of people were being pushed into ever increasing poverty; or for socialism with justice and equality for all. Imperialism disguised this main contradiction by promoting racial and "tribal" aspects as the key social contradictions in order to prevent further development of class struggle. Pinto challenged this and championed the interests of working class and for socialism.

PIO GAMA PINTO: SOME FACTS ABOUT THE LIFE OF
A GREAT LEADER AND A PATRIOTIC JOURNALIST *

by

Shiraz Durrani

24th February, 1985 will mark the twentieth anniversary of the murder of the great patriotic leader of Kenya, Pio Gama Pinto at the hands of the enemies of Kenyan people. The conspiracy of silence surrounding the achievements of our patriotic leaders of the Mau Mau War of national liberation has also kept our new generation ignorant about the achievements of Pio Gama Pinto. This is a challenge to our institutes of higher learning, especially the University, not only to undertake research on our past leaders and their achievements, but also to disseminate the results to the Kenyan people.

The following tribute to Pio Gama Pinto is an extract from a survey on the history of publishing in Kenya. We shall mainly look at his contribution in the publishing field. It should, however, be realized that mass media have played a very important role in our struggle against imperialism and were used as an organizing and uniting book by the patriotic forces fighting for liberation. Pio Gama Pinto was at the centre of the publishing activities of the freedom fighters. This publishing role did not limit his contribution to the struggle for land and freedom in Kenya. He stood foremost as an activist who clearly saw the danger posed to the young Kenyan nation from imperialism and their local allies. He devoted his whole life to the fight for a true independence for Kenya, in all spheres, economic, political and cultural. No sacrifice was too great for achieving this aim. He suffered economic hardships, detentions, and finally gave his life. His example can only fill our youth with a greater sense of dedication to the service to the people./ Pio Gama Pinto was a prominent person in publishing activities of their period (1948-65). As he was deeply involved in every aspect of the struggle for independence, Pinto was in a better position to serve national interests through his publishing activities. Oginga Odinga comments on Pinto thus:

"Pio Pinto was assassinated outside his house early in the morning of 24 February 1965. Pio Gama Pinto was a great Kenyan patriot. He leaves a gap in our political struggle for full freedom that few men - none that I know - can fill... There is no phase of our struggle in which he did not play an invaluable part. When the repression was launched against KAU, Pinto organized political defences. When fighting started from the forests Pinto maintained political liaison and supplied

* A shorter version of this paper was published in Sauti Ya Kamukunji Vol. 1 No. 8 (June, 1984)

1. Durrani: Pinto, Some Facts. Univ. of Nairobi Library Magazine (1984) .

In all the struggles in Kenya, the elephant in the room is capitalism itself. Imperialism sought to hide its very existence and to prevent discussion about the benefits and disadvantages of capitalism as compared to socialism. It removed both the terms - capitalism and socialism - from public discourse and from general consciousness. It also de-politicised people's struggles and all aspects of life, particularly in the trade union movement, which, by law, was now restricted only to industrial issues and forbidden to enter the political arena where the real solutions to workers' problems lay. It was in this arena that Makhan Singh, J. D. Kali, Bildad Kaggia, Pio Gama Pinto, and others waged incessant war with the colonial and comprador state power.

Pinto was active in resistance against colonialism as well as to neo-colonialism in the post-independence struggle. He was targeted during the former stage by the colonial Portuguese Goan and British Kenyan administrations, with the latter detaining and restricting him for four and a half years. After independence, he faced similar opposition from the ruling elites which ultimately resorted to assassination to silence him.

There is ample evidence that socialism, justice and equality were the aims of the Mau Mau liberation movement. Such were also the aims of the trade union movement as well. Pio Gama Pinto was active in both these fields and was active in promoting policies and actions supporting these aims. It was socialism that imperialism attacked by attacking those organisations and leaders that promoted socialist ideas and actions. Pinto was one of the many activists assassinated by imperialist powers. The bullets that killed Pinto may have been fired or organised by the former homeguards, now the new power-brokers, but their foreign backers were the real instigators of his assassination.

Imperialism does not allow any challenge to its hegemonic rule and viciously attacks those it sees as its enemies. The *Red Star* (2013) throws further light on such imperialist attacks on progressive forces in Kenya before and after independence:

- Although KLFA (Kenya Land and Freedom Army), known famously as the Mau Mau and KAU (Kenya African Union) did not have communist leadership, individual communists such as Pio Pinto Gama (sic) and Makhan Singh played a key role in organising urban workers.
- Kenyan communist Pio Pinto Gama (sic) was gunned down in 1965, apparently on Kenyatta's orders. Months later, Kenyatta attacked communism. The Lumumba Institute set up with the help of socialist countries to train KANU [Kenya African National Union] cadres, was shut down.
- In the early 1960s, just before independence, John Keen, a Masai independence leader, planned to form the Communist Party of Kenya with Odinga and Pio Pinto Gama. The party was never formed.

- The December 12th Movement and the March 2nd Movement grew out of the student protests and merged to become the Union of Patriots for the Liberation of Kenya, known in Swahili as *Muungano wa Wazalendo wa Kukomboa Kenya*, or Mwakenya for short. This organisation pledged itself to rid Kenya of imperialism and neo-colonialism and was based on Marxism Leninism. Although Mwakenya tended to be based on university circles and, because of repression, to have a small membership, it at times enjoyed wide popularity because of dissatisfaction with the increasingly corrupt dictatorship of Kenyatta's successor Daniel arap Moi (a former collaborator with British colonial rule).

The assassination of Pinto thus needs to be seen in its overall national and international context. Part of the imperialist strategy in Africa as a whole (and indeed around the world) was to eliminate any organisation, any leaders, and any political movements that challenge imperialism. Shivji (1988?) elaborates on this imperialist strategy in Africa and beyond:

> Many African leaders, from radical nationalists to moderate ones, found themselves being overthrown in coups engineered

or supported by the US and its erstwhile spy agency, the CIA. Patrice Lumumba was murdered in cold blood with the assistance of the CIA (Blum 1986, 174) so was Nkrumah overthrown in a CIA plot (ibid, 223). Between January 1956 and end of 1985 there were sixty successful coups in Africa, that is, an average of two every year (Hutchful 1991, 183). In 1966 alone, there were eight military *coup d'état* and by 1986 out of some 50 African states, only 18 were under civilian rule (Nyong'o 1998, 78).

Relentlessly and shamelessly, in total defiance of basic rights and in particular the right to self-determination, moderate leaders who attempted to exercise some self-determination were branded as "communists" and overthrown or assassinated. At the same time, dictators like Mobutu in the Congo, Pinochet in Chile, Marcos in the Philippines, Sukarno in Indonesia, the Shah in Iran were either created or supported by the US. The so-called cold war was cold only in Europe. It was a hot war in the Third World for which the peoples of the Third World paid in millions of lives, shattered countries and economies all in the interest of imperial hegemony. In Vietnam, one American Senator admitted, US dropped toxic chemical amounting to six pounds per head of population, including women and children (Pilger 1998, 581), destroying half the forests and leaving behind deformed children.

With the assistance of the US, the apartheid South Africa carried out its destabilisation in neighbouring countries, destroying the Angolan and Mozambican revolutions. A study by the UN Economic Commission for Africa estimated that 'South Africa's military aggression and destabilisation of its neighbours cost the region $10 billion in 1988 and over $60 billion and 1.5 million lives in the first nine years of this decade. [i.e. 1980s] (Chomsky 1991, 239). The land mines, which were planted in Angola during the civil war in which South Africa and US supported UNITA, are killing men women and children to this day. While it needs US$3 to produce a land mine, it takes over US$300 to clear it, the kind of money that Angola does not have and the corporations would not clear the mines unless they are paid!

Atrocities, force, violence and terror are inherent in the imperial system. It has been documented and documented again yet the ideological hegemony that paints imperial powers as do-gooders, humanitarian Samaritans and the defenders of human freedom and liberty are so propagandised that they seem to be accepted as non-challengeable 'eternal truths'. But people determined to … [think for themselves] have challenged them.

The particular manifestation of such imperialist attacks on progressive forces in Kenya has not been thoroughly investigated. Gregory (2016), for example, makes an important link between the assassinations of Malcolm X and Pinto, pointing to the role that Pinto played in raising Pan African consciousness in Malcolm X. He also suggests a possible link between the assassinations of Malcolm X on February 21, 1965 and that of Pinto just a few days later, on February 24, 1965 and the role that "the [USA] government" may have played in both these assassinations:

Malcolm was killed because of another brother called Pinto who was born in Nairobi. He was the one that changed Malcolm's head from Black nationalist to Pan Africanism and made the connection from here to there. And the [USA] government said we can't let that happen. He's [Pinto] the one that persuaded Malcolm when he went to Africa and stayed seven weeks and met all the real leaders. And he's the one that discussed with Malcolm bringing racism to the doorstep of the [USA]. And as Malcolm was shot dead in New York City, Pinto was being gunned down in Nairobi. Same time.

Fernandes (2016a) also refers to the links between Malcolm X and Pinto:

They [Malcolm X and Pinto] planned a common strategy to deal with the daily humiliation and indignities suffered by both, Africans and African-Caribbeans.

As the following item records, Malcolm X and Pinto had planned to charge US with "human rights violations" at the UN - reason enough to eliminate both in order to scupper the international publicity and humiliation.

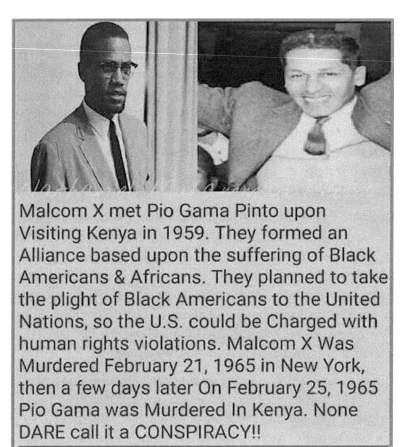

Malcom X met Pio Gama Pinto upon Visiting Kenya in 1959. They formed an Alliance based upon the suffering of Black Americans & Africans. They planned to take the plight of Black Americans to the United Nations, so the U.S. could be Charged with human rights violations. Malcom X Was Murdered February 21, 1965 in New York, then a few days later On February 25, 1965 Pio Gama was Murdered In Kenya. None DARE call it a CONSPIRACY!!

2. Malcolm X and Pinto form an alliance

There is a pattern about assassinations carried out by imperialism in that no links between the assassins and their real masters can be found. True, a number of scapegoats are made to serve sentences but the political motives of the instigators behind the assassinations are hidden. Evidence is hidden or destroyed. The assassinations of Malcolm X and Pinto fall into this pattern. This again requires more research, but the ruling classes in Kenya, USA and Britain prevent any meaningful official investigations. They also deprive funds to others seeking clarification; and if this fails to stop investigations,

Pio Gama Pinto, Kenya's Unsung Martyr

they use further threats and assassinations to suppress the truth. Pinto's assassination was one among other "mysterious" deaths: Tom Mboya in 1969, J. M. Kariuki in 1975, Titus Adungosi in 1988, Robert Ouko, Bishop Alexander Muge, Father John Kaiser in 1990. Okoth (2013) lists other deaths in "this tradition":

> Following on this tradition, more recent high-profile murders have not been resolved to date. They include that of University of Nairobi don Crispin Odhiambo Mbai, former MPs Mugabe Were (Embakasi) and David Kimutai (Ainamoi) in 2003. Others are of Virginia Nyakio, wife of former Mungiki leader Maina Njenga in 2008, human rights activist Oscar King'ara in 2009 and the controversial Muslim Cleric Sheikh Samir Khan in 2012.

Such murders have intensified in recent years, especially during elections. The murder of Chris Musando in July 2017 is among the latest.[18] Seen in this context of deaths in mysterious circumstances, Pinto's assassination acquires a new significance. It should be noted that all such deaths are those of people who have criticised government policies. Umoja (1989) documented some of these. It was such brutality - and the military and political backing of the Western powers - that enabled the very survival of the Kenyatta and Moi regimes in Kenya, which then carried out massacres and assassinations as calculated methods to maintain themselves and their class in power.

The national - Kenyan - context that is the background of the assassination of Pinto also needs to be understood. Kenya, under Mau Mau, challenged the very basis of British colonial Empire. Mau Mau fought for "land and freedom" and their organisation, militancy and armed struggle (explored further in Durrani. 2018) posed a serious threat to the very foundations of the British Empire. Imperialism saw the threat that Mau Mau, with their radical, alternative vision of an equal society, posed if they ever came to power. But colonialism was well prepared for this threat. It had, over decades, cultivated a loyal (to colonialism), petty bourgeois home-guard force that was quickly installed into power at independence while Mau Mau was reorganising for change. Any person, any organisation or political

---

18   See: *Star* (Nairobi): IEBC ICT manager Chris Musando found dead. 31-07-2017.

force, any idea that stood in the way of this transition to neo-colonialism was eliminated, some even before the actual independence. Others, like Pinto, were eliminated later, thus completing the imperialism's triumph over Mau Mau and its ideology. The dirty work of imperialism was undertaken by their local regimes of Kenyatta and Moi, who of course, got their "crumbs" in the form of political power with which to acquire thousands of acres of the best land. In addition, corruption on an industrial scale makes them, their families and succeeding generations, among the richest in the world.

Kenyan elite rulers after independence show a distinct preference for force to resolve social and political contradictions. It was this legacy that ultimately took Pinto's life. Thus it is worth looking at their bloody record to understand the increasing state violence against people. Umoja (1989:1) examines the record of the Moi government (1978-2002):

> His [Moi's] ten-year rule has been characterised by mass arrests, torture of victims, jailing on trumped-up charges, detentions without trial, disappearances and deaths whilst in police custody, and wanton massacres. In our estimate, Dictator Moi has been responsible for over 6,000 deaths in the ten-year period!

Besides naming many of those killed by the Moi regime, Umoja (1989:54) lists some massacres it carried out:

1980: Garissa: approx. 400 killed.
1982 (August): Nairobi, whole country: 2,000 killed.
1984 (February): Wajir: 1,000+ killed.
1984 (October): West Pokot: 800-1,000 killed.

But Moi's massacres were not isolated cases of brutal violence against working people of Kenya. He was following the *nyayos* (footsteps) of his mentor, Jomo Kenyatta, as documented by the Truth, Justice and Reconciliation Commission of Kenya (2013) . *Independent Kenya* (1982: 29, 30) exposes the role of the Kenyatta regime (1963-78) in suppressing any opposition to its dictatorship:

By the 1970s, few voices were raised against the ruling clique. Militant nationalism, confined largely to the back-benches of Parliament in newly "independent" Kenya, did not survive the decade in any organised sense. By 1965, back-bench critics of the government had been labelled Communist subversives. Their most forceful leader Pio Pinto was murdered in February 1965... During the decade following the banning [in 1969] of KPU (Kenya People's Union), the government moved steadily down the path to nascent fascism, using terror tactics to isolate and then eliminate dissidents.

This brief look at the national and international context of the period provides a context in which to examine Pinto'a life, work and assassination.

The Struggles Against Portuguese Colonialism in Goa

Pinto was a Goan-Indian Kenyan. This gave him diverse social, cultural and political experiences from Kenya and India. He used the experiences from one country to enrich his activities in the other. Racism affected Pinto as much as any ethnic minority member in Kenya and he was often a victim of this divisive factor encouraged by colonialism and exploited by the emerging elites. Yet he managed to rise above its disruptive influences. In fact, his background gave him a progressive internationalist approach. He supported and actively participated in the struggle of the people of Goa to overthrow Portuguese colonialism. Pinto felt in total sympathy with the struggles waged by people of Angola, Mozambique, and Guinea-Bissau against Portuguese colonialism. He often participated in the activities of the liberation movements in these countries. After Kenya's independence, Pinto was at one time seriously considering joining ranks with Frelimo in Mozambique in its battles against Portuguese colonialism, as De Souza (1966:32) observes:

Pio worked very closely with F.R.E.L.I.M.O. and the Committee of Nine of the O.A.U. and often visited Dar es Salaam to assist them. A few weeks before he was assassinated he told me that his ambition was to resign his seat in Parliament and retire to Lindi or Mtwara on the Mozambique border to assist the freedom fighters actively. His friends would not let him go - they argued that he was needed here. He never lived to help the struggle in Mozambique. But he died with his boots on.

While Pinto was in India, the Goan people's struggle was advancing rapidly. He began to play an important part in it. He was a founder member of the Goa National Congress whose aim was to liberate Goa from Portuguese colonialism. It often became necessary for Pinto to enter Goa in the course of his activities. As there was no legal entry for him into Goa, the freedom fighters organised secret safe entry for him. His activities against the Portuguese soon got him in trouble with the Portuguese authorities who issued a warrant for his arrest. However, as Murumbi (2015:213) says, there was close collaboration between the Portuguese and British colonial authorities and Pinto was the victim of both:

> It was here (Bombay), I think, that Pio got his first taste of politics. And owing to his activities against Portuguese rule in Goa, he found his position rather hot. As the Portuguese and British Governments were always in league, no doubt there were recommendations by the Portuguese to the British Government, or the Indian Government under Britain, to get Pio out of India or arrest him. Sensing that danger lay ahead, he returned to Kenya.

It was with the assistance of the freedom fighters that Pinto managed to leave Goa safely. In all, Pinto was active for the liberation of Goa for about five years. He had started agitating against the Portuguese colonialism at the young age of 17. He decided to leave Goa and chose to return to Kenya as he felt he had a contribution to make in the struggle in his homeland. He was much needed by those still active in the struggle in Goa and they were reluctant to let him go. But Pinto felt the need to be active in the struggle in Kenya.

Even when he was in Kenya, Pinto never lost touch with events in Goa and continued to support the struggle for its liberation. De Souza (1966:29-30) recalls his talks with Pinto on his early days in Goa:

Pio Gama Pinto, Kenya's Unsung Martyr

One day during our discussions Pio suggested that we should do something in East Africa to assist in the liberation of Goa. I was a little surprised and told him that while I was very sympathetic to the liberation of Goa, and indeed of the rest of the world, I thought that as we were East African we should confine our activities to East Africa. We might dissipate our slender resources and there was also the risk of being misunderstood, even by our friends. He explained that as a student and young man in India he had taken an active part in the struggle for the liberation of Goa. He had actively assisted in the formation of the Goa National Congress and had escaped from Goa only when police were searching for him with a warrant to arrest and deport him to an island off West Africa. It was our duty, he suggested, as socialists to assist all liberation fronts. Even if we did not consider ourselves Goans we had names such as De Souza, Pinto, etc. Portuguese colonialism was as bad as any other.

Pinto's early experiences in India had given him valuable political lessons which remained with him for the rest of his life. In addition, he made many friends during this period and he was to maintain strong links with them as well. Pinto's early life is summed up by *Drum* (1965:159):

> From his earliest years he was a rebel. Born in 1927, and educated in Southern India, he studied journalism there and spent 18 months in the Indian Air Force. It is said that he helped organise the Indian naval mutiny in 1946, and he is known to have been a founder member of the Goan National Congress which was founded in India to fight Portuguese imperialism.

Pinto's links with India and Goa are summed up by Romesh Chandra (1966:33) writing in the New Age:

> Pio was a bridge between India and Africa. Pio by his every act, demonstrated the oneness of the anti-imperialist battle, the solidarity of Asia and Africa, of India and Africa.

Pinto remained steadfast in his anti-imperialist stand throughout his life. On his return to Kenya, he started another phase of his life-long struggle for a world liberated from imperialism.

Return to Kenya: The Radical-Moderate Struggle

3 S. Durrani: Pinto, Conspiracy of Silence. Awaaz (2005)

By the time Pinto returned to Kenya from India in 1949, the anti-colonial fight had intensified, with land and economic rights at the top of the agenda. At the same time, clear lines were emerging between those who had favoured a peaceful approach of petitioning the colonial authorities for their rights and those who saw the ineffectiveness of such an approach and who advocated a more militant approach. In effect, these were divisions between the progressive, radical approach favoured by Mau Mau and the conservative approach of moderates which was later championed by Kenyatta and the homeguard elements nurtured by colonialism.

The radical approach was given direction by the progressive trade union movement where Makhan Singh, Fred Kubai and Bildad Kaggia had already laid the organisational groundwork and established links between workers and peasants with radical politics. They created a vision, an organisation and a strategy for achieving the political, economic and social demands of working people. Their approach proved to be successful as organised, well-led strikes had helped workers meet many of their demands. An example of this was the 62 day strike in 1936 organised by Makhan Singh which saw a successful outcome in the recognition of worker rights and better wages.

The militant strand in Kenya did not emerge overnight from a vacuum but had a long history with positive results. When the radical movement shifted from a peaceful approach of petitioning the colonial authorities to other means of struggle, their numbers swelled as the people supported this approach. This was to lead to the Mau Mau movement and its armed resistance. This radical approach was based on the clarification, among activists, of an ideological stand which embraced both national and international levels.

The success of the Russian Revolution in 1917 had inspired working people in almost every country in the world, particularly those suffering from colonial domination, to resist imperialism. It also introduced socialist ideology to anti-colonial struggles around the world. In Kenya such ideas and influences came from links with progressive movements based in India and Britain. In the latter, there was strong sympathy with the Kenyan people's struggle among trade unions and progressive politicians. There existed in Britain in the 1950s an influential Kenya Support Committee which organised public opinion in Britain and provided moral and material support for the independence movement. Pinto's links with Fenner Brockway is one indication of the support for Kenya's cause in Britain.

Another factor was the influence in Kenya of the anti-colonial and anti-imperialist influence from the Indian sub-continent. Such influences had included the strong links between Asian Kenyan activists in the 1920s with the revolutionary Ghadar [19] ("Revolution") movement which spread to

---

19   "The Ghadar Party was an organization founded by Punjabi Indians, in the United States and Canada with the aim to gaining India's independence from British rule. Key members included lala Har Dayal, Sohan Singh Bhakna, Kartar Singh Sarabha, and Rashbehari Bose" - Wikipedia. Available at: http://en.wikipedia.org/wiki/Ghadar_Party [Accessed: 29-08-14]. See also Durrani (2006).

many parts of the colonised world and sought to end British colonialism in India as well as in other colonies by an armed struggle.[20] In later years the veteran trade unionist, Makhan Singh, who was a member of the Indian Communist Party, had brought socialist and Marxist traditions from India. Pinto himself was influenced by India's struggle for independence and was closely linked with the struggle for the liberation of Goa from Portuguese colonialism. He maintained contacts with both these struggles and came to influence them in turn.

Thus, when Pinto returned to Kenya in 1949, the scene was set for a resolution of the contradiction with colonialism. The actual form it took was influenced as much by the reaction of the colonial government on finding evidence of the existence of a militant resistance movement, as by the organic development of the popular anti-colonial movement itself. Within a few years, it became obvious that continued existence of colonialism in Kenya was no longer possible. Years of resistance had bred a generation that was "ready to die on our feet rather than live on our knees". Pinto's own inclination and experience merged with this sentiment. He joined whole-heartedly in organised revolutionary work, writing memoranda and creating wider consciousness among people through the press. He was equally ready to join in the armed stage of the struggle and was active on many fronts. He never gave up hope for a peaceful solution and had been involved in negotiations for this when he was detained.

Pinto was equally active in the work of the national political party, first with the Kenya African Union and later with Kenya African National Union (KANU) founded in 1960. His work in the political work within KANU needs to be understood in the context of the ideological divide within the Party. KANU was a divided party and its right wing had been strengthened under US and British supervision when Kenya African Democratic Party (KADU) joined KANU. *Independent Kenya* (1982: 18,19) explains the internal contradiction in KANU:

> KANU contained two broadly different groups. On the one side

---

20   Some further details and references to the Ghadar Movement in Kenya are given in Durrani (2006).

were people who believed that "independence" necessitated a total break with the colonial system and a new beginning... Their voice set the tone of the 1960 KANU *Manifesto*, demanding a clean break with the past and the creation of a more egalitarian society... But the other group was ultimately to win the day. These were the moderate nationalists who stressed *continuity* with the past, and not a complete break with the colonial system.

Pinto sided with the former group and was ultimately the victim of the latter. He was was a marked man for the very reasons that made him an effective anti-imperialist warrior. His enemies saw his strength and realised that he would lead to revolutionary changes in Kenya unless he was stopped. He would have survived if he had sided with the moderate wing of KANU led by Kenyatta and Tom Mboya. But the radical wing of KANU in the years before independence and its subsequent development into the Kenya People's Union under Oginga Odinga, faced not only internal but external enemies too. The departing colonial power, Britain, now joined by the new imperialist superpower, USA, had already decided to ensure that independent Kenya would be run by the moderates. They fully supported the Kenyatta moderate wing as a way of stopping the radicals who, in effect, were carrying on the revolutionary agenda of Mau Mau. While the elimination of the radical wing was supposedly done by the Kenyatta moderates, the power behind their actions was the colonial government which dispatched a "moderate, socialist" to be the Governor of Kenya to oversee the transition of the colony to a neo-colony under the guise of independence. This is how the last Governor of Kenya, Malcolm MacDonald (MacDonald, 1976b) - self-proclaimed Moderate Socialist - explained the position of the colonial government regarding the moderate-radical contradiction in Kenya in response to the question, "I remember you saying earlier that it was wise for the British Government to support Kenyatta because he was a moderate":

I thought that if the moderates... came into power in independent Kenya they would not only be moderate in their national policies, in economic and social and political affairs, but on the side of moderation in international affairs, and for example not go communist and not come under the influence of any other communist anti-British anti-Western power.

The significance of this support by the colonial power goes beyond the control over Kenyan politics after independence. It helped to overturn the aims of the Mau Mau struggle and their quest for land, freedom and justice. The radicals were well aware of this neo-colonial danger as they pointed out in 1961 in their document "The Struggle for Kenya's Future"[21]. The British support for the moderates was crucial in ensuring that the Western-orientated government came to power. This support included the suppression of progressive political parties, radical trade unions and social movements as well as the marginalisation and undermining of radical leaders.

The imperialist manipulation of Kenya's politics provided the momentum that ultimately led to the assassination of Pio Gama Pinto. Thus, the responsibility of his death lies not only with the Government of Kenya but also with the British Government whose policy and actions supported the Western-orientated Government. It is doubtful if the moderates would ever have come to power without the Western support. While Britain was actively engaged in the internal politics of Kenya before and after independence, as shown in the MacDonald Papers, the US government and CIA supported moderate leaders like Tom Mboya who were used to create a pro-Western trade union movement to replace the militant one set up and supported by Makhan Singh, Fred Kubai, Bildad Kaggia, Pio Gama Pinto and others.

It is important to take note of the global and national political and imperialist backdrop to the events that led to the assassination of Pinto. The assassination was part of the overall imperialist plot to ensure Kenya remained in the capitalist camp managed by the key imperialist powers USA and Britain. There were Kenyan as well as international implications for this imperialist-inspired conspiracy in Kenya, as Kimena (1970:22-23) records:

> In 1964 anti-socialist elements in the cabinet of Kenyatta backed and advised by the CIA intelligence services, had

---

21   The document is reproduced in Durrani (2018).

in a most dramatic manner worked for the closedown of Lumumba Institute which was established by KANU militants to train party cadres. 27 district party officials who demanded a change to radical policies were arrested, hurriedly tried in court, and sentenced to imprisonment ranging up to a maximum of one and a half years. Expulsion of socialist journalists and diplomats became a routine matter in Kenya. Under the cloak of 'safeguarding against the infiltration of foreign ideology', the late Tom Mboya with the aid of the CIA agents worked out the notorious Kenya Sessional Paper No. 10 which was spearheaded against the introduction of any progressive policies. It became an instrument for disorientation of the intellectuals and for misleading the masses. Kenyatta's Minister of Finance, James Gichuru, spoke at a Commonwealth conference in Lagos against majority rule for the Zimbabwe Africans and the government ignored OAU's resolution which demanded the severance of diplomatic relations with Britain on the UDI.

One of the tactics used by Britain was to bring KADU into KANU as a way of undermining the strength of the militants in KANU. The coming together of the pro-Western elements in KANU and KADU was encouraged by Britain. KADU had been getting money from "the City" in London, as MacDonald (1976a) reveals and their joining KANU provided a stronger base for the business and financial interest of the West in the newly independent country. Whereas the radical wing of KANU had differences with the Kenyatta-supported KANU, there were no ideological divisions between the right wings of the two parties. "In fact," says MacDonald (1976), "they agreed on an economic policy, social policy and political policy in Kenya".

While there are many among Pinto's friends who are happy to recount what Pinto was really like - as recorded in the tribute paid to him [22] - it is

22   Pio Gama Pinto, Independent Kenya's First Martyr: Socialist and Freedom Fighter. (1966). Nairobi: Pan African Press reproduced in this book.

necessary to know what those who did not like him, or had no sympathy with his views, vision and actions, thought of him. It is their views of him - whether correct or not, whether based on evidence or not - that are ultimately likely to lead us to find the reasons for his assassination. Perhaps a clue as to why Pinto was singled out for assassination by the ruling elite was again provided by MacDonald (1976b):

> Pinto was the principal organiser of the section of KANU which was more left wing than Kenyatta... Pinto was the organiser of this left-wing group in KANU which was pro-Odinga and privately against Kenyatta and Mboya and the other so-called moderates. ... And I sometimes wonder what would have happened if he'd lived just a year longer because Odinga was having some success with the rank and file in the party. From the moment when Pinto disappeared from the scene, Odinga's chances decreased. Odinga wasn't efficient... Odinga in many ways wasn't experienced and able as an organiser, and when he was left more or less on his own after Pinto's death his chances declined... I think it was because his efforts were being successful that whoever organised his despatch, because there's no doubt he was assassinated, thought he should be eliminated before it was too late... [Answering the question if he regarded Pinto as a threat, MacDonald said]: I regarded him as the main threat in Kenya from that point of view, ["I admired his ability and felt respect for him but tremendous suspicion because he was out for the communist cause and wanted to subvert Kenya, East Africa and maybe the whole of Africa to communism"] because of his dedication, his sincerity and his ability as an organiser and his cunning as a behind-the-scenes operator... I thought there was a great risk of him succeeding because he was so clever.

Here then is the start of the process that ended in the assassination of Pinto. It is clear from the MacDonald Papers that the Governor and the British Government influenced the turn of events in Kenya and directed it to the marginalisation of the Mau Mau activists and also that of the radical groups who sought to follow the path advocated by Mau Mau. By bringing in the Cold War logic into the Kenyan situation, the Governor and the British Government succeeded in ensuring that the moderates they could trust and work with, became the new Government of independent Kenya. But this was no last-minute planning. MacDonald, upon arriving in Kenya 1962, decided to speed up the process of independence planned by London for late 1964 or early 1965. His reasons for early independence in 1963 make interesting reading as they relate to ensuring that the moderates came to power at independence. MacDonald (1976a) says:

> The reason why I thought the transition should be speeded up was that the "moderates" were in control of both KANU and KADU. Jomo Kenyatta was not supposed to be a "moderate", but I decided within a few days that he was one... I felt that if independence didn't come as quickly as they wanted, they would lose influence with a lot of their supporters, and the more extreme, less reasonable and capable politicians would take over. I thought it would be a great mistake to allow that to happen.

It needs to be pointed out that the terms, "moderates" and "radicals" can sometimes be misleading or inaccurate. In essence, the former stood for the status quo which favoured those inheriting the power that colonialists were ostensibly giving up. They were also in favour of the capitalist system that colonialism had introduced as it served their class interests. The "radicals" on the other hand favoured a change to the system that created classes and class inequality. Not all radicals favoured socialism, although many did, but all sought to create a system that did away with inequality in the society and wanted justice for all. However, the manipulation of Kenyan political process by Britain led to Mau Mau's aims, now progressed by the militant wing of KANU, losing out to the moderates. These moderates went on to become one of the most corrupt governments in Africa. Pinto had no hope of surviving this elite supported system which was egged on by the colonial power and which took over control of the independent country in the interest of capitalism.

The basic difference between conservatives and radicals was ideological. In general terms, the former favoured capitalism while the latter were inclined towards socialism. The opposition to Pinto from the moderates came from the fact that he was successful in propagating ideas and practices that would usher in socialism. Hornsby (2012:8) observes at this ideological divide in Kenya:

> Kenya has also experienced enduring tension between supporters of a more communal, egalitarian or socialist path, and proponents of a more individualised, capitalist and unequal view of what was right for the country. The tension was most visible during 1963–5, but proponents of a more egalitarian or socialist view continued to seek expression through the Kenya People's Union (KPU) in 1966–69, the unofficial opposition of the 1970s, Oginga Odinga's socialist party of 1982, Mwakenya, the struggle for multi-party democracy and even the Orange Democratic Movement of 2007. Kenya's 'left' has seldom had the opportunity to set policy or even articulate its views without harassment, but there have always been individuals ready to make a case for change, whether harking back to pre-colonial communal societies or to Marxist models of development.

The Truth, Justice and Reconciliation Commission of Kenya report (2013) also takes up the main contradiction in Kenyan society:

> The polarization of the country between the radicals and the conservatives continued to remain a threat which Kenyatta had to handle. The first attempt to deal with this situation was the development of Sessional Paper Number 10 of 1965, which was a mix of the socialist and capitalist models, rejecting both Marxism and laissez-faire capitalism, and stressing African traditions, equity and

social justice. Kenyatta made it clear in his introduction to the paper that the intent was not to stimulate discussions on Kenya's economic policy, but to end it. However, Oginga Odinga and his camp instructed Pio Gama Pinto to prepare a competing paper to mobilize for the rejection of the government sessional paper. But before Pinto could prepare the parallel paper, he was murdered on 24 February 1965 outside his home in Nairobi by people believed to have been auxiliaries loyal to Kenyatta. The killing of Pinto marked the process of political assassinations under the Kenyatta regime.

Pinto's voice and actions continued to proclaim loudly that he was in favour of the socialist approach while the conservatives, led by Kenyatta, manoeuvred themselves into positions of power. The voice of the left was thus set up to be suppressed. In the case of Pinto, it was not enough to suppress his voice; he had to be physically eliminated to stop the spread of socialist ideas. Hornsby (2012:148) describes the impact of Pinto's death:

> Pinto's death removed a key figure in Odinga's camp. The murder also shocked many Kenyans, including Pinto's close friend Murumbi. It was an end of innocence for independent Kenya and demonstrated the determination of Kenyatta's government to cling to power by any means, and of the commitment of Western countries to ensure that Kenya did not fall under communist influence. The British and US governments - in later years so outspoken on political issues - said nothing.

Manji (2015) connects Pinto's work with the struggle against the capitalist ideas pushed by the US:

> It was around *Sessional Paper Number Ten of 1965: African Socialism and its Implications for Planning in Kenya* that the polarization between the KANU and Pio erupted, exacerbated by revelations of misappropriation of

funds by the Kenyatta regime.

Authorship of this paper has usually been attributed to Tom Mboya. In fact, the key architect of the paper was an American political economist Edgar O. Edwards, who was attached to the Ministry of Planning. Edwards was part of a team of Americans who had *bona fide* credentials at the US Embassy in the 1960s. This team was put at Tom Mboya's disposal by Ambassador Atwood, to help him write economic blueprints as well as to outwit his adversaries. The paper, despite its claims of 'socialism' was a perfect articulation of the how a subservient capitalism would be developed in the post-independence period. It was in opposition to this text that Pio wrote a counter proposal which, had he not be assassinated, could very well have led, some believe, to the removal of Kenyatta as president through a vote of no confidence and the emergence of Jaramogi Odinga as the new president.

Besides his advocacy of socialism, another reason that Pinto was targeted was because of his close relations with Oginga Odinga who was unpopular with the British government because of his socialist leanings. They did all they could to discredit him and to take power from him. It was the last Governor of Kenya, Malcolm MacDonald (1972), who pushed Kenyatta to distrust Odinga and had the police portfolio removed from him when he became the Home Affairs Minister, thus driving a wider wedge between the radicals and moderates. The crimes of the British Government in Kenya have yet to be fully understood, documented and remedied.

Pinto has often been maliciously projected as a lone fighter struggling on his own against a mighty colonial-imperialist machinery. Thus, his contribution has been removed from its social, political and historical context. This is partly due to the imperialist conspiracy to present the Kenyan struggles as lacking a well-developed ideology, and a strong leadership and has sought to interpret its actions as isolated, uncoordinated acts of desperate a people. It seeks to interpret Kenyan struggles - and others around the world - as

Pio Gama Pinto, Kenya's Unsung Martyr

struggles from an imperialist perspective. They sought thus to discredit not only Pinto, but other Kenyan progressive leaders as well as the Mau Mau movement as a whole.

In the case of Pinto, another reason why it has been possible to de-contextualise him was the fact mentioned earlier: the lack of material from his personal collection which was destroyed after his assassination. Progressive historians have thus faced a situation of a lack of original material to assess Pinto and his achievements. Imperialism and those opposed to his stand among the ruling Kenyan elite have systematically blocked any attempts to interview Pinto's contemporaries and to set up a research and archive on Kenya's war of independence. The proposal to set up a National Liberation Research, Museum and Archives Centre (Durrani, 2003), if acted upon, might have addressed this lack of historical records on Pinto. While it is not possible to address this lack in the present brief article on Pinto, it is still possible to document the progressive thinking of Pinto, his actions and achievements in material currently available in the public domain.

The Activist
As soon as he returned to Kenya in 1949, Pinto joined the struggle for independence at different levels: political, social, economic, ideological and organisational. He was able to combine all these aspects skilfully without losing sight of the overall political goal of the struggle. Among the organisations he used to achieve his aims were the trade union movement, mass media and communications, as well as the above-ground and under-ground political structures. While each of these aspects had its own particularity, they were all inter-related. Thus, while he was active on the Asian front, Pinto was able to link this with his work at the trade unions and also with the overall political level where he worked with other progressive individuals and organisations.

It should be noted that throughout his political career, Pinto kept his focus on three aspects of political work: the need for a clear vision and ideological clarity - which in his case was socialism; the need for an organisation which could ensure that the vision was implemented - setting up organisations such as the Kenya Freedom Party and working with progressive KANU party are examples; and reliance on working people and party cadres to bring about social and political change - setting up the Lumumba Institute was one such example.

Durrani, Nazmi. (2017: 58) looks at Pinto's activities in a number of fields, all of which strengthened the liberation struggle which itself was being fought at different levels:

> On 20 October 1952, a very fierce battle started between Kenyan freedom fighters and the colonial government. Several African leaders and thousands of Kenyan people were put away behind bars and in detention camps. The foreign government confiscated the lands of many patriots. Even innocent people were made to suffer without any reason. Pinto and other patriots such as Ambu Patel began publications to expose these cowardly and cruel actions of the colonial government.
>
> Moreover, Pinto carried out the work of looking for lawyers willing to defend those freedom fighters who were taken to court. Many Kenyan Asian patriots came forward to defend and save the freedom fighters who had fought against the colonial government. For example, F. R. D'Souza, J. M. Nazareth, E. K. Navroji, A. R. Kapila, S. M. Akram, A. H. Malik, Sheikh Amin, K. D. Trivadi, Arvind Jamidar, and others.
> In addition to this work, Pinto joined other brave patriots in the work of transporting weapons and other necessities to the Mau Mau freedom fighters in their hideouts.

Pinto became an important person in the struggle not only because of his clear ideological grasp of the situation and his total commitment to the liberation struggle but also because he linked different aspects of the struggle and ensured that all worked together to strengthen the overall anti-imperialist struggle.

Pinto was arrested in June 1954, detained at Takwa Detention Camp on Manda Island up to 1957, then restricted at Kabernet from where he was finally released in October 1959 for his highly effective resistance activities. But he continued his revolutionary activities even in detention.

While further details of Pinto's work when in detention are given by his colleagues in *Pio Gama Pinto, Independent Kenya's First Martyr* (1966)[23], Oneko (1966:19) provides details of the information work that Pinto did in detention:

> There came a time when almost everyone was giving in, and murmuring started in the camp. The Authorities had begun to engineer confusion in the camp in order to demoralise us. We realised if we did not organise counter measures and propaganda many of us would be wrecked and give up the cause. Therefore the top group, that is, Mbiyu Koinange, now member of the Senate, Muinga Chokwe, now speaker of the Senate, J.D. Kali, now Member of Parliament, Pio and myself started a counter propaganda move. Pio was one of the "editors" and played a big role in a well organised network. It was his job to dish out information to the Lower Camp by word of mouth to our own propagandists. To the astonishment and surprise of the Camp Administration the morale of the detainees was restored and we remained hard and impenetrable but reasonable.

By the time of his release from detention and restriction in 1959, it was obvious that the liberation struggle had made independence inevitable. Pinto immersed himself once again in political work both at the South Asian level and at national level in the Kenya African National Union (KANU) and preparing for independence.

Soon after his release from restriction in 1959, Pinto founded the Kenya Freedom Party (KFP) together with Chanan Singh and K.P. Shah. *Drum* (1965) explains the circumstances:

> Formed by Asians who felt that that the Kenya Indian Congress was not sufficiently sympathetic to the African cause, the KFP

---

23   Included in this book.

advocated immediate independence for Kenya, universal franchise and social integration.

Independence came on December 12, 1963. But Pinto did not relax. The country was entering the new phase of neo-colonialism and Pinto was quick to see the danger posed by neo-colonialism as imperialism sought to retain control over Kenya in another guise. Over the next two years, he continued his struggle and kept organising to achieve the dream that had eluded the nation at independence. As events were to prove, Pinto was right to warn against neo-colonialism. His struggle extended from colonial to neo-colonial stage in Kenya.

4. *Shiraz Durrani: Gama Pinto. The Standard (Nairobi) 17-09-1984*

Pio Gama Pinto, Kenya's Unsung Martyr

5. Shiraz Durrani: Pinto Backed Nationalism. Standard (Nairobi) 18-09-1984

Some Key Aspects of Pinto's Work

The Complete Man

Details about the life and work of Pinto before and after detention are included in other documents in this book and will not be repeated here. Instead, some key aspects in which he was active are considered below. However, it is not possible to isolate specific aspects of Pinto's activism from the man. While his personality can perhaps be best understood by examining particular strengths in specific areas, it is necessary to see all these aspects as a whole to understand the person that was Pinto. This is perhaps best illustrated in some of his letters reproduced in this book. They reveal the wide range of interests that Pinto had, his understanding of different aspects of the problems that the people of Kenya faced and his activism in trying to resolve them whenever he could. At the same time, they show us his painstaking work in documenting and disseminating worldwide the reality of the situation in Kenya. Communications were at the centre of all that Pinto did. They explain how he used the cover of his work at the Kenya Indian Congress to undertake activities which the colonial government would no doubt have considered subversive. His awareness of the security implications is indicated by his use of an "innocent" address to receive mail from overseas so as to escape colonial censorship, indicating also his closeness to his wife, Emma, and brother, Rosariao. While there may be a lack of material from which to examine Pinto the political person, some of his letters reproduced under the section, "Pinto seen through his correspondence" in this book provide an indication of the real Pinto – always busy, always connecting, always aware of key developments, both local and international, always ready for action to support the struggle and those involved and affected by it. A reading of this small selection of his letters provides details of some key aspects of Pinto's work as a mature and a fully aware resistance fighter. Some of these are mentioned below:

- Contacts with a large number of people from diverse backgrounds, in India, UK, South Africa, USA and other countries.
- Such contacts included Members of Parliament, senior diplomats,

journalists, politicians as well as activists.

- Links with Embassies, for example Egypt, Morocco, India – Pinto used such links to pass messages to and from activists and supporters around the world.
- Maintaining secure communications links with overseas supporters as well as with Kenyans in UK. This included the use of "safe addresses" to ensure that messages were delivered safely.
- Providing news and newspaper cuttings to people overseas so as to keep them informed about developments in Kenya. Such reports were then used by the recipients as the basis for newspaper articles, questions in the Parliament and keeping general public informed about the reality of colonialism and imperialism in Kenya.
- Collecting information on local developments, e.g. data on the schools closed by colonial administration, prison conditions, cattle confiscated by colonial authorities, land disputes, colonial attempts to create racial and tribal divisions. These were then passed on by Pinto to his overseas contacts.
- Keeping in touch with detainees and passing on information to them and about them to others.
- Being active in all political initiatives, e.g. preparing memoranda and sending copies overseas.

It is not surprising that his family hardly saw him, so busy was he as the centre of a vast network of activities that few other leaders at the time, or since then have matched. It is indeed a heavy loss to the liberation of Kenya when his own material was destroyed as it would have provided a valuable resource on this remarkable man as well as on the struggle against colonialism and imperialism.

The Land Issue

Land was and remains a key issue for working people in Kenya. Indeed, the main contradiction between the settlers and the colonial government on the one hand, and the people of Kenya on the other, related to the appropriation of Kenyan land by the colonial administration, using legal and illegal methods. This inevitably led to the formation of the Kenya

Land and Freedom Movement which has come to be known as Mau Mau. As an activist on issues of colonialism and imperialism, Pinto was deeply involved in seeking justice for the people of Kenya for their land rights. He wrote many memoranda to colonial authorities and Commissions on the issue and also alerted progressive people in UK and other places about the land situation in Kenya as it affected peasants. Fitz De Souza (1966:28-29) remembers Pinto's role in researching and writing up memoranda on land:

> I know and history will record that Pio had a hand in the preparation of most of the memoranda and statements issued by K.AU. in those days. He often used to sit up to 5 a.m. in the Congress Office drafting political papers in the nationalist cause. For all this he never expected payment. His reward was in the contribution he made to the struggle. He never looked for personal credit.

> A couple of years later when he was the Editor of the *Daily Chronicle*, the Royal Commission on Land asked for evidence, and there was no one to put forward the African case for all the leaders were in detention. Pio resigned his job, and read through the voluminous Carter Commission Report and other documents on the land issue and took statements from Kikuyu Elders and others. He then wrote out, and personally typed and cyclostyled, always working into early hours of the morning, the 200-page Kikuyu Tribe's Memoranda for other individual Mbaris in the Central Province. Pio never told anybody about his work. I sent a copy of this Memorandum to the President at Lodwar. He was so impressed that he suggested we publish the Memorandum but for lack of funds the work was never done.

Not only did he write many memoranda digging into the land disputes with colonialism, he also recorded and campaigned in the struggles waged by peasants against the colonial land grabs. For example, he wrote to Fenner

Pio Gama Pinto, Kenya's Unsung Martyr

Brockway (Pinto, 1952a) on the on-going land take over by the colonial administration:

> **Land Evictions**. Mr. Otiende has asked me to bring the following instances of Governmental action to your notice.
>
> 1. A few hundred Kipsigis have been forcibly driven from their location called Kimilot, because they refused to shift to another area in which climatic conditions and rainfall were far from satisfactory. The Kipsigis had been contesting the legality of Government's order in Court, and I have been given to understand by Mr. Otiende that the decisions given by the Court were in the favour of the Kipsigis. Nevertheless, the Government has resorted to the use of armoured cars and prison labour to demolish their huts. The area in which they have been residing is designated by survey No. LRM7797 and is 5186 acres in extent. They have been ordered to move to a relatively dry area designated by No.LRM 7798 with an area of 7650 acres. Although the Legislative Council has sanctioned this transfer, all the African members in the Legco voted against the unjust transfer. Mr. Otiende will shortly be proceeding on a tour of up-country areas and I have asked him to take photographs of the demolished huts etc. The reason for this compulsory acquisition of land is due to the fact that it is being acquired by the African Highlands Tea Co. You will appreciate the plight of the dispossessed Kipsigis when it is remembered that the long rains are expected in the near future.
>
> 2. The second case of forcible expropriation concerns about four to five hundred Wakambas. For the past ten years these Wakamba were residing in an area situated on the Yatta plateau called Ndalani which was

earmarked for the future needs of the Wakamba people. Ndalani was sold to Harris Estates Ltd. in November, and the people who were living there have been forced to go to places where it would be impossible for them to pursue their pastoral life. Some are being enticed to go to Makueni where a man is not allowed to have more than 5 cattle owing to the extreme aridity of the area, and others are being forcibly transported to the Wakamba reserve which is known to be one of the most congested areas in the country.

It may strike you as strange that at the very moment when the delegates of the Kenya African Union are in the U.K. making representations on behalf of their people for the return of land allocated to Europeans by the Carter Commission, situated in an area popularly referred to as the White Highlands, the Government should enforce measures which, in effect, are calculated to drive Africans still further into the Bush. By their actions the Government of Kenya makes it plain that far from returning the land filched from Africans in the past, the process of dispossessing them of whatever good land still remains has not attained finality. This attitude on the part of the Kenya Government also reflects its apparent disregard for the strength of the K.A.U, and this is the problem which I feel deserves your serious consideration.

No assessment of Pinto would be complete without consideration of his active participation and involvement in the struggle for land. He continued his activism on this issue even after independence and this was perhaps one of the key background reasons for his assassination by the elite which became super-rich on the back of taking over acres of good land from the departing settlers with the full cooperation and support of British colonial authorities. The peasants lost out first under colonialism; they lost out once again under the rule of the new African ruling classes. For them,

Pio Gama Pinto, Kenya's Unsung Martyr

independence meant merely the transfer of colonial policies and practices to the "independent" government. That went against everything Pinto stood for and he was not afraid to continue his campaigns on behalf of peasants and landless Kenyans after independence.

Emma Gama Pinto (2000) recalls Pinto's work on land laws:

In 1951 Pio had enlisted the help of the Indian High Commissioner, Apa Pant for a typewriter to work on his ideas. The High Commissioner hired Pio as a secretary to the Kenya Indian Congress. Pio was given a desk at the Desai Memorial Library and he single-handedly revised the Land Reform Act to allow Africans a fair share of their country.

Information and Communication for Resistance

Pinto used social communications to unify other aspects of the struggles he was active in. Durrani, Nazmi (2017:57-58) provides some details of Pinto's activities in this field:

In 1951, Pinto started working for the East African Indian Congress movement which had its offic[24]es in Desai Memorial Building. He formed relationships with the members and leaders of African freedom movements, Kenya African Union and workers' organisations and worked towards achieving African-Asian unity. In 1950, when Makhan Singh and Fred Kubai were arrested, Pinto joined hands with workers and helped to continue with the movement's work for independence.

In order to facilitate this political work, Pinto learnt Kiswahili. He believed that it was essential to learn Kiswahili if he was going to work successfully with African leaders and workers.

In order to combat British colonial government propaganda,

---

24   The English translation varies slightly from the original Gujarati article here and as translated in Durrani, Nazmi's book in "Liberating Minds".

he started work as a journalist. He began to edit a newsletter called *Uzvod*[25] in Konkani language and wrote articles in the *Colonial Times.* In 1953 he became editor of the Gujarati-English *Daily Chronicle.* In addition, with the help of D.K. Sharda, Harun Ahmad and Pranlal Seth, he assisted in the publication of anti-government African newsletters.

Murumbi (2015:216) examines Pinto's activities in the media:

> Pinto was very active in helping, particularly young newspapermen who used to publish broadsheets in those days. And of course, they couldn't afford a duplicating machine. I think he also helped them financially in a limited way in buying them paper, but he was working in the Asian Congress Office where he had a duplicating machine and he used to type these broadsheets for them, sometimes, invariably he rolled these himself. In those days we didn't have electric duplicating machines. You had to turn them with your hand and Pinto was instrumental in getting these broadsheets out. And these broadsheets were sometimes banned. Well, in those days, if a broadsheet was banned, you had a month to cease publication. So, after that month, the same broadsheet came out in another name. They continued right throughout. And Pinto was the man behind these people, encouraging them, helping them to write these broadsheets, helping them to duplicate it, and sometimes financially he used to help them as well.

Pinto developed a communications strategy for the liberation forces to enable it to combat colonial and post-colonial attacks on its organisation, leadership, ideology and channels of communications. He was involved in setting up an independent press, writing articles and memoranda, and setting up distribution networks. He participated in all the various aspects of implementing this strategy. This included taking part in printing and distribution of anti-colonial posters and leaflets.

It was necessary for the liberation forces to counter the new imperialist

25   The correct translation should be Uzwad.

onslaught with a more powerful media strategy. In 1960, Pio Gama Pinto went to India to ask for 700,000 Kenya shillings for a KANU press. This was given by Jawaharlal Nehru, the first Prime Minister of India and thus was born the Pan African Press in 1961. Its directors were Jomo Kenyatta, Achieng Oneko, Oginga Odinga, J. D. Kali. Pinto became the general manager. Among the publications brought out by the press were *Sauti ya Mwafrika* and *Pan Africa* (Noronha, F.1987). The Pan African Press published the Kiswahili *Sauti ya Kanu* and the English *Pan African* which was edited by Pio Gama Pinto. Activists pay their tribute to Pinto on his activities in this field:

☐ **Kaggia, Bildad** (1966:12): "I can never forget his [Pinto's] help to me and other African politicians when we decided to run our own newspapers to fight the colonial newspaper monopoly. He did all he could to see that each and every small newspaper went forward. His advice and practical help in this work will never be forgotten."

☐ **Kali, J. D.** (1966:20) mentions Pinto's activities in poster and handbill production and distribution: "Mr. Pinto had many friends among the present Members of Parliament, friendships which began years ago. He was appointed by them to act as their secretary during the last General Elections' Campaign. One of his main jobs was to draft campaign slogans and print them. Pinto even took it upon himself to display them all over Nairobi. Most often he stuck the posters at the dead of night. One of the most interesting of these posters was the 'CONGO' poster. He printed posters and pamphlets for KANU candidates all over the country."

6. Pio Gama Pinto with mother (Left). Photo: Benegal Pereira

- **Chokwe, Muinga Chitari** (1966:36): "Pio joined the staff of a small newspaper organisation and started whipping up public opinion in favour of the African [cause]. Pio enlisted the help of Mr. D. K. Sharda who had a small lino press [The Tribune Press] and got him to print various papers".

- **Nowrojee, Pheroze** (2007:10): "Pio worked very hard for the Kenya African Union to let its views be known to all by writing and publishing them. He prepared most of the memoranda and statements issued by KAU in those days.... Also, together with other like-minded individuals, he started a political discussion group. This group was called the Kenya African Study Union.

Pinto wrote regular letters to colleagues to keep them - and the international community through them - informed about events in Kenya. Thus, he provided regular contact with the outside world for Mau Mau. Murumbi (2015:215) recollects Pinto's work:

Pinto sent [Fenner] Brockway regular letters, reports and these of course were sent to a cover address, Mrs. Ella Reed, wife of the correspondent of the Hindustan Times. So this information was channelled to Fenner and to Mr. Reed, who kept the Indian papers informed of activities in Kenya and who actually visited Nairobi during the Emergency… When I arrived in London, Fenner Brockway handed me a lot of Pio's reports in England. How Pio found time to do all this is remarkable. We know because he was dedicated. He believed in the cause…he used his intelligence and training very effectively in providing the right information that we needed in London and that we used as the basis for questions in the House of Commons.

Pinto's hand was behind many memoranda on land and other matters, behind many election manifestos as well as political policies but none reflect the fact that he was the author behind such work.

COLONY AND PROTECTORATE OF KENYA

Form C.

THE PRINTING PRESSES(TEMPORARY PROVISIONS)ORDINANCE, 1952

(No. 38 of 1952)

THE PRINTING PRESSES RULES, 1952

(Rule 5)

NOTIFICATION OF REFUSAL OF A LICENCE

To.....P.Gama Pinto.......

P.O. Box. 186, Nairobi.

I,.....David John Coward...................................

Ag. Registrar of Printing Presses, hereby give you notice that
in accordance with section 5 (3) of the Printing Presses
(Temporary Provisions) Ordinance, 1952, I have this day refused
to issue to you the licence requested in your application dated
the......30th.....day of.........December,....1952, on the grounds
that it appears to me that you are likely to keep or use the
printing press for the printing of documents prejudicial to, or
incompatible with, peace or good order in the Colony.

Dated at....Nairobi....this ....fifth.....day
of......March........,1953.

....
AG.REGISTRAR OF PRINTING PRESSES

7. *Colonial authorities refuse Pinto printing licence (05-03-1953)*

KNA 1. Public Meetings & the Pan African Press 1953-1964.

The anti-imperialist socialist

Pinto was a staunch socialist as his own writings and those who wrote tributes to him after his assassination show. Nabwera (1966:16) explains:

> Let me say something about Pio, the socialist. His approach to socialism was non-doctrinaire... He believed in and adhered to socialist principles. But he was intelligent enough to understand that what was required in Kenya was the establishment of a mixed economy... For Kenya, he wanted to see the Government play a major role in economic and social reconstruction.

What socialism meant to Pinto was explained in his article, *Glimpses of Kenya's Nationalist Struggle* (Pinto, P.G. 1963b). Nabwera (1966:16-17) expands on this:

> His concern about the lot of ordinary people was that we must try and build a society where differences in wealth should not penalise the poor. He, therefore, wanted to see development in all parts of our country, especially those areas that had experienced very little development under British rule. He further wanted to see the establishment of rent control in urban areas as a way of protecting the tenants from being exploited by landlords. He also advocated the establishment of free health service and free education as a method of assisting the less privileged people in our community. And finally, Pio was opposed to the practice whereby a few individuals in privileged positions were to amass excessive wealth at the expense of the masses. He believed that people in such positions should do more for the masses and that such public service would be a reward in itself.

But Pinto realised that socialism could not be achieved without addressing the power of the capitalist world which was behind the imperialism that sought to control the world. Defeating colonialism, he saw, could not by itself achieve socialism. He thus linked his socialist aims with a staunch anti-imperialist outlook.

It was Pinto's anti-imperialism and support for socialism in thought and deed that marked him out as an enemy of colonialism and neo-colonialism in Goa and Kenya. To quote Oneko (1966):

> Pio was a nationalist and socialist; a man who did so many good things for others. He put himself second to the nation in everything he thought and did. He was active, able and unassuming.

Pinto realised that socialism could not be achieved without actively propagating it and educating people to understand the differences between capitalism and socialism. While he took every opportunity at meetings and his writings to inculcate socialist thought so as to promote greater awareness among the people, he also realised that there was a need for an ideological education that could teach the tenets scientifically before they could be translated into practice. The capitalist world outlook was propagated via the entire government policy structure, the mass media (especially radio) and the educational system which it used to inculcate capitalist thinking among people. In contrast, socialism had no such avenue. The agenda of the ruling classes was to make people believe that there was no alternative to capitalism. Indeed, even socialist publications and news were banned by the Government, both the colonial one and the comprador one. Thus, Pinto worked extra hard to start an ideological school, but aimed at party (KANU) cadres so that they could then translate socialist plans and thinking into government policy. He was the brain and the activist behind getting funds for the Lumumba Institute whose aims are explained by the South African History Online (1965):

> The Patrice Lumumba Institute at Kamiti, (opened) seven miles from Nairobi [in 1964]. The school, dedicated to the memory of Lumumba, '... for his firm championship of genuine political and economic independence and socialism in Africa', will train one hundred and eight students at a time

as cadres of the party. Journalists, civil servants and promising party members will be trained in the K.A.N.U. party spirit in theory and practice of African socialism The school was paid for by donations from Afro-Asian and socialist states.

It should be remembered that the initiative for Lumumba Institute came from the left wing of the KANU Party. It was closed in April 1965 by the Government.

The Internationalist

Pinto was involved in struggles in two countries and two continents - Goa and Kenya. In addition, he actively supported liberation struggles in the Portuguese colonies in Africa - Angola, Mozambique and Guinea- Bissau. Pinto also kept in close contact with activists in South Africa and other parts of East Africa as well as around the world. All these connections gave Pinto a unique internationalist perspective. *Drum* (1965) looks at his internationalism:

> Nor did Pinto forget the struggle of freedom fighters in other countries when Kenya won her own independence. Many a refugee from South Africa and the Portuguese colonies counted him as an adviser and a friend, and campaigners for civil rights from the [United] States, such as Malcolm X, did the same. A few months earlier, Malcolm X had stayed in Pinto's Nairobi house. They had a lot in common.

Among the communities that Pinto was active in were South Asians. Just as there was a division among African communities into the so-called moderates and militants, there were similar divisions among the South Asian communities, mostly based on class positions and possession of wealth. However, there were issues that transcended these divisive factors and created a common identity among them. Pinto saw the broader picture of the issues facing South Asian communities and helped create conditions for ensuring that colonialism did not divide African and South Asian communities from each other. Pant (1987:26) sums up another aspect of Pinto's contribution:

Pio Pinto was deeply involved with the African freedom movement in Kenya and knew all the important underground leaders. But what diminutive, brilliant highly affectionate Pio Pinto did for India and for the Indians community in Kenya during those critical days of Mau Mau rebellion can never be forgotten. The South Africans, the colonial powers and even Israel would have liked the anger, frustration and hatred of the Mau Mau to be diverted against India and the Indians. Serious and persistent attempts were indeed made to do so. Even the Church joined in smear campaign, with sermons in Swahili and passion plays depicting Africans as criminally exploited by Indians.

Pio Pinto was largely responsible for having prevented the wrath of the Mau Mau from being vented on the Indian community. Had he not been able to enter the secret conclaves of the freedom fighters unnoticed, and had he not won the trust of leaders such as Stanley Mathenge, Jomo Kenyatta, Senior Chief Koinange and Tom Mboya for his sound and clear advice, thousands of Indians may well have been murdered and their property looted.

After independence of Kenya, destiny's strange way led to Pio being murdered in broad daylight. It is appropriate to offer homage to Pio Pinto -- a great freedom fighter, a staunch friend, and a humanist.

Pinto's vision was an internationalist vision and he looked beyond the borders of Kenya and Goa, as indicated by Emma Gama Pinto (Noronha, F. 2000):

Mentally, Pio wore blinkers like a racehorse - his total focus was on working for the liberation of countries under foreign rule. He received newspapers from these countries and seemed glued to his typewriter sending off letters or articles to the leaders of the freedom movement.

His aim was a unified approach across Africa. He enlisted the help of other African countries which had attained Independence...

As soon as we moved into 6 Lower Kahete Road, Pio set up office in a spare room. He typed until the early hours of the morning when there were no interruptions. I did, of course, miss out on normal family outings, and so on, but Pio's earnestness of purpose gave me the understanding to let him have the freedom to follow his ideals.

Fernandes (2016b) says:

There have been few, if any, internationalists in Kenya to match Pio Gama Pinto in terms of commitment and actions to this day.

Mau Mau and Trade Unions

An important aspect of Pinto's work tends to be hidden or not addressed at all. This was to do with his involvement in trade unions and Mau Mau. There is some evidence, as yet unconfirmed, that he had taken the Mau Mau oath. Durrani (2018:206-7) quotes "Mzee WM":

Pio Gama Pinto and I were in one *kundi* (Mau Mau cell). Issac GW gave me the Mau Mau oath in 1946. My sister and mother knew Pinto. Pinto's work was to *kuunganisha makabila* [bring together different nationalities], establish links with like-minded people who shared goals.

Other evidence may be needed to confirm this, but the facts indicate that he was an active supporter of the movement. He could not have been involved in the formation of the Mau Mau War Council in Nairobi nor in the procurement of arms had he not been part of the central leadership of Mau Mau. His involvement ranged from supplying weapons to the fighters, providing medical and other care to fighters and their families, organising legal aid to those condemned to jail by the colonial system to jail terms, researching and writing documents and gathering international support for the liberation struggle. It was such actions and consistent level of active support which demonstrated very clearly his political stand in the struggle against neo-colonialism and imperialism. Like many other activists, he was detained and restricted by the colonial administration based on its intelligence and surveillance activities.

Another indication of Pinto's position regarding Mau Mau and the liberation struggle was his ideological stand, both before and after independence. It is no coincidence that his views, vision and ideas were always in line with those who stood for real liberation of working people and against the colonial or neo-colonial position of capitulating to capitalism. He stood firm against personal gain made at the expense of working people. These can broadly be seen as the Mau Mau position too.

The loss of Pinto's papers and documents at his assassination robs us of the original material on his political position and stand regarding Mau Mau and the liberation struggle. However, given the need for secrecy among Mau Mau activists, it is unlikely that there would have been any documentary evidence to indicate his membership of the movement. At the same time, other factors have also contributed to the silencing of Pinto's real record. Two powerful forces were at work here. First, the colonial authorities, in keeping with their political and economic interests, always sought to discredit or distort anyone or any idea that provided an alternative to capitalism and imperialism. Secondly, the elite that came to power after independence would be happy to keep Pinto's record secret, given that Pinto represented a grave danger to its looting activities. They had amassed vast resources of land, business interests and power to add to those it was given by the colonial administration as part of its departing independence gift to ensure capitalism and imperialism did not lose out after independence. Pinto was among others in the liberation struggle who was targeted by the new ruling class. Pinto was also active in the militant trade union movement, another institution targeted by the ruling class.

Some historical records are nonetheless still available to show Pinto's stand and contribution to Mau Mau and to total liberation after independence.

Ness (2009) records Pinto's involvement in Mau Mau:

> On his return to Kenya, he joined the East African Indian Congress, the Kenya African Union, and the trade union movement. He became actively involved in the Land and Freedom Army, better known as the "Mau Mau," which engaged in armed struggle against the colonialists. He supplied the freedom fighters with weapons, funds, and information and cared for the families of those killed or arrested by the British colonial forces. He helped to set up a Mau Mau War Council in Nairobi and played a key role in sending out information to, and sourcing support from, foreign countries, especially India. Because of his activities, Pinto was detained from 1954 to 1959, just five months after he got married.

Durrani (2018) shows that there were very close links between the militant trade union movement in Kenya and Mau Mau. Pinto was active in both. Kaggia (1966:12) commented on Pinto's work in the trade union movement:

> In the early years of Kenya Trade Unionism, Pio acted as advisor and gave practical help to every Union to establish sound Trade Union principles and practices. As he was not an officer of any one of them, he was free to help all of them without any rivalry - a thing that no other trade unionist could do. All early trade unionists will never forget Pio's work to establish trade unionism.

Kinyatti (2008:148-149) records Pinto's role in supplying arms to Mau Mau:

> The progressive, anti-imperialist elements in the South Asian community, men like Pio Gama Pinto, Jaswant Bharaj and others, played a very important role in supplying KFLA with firearms, intelligence information, fund, medicine and helped the movement to produce revolutionary literature. Pinto in particular established contacts with the illegal South Asian gun-traders who secretly sold firearms and ammunition to KFLA.

Pinto provided active support to the Mau Mau fighters, as Odinga (1967:128) recalls:

In Nairobi Pinto was an invaluable supply man, working with the Nairobi War Council that siphoned food, money, arms and intelligence information through to the forests, and smuggling out of Kenya and into the world's press reports and photographs of atrocities by the security forces, until his activities were discovered and he, too, was detained.

Fernandes (2016b:132) records Pinto's support for Mau Mau:

Pinto not only financed the Mau Mau chapter in the village of Mathare Valley in Eastleigh, metres away from the St. Teresa's boys and girls schools, but he also armed them...... with the work that Pinto had done in organising and arming the Mau Mau and the wide-ranging freedom movements in Africa, especially those fighting Portuguese oppression, it was clear that he was the strategic brains behind any socialist drive towards power in Kenya.

Akumu (1966:26) provides an overview on Pinto, the trade unionist:

In his many roles as a nationalist, Pinto played a very key role in the formation of the Trade Union movement at a time when the movement was still illegal and enjoyed no legal status. He, together with people like Makhan Singh, Chege Kibachia, Fred Kubai and Aggrey Minya, can never be forgotten when the History of Trade Union movement is being discussed.

Pinto was detained during the Emergency because of his nationalistic support for the masses and because of the role he played in the formation of the anti-imperialist East African Trade Union Congress, which was later banned

While under detention, Pinto used to give encouragement to nationalists and trade unionists who were continuing the fight against colonialism. When trade unionists and politicians called for a boycott of buses, beer etc, during Kenyatta Day, Pio wrote to our union congratulating us, but added that "next time organise better and if possible, it should be a national strike demanding Mzee Kenyatta's release".

The key role that Pinto played in the trade union movement is hinted at by James Beauttah when he says that during Makhan Singh's absence in India, Pinto was "the only Asian any of us had real confidence in" (Spencer, 1983). Yet his name rarely makes it to the top when the history of the trade Union movement is being discussed today. Evidence from some of his correspondence also points to his working behind the scene for trade unions. Here is a quote from his letter to Fenner Brockway dated March 10, 1952 where, among other issues, he discussed the condition of the trade union movement in Kenya (Pinto, 1952a):

> T.U. Bill. You must be acquainted with the provisions of the new Trade Union Bill. In collaboration D.K.[Sharda], I have been able to prepare a memorandum for the Labour Trade Union of East Africa. A copy or this memorandum will he sent to you by air mail in the course of the next 3 to 4 days. I do not know whether you have a copy of the Bill with you, but in case you have not got one I shall be only too pleased to send you a copy. We have sent a copy to the Fabian Colonial Bureau. I do not know whether you can do anything about the extremely restrictive clauses which are a feature of the Bill. Under the proposed Bill trade unions are under the complete mercy of the Registrar.
>
> I was wondering whether you could assist the trade unions here to secure their affiliation to the International Confederation of Free Trade Unions. It would be very much appreciated if you could give us some advice on this matter. Following the disturbances which took place in May 1950, trade union activity has slowed down considerably but efforts are now being made to resuscitate these unions.

As with other aspects of Pinto's life and work, his role in the Mau Mau movement remains undocumented. Until the entire history of Mau Mau is allowed to be researched and written, Pinto's role in the movement will remain incomplete. There is, however, no doubt that Pinto was active in Mau Mau. Ngunyi (2015) records his activism in Mau Mau:

> Before independence, ...Pinto had been at the forefront of the formation of Mau Mau Freedom movement. Secretly, he had acquired a cache of arms for 1,500 youth who had joined freedom fighters in Mount Kenya forests.

Nowrojee (2007:11) provides a brief look at Pinto's involvement in the Mau Mau movement:

> Bildad Kaggia and others had formed the Central Committee of Mau Mau. Pinto worked with this important committee. They transported people and supplies, sent information back and forth and raised money for the fighters in the forests and towns.

Again, Nowrojee (2007:2;17-18;20-21), shows Pinto active in the movement's activities after the declaration of Emergency in 1952:

> Pio's work under the Central Committee of Mau Mau was especially important during the Emergency. The Committee needed money, food and arms for the fighters. Most of the leaders were in prison...Despite these difficult conditions, money was collected from supporters... These were carefully collected in sacks and taken to certain trusted persons. Pio was one of these. He would then take the money to wherever he was directed by the Central Committee.

> Hundreds of people were charged in courts with offences under the Emergency Regulations. These people needed

lawyers to defend them... Pio collected money from sources outside Kenya as well, so as to pay the lawyers. He also interviewed people and prepared petitions for the release of persons illegally arrested by the police.

...

Pio's work in support of the freedom fighters grew as the struggle became more intense. The Emergency meant that for many Kenyans, there was military rule in the country...Pio now had to help the freedom fighters in the forests of Mount Kenya and the Aberdares. He also had to look after their families and the families of those who had been killed. He continued to gather food, equipment and medicine for the soldiers in the forests, as well as for families left behind. (p.20).

All this work was extremely dangerous work. Had Pinto been caught with guns or any supplies for the freedom fighters in the forests, he would have been sentenced to death. The same could have happened if he had been caught talking to a freedom fighter! (p.21)
...

Pinto was active in Mau Mau, the movement fighting for independence. He collected and transported money, food and other supplies that the freedom fighters needed all the time. He also made sure that the fighters remained in touch with other leaders and with their supporters while they fought their battles in the forests and towns. (p.2)

In addition to such open activities, Pinto was active behind the scene too. He joined others who had also decided that it was not possible to dislodge colonialism from Kenya through the British-instituted seemingly democratic methods. These were always set up to favour the rich settler minority. Pinto became active in the Mau Mau movement in various ways, ranging from securing arms and other necessities to the fighters to supporting those who landed in the colonial jails and who needed legal support. On another level, he gave full support to the communications aspect within Mau Mau. Here he joined hands with yet another activist supporter of Mau Mau, as Kinyatti (2008:149) explains:

> Ambu Patel also played a significant role in Mau Mau movement. He collected funds for the movement and made his house in Nairobi, a safe haven for the movement. He and Pinto were involved in the production of the Mau Mau organ, *The High Command*.

Mau Mau High Command (1952-57) was the underground paper of Mau Mau. Durrani (2006:217-218) provides further information:

> The liberation forces took various steps to overcome the colonial-imposed embargo on free flow of information. These steps included the use of an oral medium to exchange information with its armed forces and progressive people; the establishment of their own presses which printed Mau Mau newspapers; and issuing of handbills and posters which were circulated widely throughout the country. The success of these steps depended on a wide distribution network, which was duly created by the High Command. Such measures overcame the communications embargo imposed by the colonial forces

> The main newspaper established by the liberation forces was appropriately called the *Mau Mau High Command*, published between 1952 and 1957. This was initially printed by South Asian Kenyans in Nairobi. Later, the Mau Mau established new printing facilities at their Mathare Headquarters in Nairobi. The *Mau Mau High Command* was anti-imperialist in content. It was an underground paper circulating among 35,000 freedom fighters Articles were signed by responsible leaders and communicated within the liberated areas and in

Pio Gama Pinto, Kenya's Unsung Martyr

semi-liberated and enemy controlled areas (to selected units in the latter two).

During the active war years of 1952-57, it was important for the people to know the real activities of Mau Mau. The paper carried information about colonial atrocities and explained the Mau Mau stand, as a lot of killings and destruction of peasant property were done by home guards and blamed on the Mau Mau. The Mau Mau position was to oppose colonial authorities and collaborators who worked with colonial administration, not random destruction of lives and property. The truth of these atrocities had to be communicated. Ambu Patel recalled writing various articles encouraging people and Kenyan armed forces to continue the struggle, as well as articles explaining the nature of imperialism. [26]

Whether Pinto had taken a Mau Mau oath or not, whether he can be called a Mau Mau by those more interested in shadows than substance, the above facts are undeniable. And they show clearly that Pinto was part of the Mau Mau movement. If Kenyan history does not record or acknowledge this fact, then it is the history and those who write history who can be considered responsible for misinterpreting history.

Pinto had a clear understanding of the conditions that gave rise to the growth of Mau Mau as an underground movement. He explains this in his letter dated April 8, 1952 to Fenner Brockway (Pinto, P.G. 1952a).

I believe it is generally recognised that secret societies flourish, often at the expense of legal political institutions, when the conditions are such that it is impossible to function in public without incurring the wrath of the authorities. This is apparently what is happening in certain parts of Kenya. The Government in its efforts to eradicate secret societies is indirectly creating conditions which are conducive to their growth. This is affected by denying the

26   Oral source: Nazmi Durrani, based on information supplied by Ambu Patel.

people in the Reserves civil liberties or the right to express their grievances at public meetings, with the result that the people at large are compelled to resort to secret societies which lend themeless admirably to extremism. If the Government can go to the extent of forbidding a meeting of the Congress and the Kenya African Union in Nairobi without assigning any reason, one can imagine the policy which is being pursued in the Reserves and areas occupied by squatters. It would be interesting to note that the Mau Mau has for a long time been active in the Naivasha district, an area located in the White Highlands, where the greatest reluctance will be exercised in granting permission to hold meetings, etc.

You may think it advisable to draw the attention of the public or the Authorities to the above. It may be pointed out that the existence of Secret Societies in a particular district should not constitute an excuse for the Police to ban meetings etc. On the contrary, if the Government is anxious to do away with Secret Societies, its objective can only be attained by giving all possible encouragement to legal political institutions like the K.A.U. and by ensuring that the people are given the maximum opportunity to give vent to their feelings.

In Malaya the Government has at last come to the realisation that it cannot achieve success in its efforts to stamp out Communism (which has to adopt the tactics of secret societies) without affecting political reforms and encouraging nationalist forces. I wonder whether you consider it advisable to draw the attention of the Government to the similarities in the situation. It would, of course, be impossible to get the Settler-dominated government in this country to look at it from that angle.

Pinto was very astute in his analysis of the situation regarding the treatment of the Mau Mau issue by the colonial government. He saw the government using the Mau Mau resistance as an opportunity to bring in excessively repressive measures against whole populations through its villagisation and other programmes. In his letter (Pinto, P. G. 1952b, 08-04-1952) Pinto says

> Since the last two months or so, the Government has banned meetings and public demonstrations in the Nyeri and Fort Hall districts. Among the reasons given are the disturbances which followed the refusal of cattle—owners to have their cattle inoculated, and reports of widespread arson for which the Mau Mau is held responsible. The Mau Mau, as you are probably aware, is a secret organisation which has been proscribed. The East African Standard has been writing editorials advocating strong measures against the Mau Mau. As the Standard is regarded as the semi-official organ of the Government, we can expect the forces of "law and order" to take their clue from the public indignation expressed through the Standard to launch a movement in which they will not be very discriminating in distinguishing the Mau Mau from the K.A.U. In fact, as is evident from the report of the trials, a move is afoot to involve the K.A.U. so that there can be an excuse to either ban it altogether in a particular area, or to make it impossible to function actively by imposing all sorts of restrictions necessary for holding meetings.

Involvement in trade union and Mau Mau activities were the principal aspects which define Pinto and make him the outstanding warrior that he was. He did not give up the struggle for trade union militancy after independence. He actively supported Dennis Akumu to form the Kenya Federation of Progressive Trade Unions in 1984 and arranged for it to be affiliated to the Ghana-based All African Trade Unions Federation. This move clearly challenged the neo-colonial trap of setting up trade union organisations friendly to Western corporations and powers.

Politics, Ideology and Organisation

Murumbi (2015:214) gets to the crux of Pinto's work and approach in response to the question of what motivated Pio to help and honour the people. He responded:

> It was really his principles. As I said in my appreciation of Pio, "Politically his views were beyond many of us in his depth of political understanding and social consciousness. To him socialism meant its true application". Pinto lived his socialism. He lived by his principles, and he died by his principles. He was quick to react to any injustice, and he spent long hours helping other people, but he never helped himself.

Pinto was under no illusions about the difficulties of defeating colonialism and imperialism which had global resources to overpower struggles for independence and for socialism among colonies and among newly independent nations. But Pinto had also witnessed people's victories in Goa and India and learnt through his contacts and study the reality of how people have managed to organise and win against vastly superior forces in other countries and regions. Three weapons were essential in their struggle. First was an ideology that would be in the interest of the majority of people and aimed at equality and justice for the majority of people. Secondly, a strong organisation was necessary to mobilise the people and to ensure that the ideology was put into practice. Finally, an equally essential requirement was a committed leadership. The resistance of people against colonialism and imperialism could win if these three weapons were available to the liberation forces.

The ideological aspect was clear to Pinto. He made this clear in action and writings, for example, he said (Pinto, P.G. 1963b):

> The sacrifices of the hundreds of thousands of Kenya's freedom fighters must be honoured by the effective implementation of the policy - a democratic, African, socialist state in which the people have the right to be free from economic exploitation

and the right to social equality. Kenya's uhuru must not be transformed into freedom to exploit, or freedom to be hungry and live in ignorance. Uhuru must be uhuru for the masses - uhuru from exploitation, from ignorance, disease and poverty.

Pinto worked behind the scenes in every organisation he was involved in so as to strengthen its structures and to make it more efficient and effective. Sidenberg (1983:117) recalls Ambu H. Patel's assessment on Pinto:

> By March 1952, Pinto had become a driving force in KAU politics, and he was to remain active in that body until his arrest in June 1954.

However, Pinto was aware of the weaknesses in the Kenya Indian Congress, KAU and KANU both before and after independence and he worked tirelessly to strengthen each one of them. For example, he was keen to ensure that KAU became strong through its organisational structures and sought the support of Fenner Brockway to make this possible. His letter to Brockway (Pinto, P.G., 1952 a, b) makes this clear

> Although you may not be aware of it, the organisation of the Kenya African Union is very poor. It can, no doubt, call mammoth meetings whenever it pleases, but this is to a large extent a reflection of the dissatisfaction and social unrest that prevails among the people, and it would not be unexpected if another political organisation, if it existed, would not achieve similar results. The day to day organisation of the KAU leaves very much to be desired. The village, location or district branches function in a very haphazard manner. This is not due to the fact that the people are averse to such organisations, but due to lack of attention and interest which has hitherto existed among some of the leaders in their approach to this problem. If the K.A.U. could be modelled somewhat on the lines of the Convention of Peoples Party in the Gold Coast, or

the Indian National Congress of India, possessing a mass membership, it would be in a position to exercise a very good influence on the Kenya Government. Given proper encouragement I am sure that it will not be difficult to organise the K.A.U. on a proper basis.

I know that you possess a lot of influence over leaders of the K.A.U. I have had many talks with officers of the K.A.U. and they all feel the need of proper organisation. I feel that if you impress upon those with whom you are in contact of the absolute importance of organisation, things will take a turn for the better. You could make them realise that without proper organisation, they would only be inviting more trouble from Govt. because it is evident that the Kenya Govt. only respects strength. The problem of organisation could be given first priority.

You can expect me to do my best on this side. If necessary I am prepared to work for the K.A.U. I am trying to get them to establish some form of liaison with African political organisations in other territories. Relations between the Congress and the K.A.U. are very satisfactory. I have no illusions about the role which many Indians will play, but at the present juncture, I feel that it is in the interest of the Africans to get as many allies as possible.

Pinto demonstrated the qualities required in leaders by his own example of how he expected leaders to behave. He lived a simple life and devoted resources, time and emotions to meeting the needs of those in need. He also acquired funds and set up the Lumumba Institute which was to train party cadres in organisational and ideological aspects so as to enhance the strength of the organisation and also to ensure that a correct method of leadership was developed.

Pinto was aware of the tactics used by colonialism and imperialism to divide and rule people in different ways. They created divisions and hostilities

Pio Gama Pinto, Kenya's Unsung Martyr

among Kenyan people, for example, on the basis of their nationalities which they called 'tribes'. This was the approach adopted by colonialism in allowing the formation of regional rather than national political parties in order to prevent united nation-wide political action. Pinto (Pinto, P. G. 1953) highlighted this colonial tactic in a letter to Fenner Brockway:

> From the cuttings and my personal talks with Mr. John Tameno, M.L.C. the most disturbing feature is the attempt on the part of the Government to create antagonisms between the Masai and the Kikuyu by encouraging the Moran to take part in raids on the Kikuyu in the Aberdares and other places. Tameno has actually toured several areas and protested to the District Commissioner, Sweetman, at Ngong against the attempts to stir up trouble. He tells me that he was responsible in getting the administration to send back Masai Moran from Loitoktok. The Masai Elders told him that they had been told by Government Officials to fight the Kikuyu, and when they refused they were warned that their sections would suffer. The Elders therefore thought it wise to advise the Moran to do what the Administration desired of them. Tameno, as you will observe from a perusal of the *Standard* reports of the proceedings of the Legislative Council, raised the matter in the Council.

It will be obvious from the above and other correspondence from Pinto that without his diligent reporting on the events in Kenya, his cuttings and his own commentaries explaining the context and significance of events, the support for the Kenyan cause in UK and India would not have been as powerful and effective as it was.

Pinto's organisational skills and awareness of colonial tactics are indicated by Nazareth (2014):

> The joint meeting of the executive committees of the Kenya African Union and the Congress was duly held at the Desai Memorial Committee Room on December 7, 1951. It was well attended. Pio Pinto had done effective work in canvassing members of the KAU

executive committee. They fully realised that the principle of "divide and rule" which Mitchell was pursuing to divide and weaken the Indian community might be applied in time, as indeed it soon was to be, to divide and weaken the Africans on a tribal basis. They came to the joint meeting convinced that on this issue of religious separate electorates they must join hands with the general body of the Indian community against the Indian Muslims and their European supporters and supporters in the Kenya Government. As president of the Congress, I proposed Kenyatta to the chair and he was unanimously elected chairman of the meeting.

Pinto's role in supporting the KAU leaders detained and charged by colonial government was exemplary. Sidenberg (1983:115) points to the achievement of Pinto and others with him in supporting the detainees:

> ...De Souza and Pinto took a house together in Parklands [with others] to facilitate organising the defence of the six detainees. Telegrams were sent by the group all over the world to secure a good team of lawyers.

It was Pinto's total grasp of organisational aspects of a liberation struggle that marked him as a remarkable politician.

The Class Activist: "Organised Violence the Only Answer"

Pinto's enemies misrepresented his political stand by de-emphasising, or removing altogether, important strands of his work. His work has been depoliticised and its clear class stand removed. He is thus shown as a person without a socialist vision, merely as a nationalist. Pinto's anti-capitalist and anti-imperialist stand does not feature in this artificial image of Pinto. This de-politicisation of Pinto is then reinforced by destroying or hiding his work and removing him from history. That his own material was destroyed by his friends after his assassination, with the best intentions, makes it even more difficult today to recreate the history of the real Pinto.

However, an assessment on his life and work by "those who knew him well and participated with him in the struggle" (Patel, Ambu, 1966) was recorded in the booklet *Pio Gama Pinto, Independent Kenya's First Martyr: Socialist and Freedom Fighter* (1966). They point to Pinto's contribution to the liberation struggle in Kenya. This booklet is reproduced in this book. However, it is a matter of concern that the person who initiated this tribute to Pinto and who published it, Ambu Patel, himself remains marginalised in Kenya's history just as Pinto has been. His achievements remain hidden from public view.[27]

Perhaps one way to understand Pinto's stand is to examine his writings which have survived. While not much material is in the public domain, an important document is still available. This is his article entitled, "Glimpses of Kenya's Nationalist Struggle" (Pinto, P. G. 1963b) published in the Kenya Uhuru Souvenir issue of *Pan Africa* dated December 12, 1963, Kenya's Independence Day. This has recently been reprinted as a booklet and is also reproduced in this book. While this article provides a useful insight into Pinto's thinking, it should be remembered that the document was written at the time of independence and Pinto, while fully aware of the contradictions in Kenya, would not have wanted to expose in public the two-line struggle taking place within Kanu and the Government. In this sense, this document has its own limitations in revealing the complex character of Pinto. However, this shortcoming can be mitigated to some extent by listening to what others working with him have said about him.

In the article, Pinto provides a glimpse not only of Kenya's anti-imperialist struggles, but also an insight into his own remarkable grasp of Kenya's colonial history. Although he says, "it is impossible in an article to do justice to the heroic efforts of individuals and organisations who participated in the struggle for the liquidation of colonialism," he manages to provide a progressive record and interpretation of the entire history of colonialism and resistance in Kenya from 1902 to Independence Day, December 12,

---

27 Some aspects of Ambu Patel's contribution to the liberation struggle in Kenya are recorded by Nazmi Durrani in Durrani, Nazmi, Naila Durrani, and Benegal Pereira (2017). Nairobi: Vita Books.

1963.

Pinto shows his total grasp of imperialism in the very first sentence of the article by addressing the issue of land and labour which remain important issues in Kenya to this day. He provides succinctly the essence of colonialism and imperialism and provides the background to decades of resistance by people of Kenya. Few history books on Kenya provide Kenyan history from the perspectives of working people with such clarity. It is worth taking a brief look at this document. Pinto (Pinto, P. G., 1963b) writes:

> In 1902 Commissioner Elliot declared Kenya a fit place for European settlement.
> …
> What followed has been aptly referred to as the "Great Land Grab". Adventurers and speculators displayed considerable enterprise in acquiring huge areas of land for little or nothing, and then parcelling it out to their fellow countrymen at considerable profit to themselves. The whole process was accompanied by astute jingoism with demands for "responsible government' under European hegemony alternating with demands for the introduction of laws existing in South Africa which were found eminently suitable to ensure an abundant supply of cheap labour.

Pinto then goes on to provide a brief record of events of colonial oppression and resistance by people, covering key areas such as the formation of Independent Schools, noting, "at the time of the declaration of the State of Emergency in October 1952, over 175,000 children were receiving their education at these Independent Schools, and many of the best fighters and nationalists graduated from them".

Colonialism intensified its control over Kenya and became more repressive by the time of the Second World War when, Pinto records, the foundation of a war of resistance through armed struggle was being laid:

Pio Gama Pinto, Kenya's Unsung Martyr

In May 1940, the K.C.A. [Kikuyu Central Association] was proscribed ... Twelve Kikuyu, eight Wakamba and two Taita were arrested and detained ... Africans had by now come to an understanding that non-violent, constitutional agitation had serious limitations and that new methods must be evolved to avoid the collapse in political organisation which characterised the banning of the political association and the arrest of its leaders.

This marked a significant shift on the part of Kenyan activists in the strategies to defeat colonialism in Kenya. Pinto then summarises the grievances of Kenyan people against colonialism, grievances that could only be addressed seriously through a violent struggle such as the one by the Mau Mau in which Pinto played an important part. In a brief paragraph, Pinto sums up the contradiction between colonialism and people of Kenya:

The disabilities from which Africans suffered might be listed as the wholesale alienation of their lands, highly discriminatory scales of pay in the Civil Service, the ban on the growth of cash crops, the transformation of Reserves or "Native Land Units" into reservoirs of cheap labour, the imposition of a tax structure which compelled Africans to seek work on terms and conditions dictated by their employers, an educational and economic system which discriminated in favour of the rich and powerful and against the poor, a change from a subsistence economy and shifting cultivation to a money economy and static farming without the provision or acquisition of new technologies, resulting in a considerably lower standard of living, and the disintegration of the tribal society without the benefit of new values, and the absence of any voice in the Legislature or any of the policy-making institutions.

It is interesting to note that Pinto did not want change for its own sake but wanted change to be democratic and in the interest of working people. He makes it clear that the struggle against colonialism was also an aspect of class struggle. Pinto thus shows that he was not only an astute politician, but had an understanding of sociology and economics. It is no surprise that it was not only colonialism that saw him as their enemy; the new Kenyan elite that came to power at independence and who carried on the practices of colonialism by merely replacing white settlers and colonial rulers with themselves, saw Pinto as their enemy. Nor did the new Kenyan elite address the grievances that Pinto highlighted above. Eliminating Pinto became their only option to silence this class warrior.

In the same article, Pinto then focuses on the crucial role played by the trade union movement under Chege Kibachia, Makhan Singh and Fred Kubai. He lists some key trade union actions, for example the Dockworkers Strike of 1948 led by Chege Kibachia, the 1950 Nairobi General Strike following the arrest of Fred Kubai and Makhan Singh. The key attack by colonialism was on all organisations which could lead to resistance against colonialism, whether political or trade union. It now banned the East African Trade Union Congress. The suppression of peaceful political and social organisations and movements by colonialism could lead to the only conclusion possible, as Pinto summarises here:

> It had become increasingly obvious that "constitutional," "non-violent" methods of fighting for one's rights was absolutely futile in dealing with the Settler-Colonial combination which was charged with the administration of the country. ORGANISED VIOLENCE WAS THE ONLY ANSWER TO SUCH A SITUATION.[28]

And indeed, it was organised violence that brought about Kenya's independence. The above document gives a brief glimpse of Pinto's deep understanding of Kenyan struggle and clarity with which he saw the liberation struggle.

Pinto wrote other material for the political organisations he was active in. For example, he wrote the Memorandum from the Gikuyu nationality to the Royal Commission on Land. Dr. Fitz De Souza (Pio Gama Pinto, 1966) recalls some of his writing activities, as we have noted elsewhere in this article

---

28   Capitalisation in the original.

... I know, and history will record that Pinto had a hand in the preparation of most of the memoranda and statements issued by K.A.U. (Kenya African Union) in those days. He often used to sit up to 5 a.m. in the [Indian] Congress office drafting political papers in the nationalist cause. For all this he never expected payment. His reward was in the contribution he made to the struggle. He never looked for personal credit.

Emma Gama Pinto (1972), Pio's widow, reflects on another aspect of his political writings:

My husband's views on current affairs were often published in Letters to the Editor in the *East African Standard* under a pseudonym, and which never remained the same over the years. On occasion he used his own, but in most cases, he favoured an African name. He was a prolific writer but remained the hand behind the curtain. He felt he could achieve more by not contesting in the race to jump on the bandwagon. His was a dedication to uncover the injustices perpetrated on innocent Africans who, although politically very mature, could not articulate in the lingua franca of the world, their grievances. They were men who were often hamstrung by the inability to retort rhetorically to the arguments that came thick and fast, and eventually had to resort to brute force.

In another context, Emma provides similar views (KNA):

It is sad for me to say that most of my husband's briefs on the situation in Kenya and the East African Territories (as it was then known), were destroyed immediately after his assassination. Unfortunately, in an atmosphere of suspicion, even a patriot's best intentions can be twisted and his memory nailed to a cross.

The complex nature of Pinto's personality is revealed by an examination of what others have said about him. Some material included in this book provides an insight into this extraordinary man.

Pinto the Man

Pio Gama Pinto was a totally political man. The political Pinto is so large that it dwarfs Pinto the man. It is thus easy to forget that he had a personal life that is not easy to depict so many years after his death. While many of his political colleagues have given some insight on Pinto the person, there remains a big gap in completing his real image. One way to look for the man through the political clothes that hide him is to see the impact he has had on his family members, particularly his daughters, the eldest one of whom, Linda, was just seven when Pinto was assassinated. It is not only the impression that Pinto left on his young children that is of interest, but also the values, the outlook and the principles that they take from their father's example that indicates some aspects of Pinto the man. Linda Gama Pinto's recollection (Ngunyi, 2015) of his father provides an insight:

> It is clear that my father was a man who was profoundly dedicated to fairness. At a time when many people were measured by extrinsic qualities, such as race or wealth, he saw only the intrinsic dignity of all humanity. This deep awareness of our shared dignity motivated him, I believe, to work for greater fairness in the world. Poverty and violence are great insults to human dignity and I understand that he worked towards land reforms and supported the rule of law that would alleviate those afflictions. That fairness meant that he did not seek to enrich himself or to benefit before others who were less fortunate. This commitment to fairness and dignity are in my mind a powerful legacy and challenge.

It is indeed ironic that the two principles that guided Pinto - rule of law and fairness - are the very ones that Kenya needs even more today. Lack of respect for rule of law deprived Pinto of his life as it does to hundreds of youth today who become victims of state violence and terrorism; lack of fairness among ruling classes in Kenya deprives all working people of their lives and means of survival. Pinto was needed not only in 1965, he is needed even more today as the rampant corruption and cronyism roam freely over the land that gave birth to Mau Mau. Pinto's ideas, actions, advice and commitment, if adhered to, could have avoided this unequal and unjust society created by capitalism and imperialism and driven by greed of the comprador ruling class.

Linda Gama Pinto, basing her comments on the teachings of her father, shows a rare maturity in understanding social and political reality that are needed urgently in Kenya today:

> It is important that his example be remembered. I believe people like my father, people of integrity who put the well-being of others and the nation ahead of personal ambition are tremendous role models for all of us. We need to be reminded that such behaviour has been demonstrated, not only because such behaviour is possible in all of us, but because we should expect it of those who wish to be considered leaders. The greater the fairness between citizens, the more that human dignity is respected, the richer is the nation— by all measures. - Linda Gama Pinto, quoted in Ngunyi, 2015).

That Pinto's actions, vision and commitment are being echoed in Kenya over 50 years after his death is a testimony that here was no ordinary man. His enemies struck a blow that is being felt by children born decades after his assassination. The true impact of the loss that the nation suffered from Pinto's assassination cannot be assessed only in monetary terms. It was the loss of a vision of a society that was within the grasp of Kenyans when they defeated colonialism. Pinto came to symbolise that vision of a fair, just, equal society at peace with itself. He came close to making such a society a reality. It is no surprise that his enemies, who are also enemies of the people of Kenya, decided to end his life. His death meant the death of all that is decent in life, it meant the death of all that people desire and deserve as human beings. Pinto's struggle has now become the struggle of all working people opposed to the capture of the Kenyan state by looters. The struggle goes on, guided by Pinto's ideas and ideals which cannot die.

Pinto Must Die

As you can imagine, Pio's death has greatly impacted our family and my late father's [Rosario Da Gama Pinto, Pio Gama Pinto's brother] health and wellbeing in particular - Audrey Da Gama Pinto, Personal Communications, Editor, 15-07-2018.

Gama Pinto was shot dead in Nairobi on February 24, 1965. Branch (2011:45-46) describes how Pio Gama Pinto was assassinated:

On the morning of 24 February 1965, Pinto followed his regular routine of driving his daughter, Tereshka, up and down the driveway outside the family home in Nairobi... While he waited for the gates at the bottom of the driveway to open, three men approached the car. Pausing only to greet Pinto, the men fired shots through the windscreen. Pinto died in his car.

Branch (2011:44) provides some clues as to the reasons for his assassination and about those responsible:

The first move was made against Odinga's most important supporter, Pio Gama Pinto. Pinto was, so the US embassy thought, Odinga's 'brilliant political tactician'. The British agreed. MacDonald described Pinto as 'a dedicated Communist, and the principal brain behind the whole secret organisation of Mr. Odinga's movement'. The high commissioner credited Pinto with having mobilised backbench opposition in parliament to Kenyatta and with leading 'other anti-Government movements'. But Pinto was more than that. He was an important figure in his own right.

The crucial point regarding Pinto was that his vision went beyond the achievement of political independence. He wanted revolutionary changes in economic and social relations so that historic imbalances imposed by colonialism and reinforced by imperialism were addressed. Nowrojee (2007:53-54) explains his stand:

"Soon after Independence, the Government began moving away

from those ideals. It did not honour the freedom fighters and did not look after their families. It forgot its duty to ensure social justice.

Prominent individuals grabbed public land for themselves, while many of those who had suffered in the struggle for freedom did not have enough to live on.... Emma [Gama Pinto] remembers that "Pio was torn with concern for the needs of the man-on-the-street".

Pinto's concern for the man-on-the-street was what defined him, and it had been his lifelong belief and commitment to ensure their wellbeing. He realised that this concern was not in favour with the ruling classes or their imperialist backers. Nowrojee (2007:54) shows Pinto's awareness of the danger of replacing one set of (White) elite rulers with another, black this time, without any fundamental change to the system of inequality and injustice:

Pio had foreseen that this might happen. Even before Uhuru he had said to one of his close friends in Parliament the following poignant words: "If, when we get independence, we only have black Lord Delameres instead of white Lord Delameres, we will have achieved very little". Pio did not want our freedom to mean simply transferring unfair land ownership, wealth and privilege from British people to a few prominent Kenyans, while the majority of the people were neglected.

Thursday, February 25, 1965   5

Mombasa shocked at killing

By NATION Reporter

MANY people in Mombasa were "completely shattered and shocked on hearing that Mr. Pio Pinto had been assassinated in Nairobi — for only a few days ago he was accompanying Kenya's Vice-President, Mr. Oginga Odinga, on an official visit to the Coast.

While in Mombasa he stayed with a long-standing friend, Mr. Inamdar, who said yesterday: "The assassin's bullet has robbed Kenya of a very great patriot and nationalist, and I have lost a close personal friend."

Mombasa's Deputy Mayor, Councillor Dr. S. S. Dhillon, said: "I am shocked. In his death Kenya has lost one of the staunchest nationalists and a youngster who would have rendered useful service to the country."

Councillor Mr. B. T. Parkar said: "Pinto's tragic death is a definite loss, not only to the Asian community, but to Kenya as a whole."

The general secretary of the Mombasa Dockworkers' Union, Mr. Denis Akumu, said: "We have lost a sincere, dedicated and militant fighter for the rights of the oppressed. It is only a few days since union officials met him to exchange views.

"I condemn the cold-blooded murder of Pinto, who was a dedicated nationalist. He suffered detention for nearly ten years and was highly respected by all true nationalists."

The union has sent condolences to his wife and children.

DAILY NATION

No. 1367 Thursday, February 25, 1965 30 Cents

M.P. SHOT DEAD

Massive manhunt follows city assassination

By MICHAEL CHESTER and WARREN McMAHON

KENYA POLICE yesterday mounted a massive manhunt for three gunmen who ambushed and murdered Mr. Pio da Gama Pinto, a Member of the Kenya House of Representatives, as he was driving away from his suburban home at Westlands, outside Nairobi.

Mr. Pinto was shot dead in full view of his year-old youngest child, Tereza, whom he was letting out of the car in the drive of their bungalow home.

The killing shocked the whole of Kenya. President Kenyatta lamented in tribute that the death had roused the Republic the loss of "one of the construction workers for freedom who suffered many years in detention for his uncompromising stand in politics."

The President promised that the Government "will exert every effort to hunt down and bring to justice the perpetrators of this outrage."

Both the Senate and the House of Representatives, stunned by news of the killing, adjourned in mourning yesterday afternoon.

'Deliberate, cowardly'

Mr. Achieng Oneko, Minister for Information, Broadcasting and Tourism, called the murder "deliberate and cowardly move in what I believe to be a planned assassination."

Underscoring the widespread suspicion of a political murder, Mr. Oneko added: "Any attempt to introduce gangsterism into Kenya politics must be dampened in the strongest possible terms."

Mr. Joseph Murumbi, Minister for External Affairs, and Dr. Njoroge Mungai, Minister for Internal Security and Defence, were among the many Cabinet Ministers and MP's who called at the Pinto home with condolences to the widow and three children of the slain MP.

Mr. Pinto, who served several years in detention during the Emergency years in Kenya, was an outspoken critic of colonialism and a staunch supporter of liberation movements elsewhere in Africa.

He was the only non-African to suffer detention.

His close friendship with President Kenyatta.

TURN TO BACK PAGE

With Mzee Kenyatta at Maralal in 1961 shortly before the restriction order on the former was lifted. Mr. Pinto was a member of a deputation from the East African Osmn League which called on him.

SHOCKING CRIME, SAYS PRESIDENT

THE President, Mzee Jomo Kenyatta, said in a statement yesterday that he had been deeply grieved to learn of the death by assassination of Mr. Pinto.

"By his death our country has lost one of the conscientious workers for freedom who suffered many years in detention for his uncompromising stand in politics," he said.

"This is a shocking crime, which by its nature must plunge the country into sadness.

"I wish now only to state that the Government will exert every effort to hunt down and bring to justice the perpetrators of this outrage."

Mr. H. D. Waritihi, chairman of the Parliamentary Group of the National Assembly, and members of Parliament who had worked closely with Mr. Pinto "are most appalled by this cowardly act of gangsterism."

He added: "The ghastly murder of Mr. Pinto must shock all the people of Kenya. His death removes from our midst a devoted, dedicated and faithful worker for Kenya. It will be recalled Mr. Pinto was one of the nationalists personified by the imperialists because of his beliefs and his activities during the nationalist struggle.

"His untimely death has robbed Kenya of a great fighter and servant."

INQUIRY

He added: "This is a murder which cannot be left surrounded with mystery or without public inquiry and explanation through the process of law."

MPs demanding that no effort be spared by the police in their effort to investigate the crime, and they called for public co-operation to bring the culprit to justice.

The Minister for Information, Broadcasting and Tourism, Mr. Achieng Oneko, said:

"The untimely death of

TURN TO BACK PAGE

8. *"MP Shot Dead" Daily Nation (25-02-1965)*

It was such views and actions on the part of Pinto that led to his assassination by those who benefited from the transfer of national wealth to themselves and who saw Pinto as a threat to their power and wealth. De Souza (2014:401) sums up Pinto's life and the reason for his assassination:

> He worked with the Kenya African Union. He was incarcerated for a long time… as his loyalties were entirely with the Africans, and he suffered a great deal. Eventually he got out of jail and he stood for MP and won. He had a falling out with the Powers that Be and he got into a shouting match with Kenyatta over what he perceived as land grabbing by those in power. He refused to participate in such things as he was all for equality. He was a very good man. He did not consider himself a Muhindi or an Arab, he considered himself an African.

The land grabbing by the successive KANU regimes of Kenyatta and Moi has been confirmed in recently available documents of the last Colonial Governor of Kenya, Malcolm MacDonald and those of the former Vice President of Kenya, Joseph Murumbi. Ng'otho (2008), using material from from both sources, reveals the conspiracy which resulted in the new ruling class stealing peasant land:

> Fresh evidence pieced together by the *Sunday Nation* confirms widespread speculation that Kenya's first president Jomo Kenyatta entered a secret pact with the British government not to interfere with the skewed land distribution at independence.
>
> In return, the British would clear his way as independent Kenya's first leader which looked impossible only three years to freedom. Kenyatta would later extract a similar pledge from his successor, retired President Daniel arap Moi.

Pinto's opposition to Kenyatta was thus based on the reality of imperialist imposition of the Kenyatta regime in return for favourable land deals for the White settlers. This was again confirmed by Joseph Murumbi, as Ng'otho (2008) confirms:

Pio Gama Pinto, Kenya's Unsung Martyr

[In] another entry in Murumbi notes just before he resigned as vice president in 1966 he expresses disappointment that President Kenyatta "had no political will to direct the Settler Transfer Fund (STF) to benefit millions of landless Africans as had been stated in the Kanu manifesto at independence".

Instead, Murumbi noted, the STF scheme "had been hijacked by few African elites who were loaning themselves money meant for the landless and acquiring huge tracts of land at the expense of the majority poor".

Pinto had fought for the rights of Kenyan people all his life. The right to land was among the primary rights he wanted to see established in Kenya. His opposition to imperialism and their imposed neo-colonial government in Kenya was a principled one to see equality and justice in practice. But he stood in the way of the powerful enemies, both internal and external, who opposed him at every step. In the end, he gave his life fighting to achieve his vision of justice and equality under socialism.

The contradictions between progressive and reactionary forces - the radicals and conservatives - had been going on for a long time before Pinto's assassination, encouraged as it was by colonialism as part of its divide and rule policy. As far as can be established, it was only in the case of Pio Gama Pinto that the reactionary forces resorted to assassination. And the timing of his assassination is also significant. It is not possible at present to determine the full extent to which UK and USA were involved in the decision to attack the progressives by eliminating their "ideas and action" person, Pio Gama Pinto. Given the extent to which these external parties were involved in Kenyan politics, it would be surprising if they did not know about it, let alone initiating it. The reason for the attack on Pinto is hinted at by the Truth Justice and Reconciliation Commission of Kenya (TJRC, 2013), as mentioned previously. To recap: the Kenyatta government presents a Sensational Paper No. 10 of 1965 charting a capitalist path: Pinto prepare an alternative socialist policy paper on behalf of the radicals led by Oginga Odinga; Pinto tragically assasinated before the task could be completed.

What was at stake here was not a mere policy document. Fundamental issues about the future direction of the country, its government, its policies on land and its position on corruption and looting national resources were all involved. Pinto's involvement with the radical trade union movement was yet another reason his enemies wanted him eliminated. At the same time, Pinto's "competing paper" was very likely to be passed in the Parliament and thus force the Kenyatta government to resign, opening the way for the radical group to form a government. The ruling class certainly found the prospect of such developments extremely alarming, as did their backers among the imperialist camps. As the TJRC, Vol. IIA, 2013) says:

> The Pinto assassination demonstrates all of the complexities and tragedy of political assassinations in post-independence Kenya. Its context included: a global cold war that was mirrored in domestic political debates; a domestic struggle to consolidate power and narrow dissent; and a resort to violence to address political differences. (p.436).

And again:

> It was during the heat of these early debates about the direction of Kenyan economic and political policy that Pinto was assassinated. (p. 437).

The relevance of Pinto's trade union link is mentioned in a *Daily Nation* report dated 18-06-2000 by Kamau Ngotho as reported by TJRC, Vol. IIA (p.439) which also records the refusal by the Government to release key documents for reasons that can only be subject of speculation about government involvement in Pinto's assassination:

> The Daily Nation asserts that Kisilu in fact did not kill Pinto but was instead set up by the Directorate of Security Intelligence. According to the Daily Nation, the plan to assassinate Pinto began three years earlier. A memo by the Kenya Intelligence Committee dated 13 December 1962 had labelled Pinto as a "man to be watched very

closely." By 1965, Kenyatta felt threatened by Pinto's strong trade union base. Pinto's positioning as a substantial threat to the existing Government ultimately led to his elimination. The subsequent cover up, according to the Daily Nation, included keeping Kisilu behind bars against numerous recommendations by the Prisons Review Board for fear of the dossier that he might spill on the Pinto murder. The Commission was unable to verify or disprove the allegations made in the Daily Nation report. Indeed, although the Commission heard testimony on the assassination of Pinto, it was unable to discover any additional evidence that would shed light on any of the theories concerning Pinto's death. As noted elsewhere in this Report, the Commission was not allowed access to many of the documents held by the Government that would have assisted in investigations such as this, including the archives of the National Security Intelligence Service.

Another key issue that Pinto and those around him challenged is that related to land ownership. The radical group saw the danger of the former loyalists taking over land from the White settlers, depriving peasants of the land for which they had fought in the war of independence. That was a key demand of Mau Mau activists but here was a minority taking over where colonialism left off. Ngunyi (2015) looks at the land issue:

> But a group associated with Pinto and whose *de facto* leader was Vice President Jaramogi Odinga Odinga was opposed to the move. They were angry that after taking over power from the British, the independent government continued to entrench British and American interests in the country at the expense of Kenyan citizens...[The] Pinto group was especially concerned about land ownership and distribution in the country. They demanded that the government put a ceiling on how much land an individual could own as well as effect an affirmative action to ensure that every Kenyan had some form of ownership for sustenance and production.

This was going too far as far as the inheritors of the colonial legacy on land were concerned. Kenyatta and those around him had already acquired vast tracts of land and were busy gobbling up other resources in the name of Africanisation and independence. They would not have minded much if Pinto and others just made demands for land and equality. But the group moved beyond just talking and planned action to seize the initiative and power to bring about change, as Ngunyi (2015) narrates:

> ...it was agreed that on the day the government was to introduce the sessional paper [Sessional Paper No. 10 on African Socialism], Odinga would also introduce a counter version of African socialism that had been drafted by Pinto and Okello-Odingo and which was radically different from that of the government.

So here was an alternative programme from the capitalist one favoured by imperialism and their supporters. There was a real possibility that the alternate version would have been passed in the parliament as the radical group had support from 98 of the 158 Members of Parliament (MPs). Here was proof that the country and their MPs were not in favour of the capitalist road imposed by Kenyatta and his gang. The defeat of the government on this vital issue would have led to a vote of no confidence in the government. The situation was desperate for the government - and the imperialist backers. There was every possibility that Kenya would slip out of the capitalist and imperialist prison to chart out a new, truly independent path which could affect not only Kenya, but the rest of the colonial and post-colonial world. Just as Mau Mau had a global impact on colonialism, this development would have had a similar impact on neo-colonialism. Imperialism and the government they had facilitated into power in Kenya could not allow that. They picked on the key architect of the move - Pio Gama Pinto - for elimination and as events were to prove, his assassination put an end to the introduction of the alternative programme in the Parliament. The complicity of the Kenya Government in the assassination of Pinto is no longer a matter of speculation. It was confirmed by the Truth, Justice and Reconciliation Commission (2013) after careful scrutiny of facts and events:

The Commission gathered information, undertook research and investigations, and solicited testimony to understand the context in which such killings took place; the circumstances and thus probable causes of such killings; the impact of such killings, particularly on the family and friends of the victim; and the failure of investigations to solve the mystery of why a person was killed and who was responsible. The Commission's work in relation to political assassinations confirms that the state was complicit in the assassination of Pio Gama Pinto, Tom Mboya, Josiah Mwangi Kariuki, and Robert Ouko.

The Commission is also precise in using the term "assassination" which it defines in the following terms:

Political assassinations are a special type of killing defined by both the nature of the victim and the motive of the perpetrators. While legal authorities differ over what constitutes a political assassination, we adopt here those elements that are common to most definitions: (a) The killing; (b) of an individual with leadership or other symbolic importance (c) For the purpose of sending a strong political message... Assassinations are intentional killings...Assassinations... target a specific individual whose death, because of his or her status, will have a significant political impact.

This confirms that the government saw Pinto as a leader with "symbolic importance" and that his assassination, besides scuppering the policies and activities he was involved in, was intended as a "strong political message" to the others working with him on an alternative approach to Kenya's future. It is a matter of speculation why it was Pinto who was targeted and not any of the others. There can be various explanations for this. He was the one with the clearest ideological understanding of the issues involved, was articulate in translating his ideas into policies and practice, had national and international standing which gave him extra confidence in the path he took, he was also part of the Mau Mau movement and thus carried on its policies and experiences into action. At the same time, it may be inferred that his assassination would not arouse as much resentment and opposition from his own nationality or ethnic group as he was from a minority ethnic group and thus did not have massive support that others from other nationalities may have had. It is also instructive to see that the TJRC (2013) recognised that the perpetrators of the assassination realised that so serious was the step they had taken, and the events could get out of hand that they used divisive tactics to cover their tracks to divert public attention from facts, indicating that this was a well-planned and executed programme:

> The Commission found that the assassination of Pio Gama Pinto was motivated by ideological differences that were at the heart of the global Cold War but also mirrored in domestic Kenyan politics. The Commission further found that the arrest and prosecution of Kisilu, Chege Thuo, and a third unidentified man who disappeared, was used to divert attention away from the true motive and the more responsible perpetrators of Pinto's assassination.

That those behind the assassination in the Government of Kenya was able to go unpunished for the assassination of Pio Gama Pinto, has had long term impact in Kenya. The assassination became a test case for the ruling class in how to bypass the rule of law and resort to the elimination of those who disagreed with their policies. The day that Pinto was assassinated was the day that any prospect of justice, rule of law, democracy also died.

The Kenyatta government faced increasing challenges in the first years of independence in spite of all the measures outlined above. As the situation began to get critical, it became clear to the Kenyatta government and its Western backers that Pinto was at the centre of every challenge facing the government. Pinto did not have the power of a government, but his activism gave him political power way beyond a governmental one: he had influence on public opinion via his press activities; his trade union activities linked him to key people and policy fora in trade union matters; the Lumumba Institute gave him the power over learning and teaching curricula and training future civil servants and leaders; in Parliament, he set up the powerful Backbenchers' Committee which had considerable influence; his support for many KANU candidates in the elections had given him wider support from many politicians. Pinto was popular among Mau Mau activists for whom he had acquired arms, funds, medical care as well support for their families. In essence, he had power over all the three pillars of resistance that ensured independence for Kenya: Mau Mau, trade unions, and people.[29] There was no way that the Kenyatta Government could silence him or reduce his influence as he had a dynamic profile which would have to be attacked at all the levels that Pinto was active in.

An important development that exposed further the rift between Pinto and the Kenya government was the opposition from the radical wing in KANU to the introduction of the Sessional Paper No. 10 on African Socialism. As mentione earlier, Pinto was to draft an opposition socialist-orientated position to challenge the Sessional Paper in Parliament. It has also been stated how, given the wide support that the radical wing of KANU had in Parliament, it was very likely that the Kenyatta Government would be defeated, leading to fresh elections which could easily have been won by Odinga and his radical supporters. This was a formidable situation which would have threatened Kenyatta. As Pinto was a key player behind this move, he became target number one for those who supported the Sessional Paper which in effect would have entrenched capitalism in Kenya.

Another arena that increased the conflict between opposing forces of socialist-oriented and conservative-oriented groups was the creeping government corruption and marginalisation of those who fought for independence. The persistent campaigns by Pinto and others to expose and stop corruption at the highest levels the Government hightened this conflict. A key event was the information that Pinto received from Cairo that the British Government had given £12m to Kenya for the support of freedom fighters and those returning from detention. The money reached the Kenya government, but it went no further. Pinto saw a gross betrayal of the aims of the struggle. He had a clear vision of what should happen after independence, and saw the government taking the opposite route.

---

29 These three pillars are examined in the Kenya Resists Series from Vita Books.

Nowrojee (2007) comments on Pinto's position:

> Pinto believed that with the achievement of independence, the government had the opportunity to bring about great improvements in the lives of millions of Kenyans. His actions were based on the belief that we should not forget the history of our struggle for freedom and that we should always remember and honour those who had fought so hard for *uhuru* and suffered on our behalf. These men and women had been ready to lay down their lives so that Kenya could one day be free. They should never be forgotten.

Yet the ruling class has ensured that they have been forgotten on a massive scale.

It was broad daylight. The sun was shining innocently.
Pio Pinto was taking his little daughter for a drive
in the car. Suddenly some men stepped out of the bushes.
They fired. Pio Pinto, a man dedicated to the African
        cause, slumped at the wheel. It was a human tragedy,
an outrage to all Kenya and a terrible precedent.
When the sound of the last shot faded into the stillness
of the suburbs Africa had another martyr.

DRUM MAY 1965

ON a Wednesday morning last February, a young man drove his wife to work and then hurried home for a quick breakfast and a few minutes play with his three small daughters.

For Tereshka, aged 18 months, her father had a special treat, and one he did not often have time to give her . . . a drive in his car from the front door to the gateway of their home. The little ritual cost Pio Gama Pinto, one of Kenya's greatest freedom fighters, his life. For as he stopped the car to let Tereshka out, a man stepped out of the bushes near the front gate and a second man approached him from the right of the driveway.

While the little girl crouched in wide-eyed terror in the back seat, Pinto was riddled with bullets from the guns of assassins.

Winding down
car window

It seems likely that he knew one of the men who killed him. He was trying to wind down the window of the car when the killers shot through it. One thing is certain. Pio Gama Pinto was a man whose activities in Parliament, the Pan-Africa Press, the Lumumba Institute and KANU had made him a stranger to routine. The killers who struck him down must have been determined—even desperate—to have risked assassinating him in broad daylight, in a busy thoroughfare.

It is thought they even followed him as he drove his wife Emma to her office—she is personal secretary to the Minister for Information—and back again, seeking any opportunity to kill.

While police, called to the scene of the murder by horrified neighbours operated the biggest man-hunt in Kenya's history, the great men of the land mourned one they looked on as a brother.

A grief-filled statement from the President was followed by countless tributes from ministers, members of Parliament and nationalist leaders. When Pinto became a specially elected member of Parliament in July last year, many people protested at the presence of another non-African in Parliament. It is to his credit that he never once answered his critics. He could have told them that he spent years in detention with their leaders—and in fact was arrested only four days after his wedding in 1954. 5 months

From his earliest years he was a rebel. Born in Kenya in 1927, and educated in southern India, he studied journalism there and spent 18 months in the Indian Air Force. It is said that he helped organise the Indian naval mutiny

in 1946, and he is known to have been a founder member of the Goan National Congress which was formed in India to fight Portuguese Imperialism.

From India he went to Goa, where his activities against the Portuguese resulted in his nearly being arrested. Escaping in the nick of time, young Pinto came back to Kenya and started work on the progressive Daily Chronicle.

Early in the fifties, Pinto met and courted the girl whom he married in 1954—Emma. At the same time he was an active member of the Indian National Congress which campaigned against racial segregation.

During those early days of the struggle, he met and influenced many men who today recall, like External Affairs Minister Joseph Murumbi ". . . it was through Pinto that I became interested in politics . . . if ever the country and the party had a friend, it was Pio."

They riddled this car window with bullets when they killed Pinto.

5 Months

Four days after his wedding, Pinto was arrested. Although he was never charged in court, the Executive Officer of the Advisory Committee on Detainees gave several reasons for his detention. Among them were that Pinto assisted in Mau Mau subversion, possessd knowledge of illegal fire-arms traffic and concealed a terrorist.

Pinto himself claimed that he had been active with the Indian High Commissioner in negotiating between the Mau Mau and the Kenya Government, but that the latter had suddenly abandoned the negotiation and arrested him.

For over three years Pinto was imprisoned in a Mau Mau detainee camp at Hola Hola, alongside African leaders such as Muinga Chokwe—one of the nati

9. *"It was broad daylight" Drum magazine reports on Pinto's assassination (May 1965)*

Some Questions Asked by Special Branch in Nairobi.

INTERROGATOR - FREDRICK MULANGU

1. What is your name, nationality, age. Give details, of your employment, businesses, sources of income; how much do you earn? How much have you studied. What property do you own? A house? how many cars? Are you hard up financially? Why are you not doing business? Are you married? What does your wife do? How many children do you have? How old are they? Do they go to school?
Are you a Kenya citizen by birth? Where are your parents? How many brothers and sisters do you have? Where are they? What work do they do?

2. We have called you here (at the Special Branch, 24th floor, Nyayo House, Nairobi) because of the article you wrote in "the Standard" of 17 & 18th September 1984 on Pio Gama Pinto. Are you the one who wrote the article? Why did you write on Pinto? Are you a historian? Even historians at the University do not write about him. Then why are you writing about him? Is somebody paying you to write it? We want to know who are the groups who are making you write the article. You cannot hide it from us. Your answer, that you were doing research on publishing, is not satisfactory. You had better reveal the "real" reasons why you wrote the article. We have our own ways of getting the "truth" from you. You will get into more trouble than you already are if you do not tell us everything. Who are these people asking you to write?

3. Why are you not writing about Kenyatta? You do not

Pio Gama Pinto, Kenya's Unsung Martyr

believe that he contributed anything to getting independence, do you? Why is it that you wrote about Pinto and Kimathi? Do you not know that Pinto's was a political murder? So then why write about him? What you have written touches on the security of the state. Very high people in government have been affected by your article and they are very concerned. They want to know why you wrote the article.

4. Where did you get the facts for writing the articles? Who gave these to you. Can you assure me (asks the interrogator: a Mr. Fredrick Mukangu) that every word you have written is taken from books and that are not your views. Can you bring the references from where you took the facts. Point these out paragraph by paragraph. Where did you get the photographs that were published in the article on Pio Gama Pinto in "the Standard".

5. Which lecturers do you know at the University? at the Main Campus and at Kabete Campus? Write down their names. Which library staff do you know? Write down their names. Do you know Oginga Odinga? Do you have any connections with him? Do you know Ngugi wa Thiongo?

6. What is your ideology? Do you think the present Government is "delivering the goods"? Who is a peasant? and a worker? If a person is not a peasant or a worker, what is he? let us look at the definitions of 'worker' and 'peasant' in the dictionary. Am I (the interrogator: Frederick Mukangu) a worker?

10. Shiraz Durrani: Some questions asked by the Special Branch (October 1984)

This is where a deep gulf had formed between those who worked with Pinto like Oginga Odinga, Achieng' Oneko, Bildad Kaggia, and J. D. Kali, among others and those who worked with the Kenyatta government which used state power to force through policies which favoured the elite at the expense of the "millions of Kenyans".

The particular event that escalated the conflict between Pinto and Kenyatta, as stated previously, was related to the money given by Britain for freedom fighters and detainees which was given to Kenyatta. It never reached those it was intended for. It was this serious matter of corruption - with the land issue as the primary one - that Pinto was very unhappy about. The contradiction between him and Kenyatta sharpened, revealing its true essence as socialist and capitalist paths. Pinto stood his ground on these differences with the Kenyatta government. Nowrojee (2007:56) provides the background to this:

> ... After independence, money had been sent from abroad to assist the freedom fighters and detainees...This money was received by the Government, but it was not distributed to these ex-freedom fighters and ex-detainees for whom it was intended. Instead a few powerful persons pocketed it. Pio vehemently opposed this. He spoke out against these betrayals of the freedom struggle. He said he would raise the matter in Parliament to ensure that the sums be paid over to the ex-freedom fighters and ex-detainees. The powerful persons saw such an exposure as a threat to their wealth and their positions. They decided to get rid of Pio.

The money referred to here was "grants and loans for development, land settlement, compensation for overseas officers and administration (£12,400,000)" from Britain.[30] The Kenyan newspapers did not print news about the gift from Britain to Kenya. Pinto's threat to raise this matter in the Parliament appears to have been straw that led to finishing the plan to assassinate Pinto. While De Souza (2015:401) sees the land issue as the aspect that got him into trouble, it is likely to be a combination of issues that was to lead to his assassination:

> He had a falling out with the Powers that Be and he got

---

30   *The Times* (London). 04-07-1964.

into a shouting match with [Jomo] Kenyatta over what he perceived as land grabbing by those in power. He refused to participate in such things as he was all for equality.

Nazareth (2016) comments: 'Prominent politicians' and the 'powers that be' is the euphemism used to camouflage Pinto's killers. He quotes Rosario de Gama Pinto:

Pio was often threatened and even a month before his death was aware of the plot to kill him by prominent politicians. Although upset about the plot, he carried on as normal until his assassination.

Bildad Kaggia (Kaggia, W. de Leeuw and M Kaggia, 2012:262) recalls the betrayal of Pinto that seems to have contributed to his death:

Pinto was one of my best friends. Shortly before he was killed he had confided in me that he had gathered information about money from foreign countries that had been meant for the freedom fighters and had been used by [Jomo] Kenyatta. This information was extremely damaging to the President and he was sure it would cause outrage if he would raise it in Parliament. Pinto also shared this information with a few other Kikuyu friends and one of them betrayed him. Shortly afterwards Pinto was killed.

Sensing the danger that Pinto was in, Odinga, Murumbi and Oneko persuaded Pinto to leave Nairobi. Indeed, Pinto did go to Mombasa on February 19, 1965 and met Muinga Chokwe and Sayu Anjarwalla (both were MPs). On his return to Nairobi, he immediately left for Kisumu for a meeting with Pranlal Sethi who was Odinga's legal adviser. It was the day after his return from Kisumu that he was assassinated on February 24. It would seem that it was just a matter of time before Pinto would be assassinated for daring to challenge the "powers that be" over land, government policy and corruption. According to Mwenda (2017), Murumbi realised that he could have saved Pinto from assassination:

Murumbi soon resigned on August 31, 1966, shortly after he discovered — years after it had happened — that he was partly responsible for Pio Gama Pinto's murder 18 months before by confidently calling him out of hiding.

Unhappily, at the time of the assassination, none of Pio's colleagues had the courage to reveal the truth and rock the political boat or risk the same fate at the hands of the men at the top. And that lack of courage is felt even now, over 50 years after Pinto's assassination, so powerful is the ring of silence imposed on the nation by the ruling class - even more so since their rule has been further consolidated after the assassination of Pinto. It has proved almost impossible to get evidence as to who was really responsible for his assassination, particularly in the face of successive governments' failure to reveal facts hidden in the vaults. However, facts cannot be hidden for ever and come to be released in one manner or another. Hechio (2018) quotes a tweet by the lawyer Miguna Miguna:

> "Jomo Kenyatta murdered Pinto Gama, Kodhek, Kunga Karumba,Tom Mboya and JM Kariuki. Daniel Arap Moi murdered Ochuka, Adungosi, Dr. Ouko and Alexander Muge. Mwai Kibaki murdered Dr. Odhiambo Mbai, King'ara and Oulu. UKenyatta has murdered Thuo, Saitoti, Mutula,Juma, Msando,etc," Miguna's tweet read.

However, as Hechio (2018) makes clear, "his [Miguna's] tweets are allegations since none of the above murders have been proved in the court and therefore, he might be asked to give evidence of his allegations. It remains for the future to see if any real evidence emerges to show who was to be blamed for these murders.

COMMENTARY

Houses of Parliament pay tribute

'Fighter for freedom'

WITH the tragic assassination of the Hon. P. G. Pinto, Kenya must hang her head both in sorrow and shame.

In sorrow because she has lost an honest and outspoken politician whose entire adult life was a courageous dedication to the cause of freedom and unity in his country.

When most people of his own community were afraid or unwilling to support the African cause for freedom during those dark days of the Mau Mau rebellion, he chose his destiny among the Africans, serving many years in detention along with many thousands of Africans whose lot it was to submit to the temporary suppressive measures of the colonial government of the time.

STALWART

And when the freedom for which his detention had been a sacrifice had been achieved he continued to identify himself wholly with the Africans, working closely with them b o t h in Kanu and later in Parliament.

A stalwart supporter of East African unity his name will be remembered among all those East Africans who have helped lay down the foundations of a f u t u r e East African Federation.

Whatever the motives behind the killing, his death is a cause of shame for the whole Kenya nation, for it is a big blot on the spirit of give and take which most people in and outside Kenya had come to believe to be the guiding force in the country since independence.

THE LEAST

His death reveals the existence in Kenya of a degree of intolerance w h i c h threatens to negate all the great advances in human relations which have been in the past year or two under the guidance of a responsible political leadership.

The least Kenya can do to express her sorrow and shame and to discourage the kind of intolerance which was behind Mr. Pinto's assassination is to bring to swift justice all t h o s e who were connected with the horrible crime.

— HILARY NG'WENO

TRIBUTES to Mr. P. G. Pinto were paid yesterday in b o t h Houses of Parliament.

The Speaker of the Lower House, **Mr. Humphrey Slade,** opened the proceedings with a s p e e c h of tribute "to this friendly and courteous man of great public spirit and considerable ability."

Mr. Slade said that Members were horrified beyond measure at the news that "our colleague and friend was murdered this morning."

He added: "I can't imagine any sane motive for the murder of such a man. We must await the findings of the police."

He expressed sympathy to Mr. Pinto's widow and children in their "terrible bereavement."

Mr. Slade said that, though Mr. Pinto had been a Member of Parliament for only a short time, he had made his mark. "It is indeed a tragedy for this House and for the country that we should lose such a man in the prime of life."

'Brother'

Kenya's Vice - President, **Jaramogi Oginga Odinga,** speaking on behalf of the Government and people of Kenya, expressed deep shock "at the murder of our brother."

He went on to suggest that, in view of what had happened, the House adjourn till Thursday.

The suggestion was accepted unanimously.

The Senate adjourned after the Speaker, Mr. Mulngs Obokwe, delivered a communication from the Chair in which he recalled the tireless work of Mr. Pinto and his devotion to the cause of human dignity throughout his life.

Mr. Obokwe said: "Hon. Senators must have learned with horror of the tragic end of one of our colleagues, the Hon. Pio Gama Pinto, who met his death this morning at the hands of gunners.

"Needless to say how much Pio Gama Pinto was loved by many, young and old. He was a tireless worker devoted to the cause of human dignity throughout his career.

"While appreciating that Members would like to pay their tribute to the gallant Member, I must say that his passing away is a personal loss to many of us and to our country too.

'Shame'

"Let us all together extend our condolences to his wife, children and relatives and may God rest his soul."

Mr. Obokwe then asked Members to stand in silence as a mark of respect to Mr. Pinto.

The Assistant Minister for Commerce and Industry, Mr. James Muchlo, then moved that the House adjourn till Friday as a mark of respect.

Tributes to Mr. Pinto poured in from persons in all walks of life.

The Minister for Commerce and Industry, Dr. J. G. Kiano, said he was "horrified that such a thing can ever happen in this country."

Visibly shocked and shaken, he said: "It is a shame. I can assure you the Government will

leave no stone unturned until these men, these gangsters, have been brought to justice.

"We have been enjoying extremely pleasant relations in Kenya and we will not tolerate any incident that can create fear, worry and unrest among the various peoples."

Sir Derek Erskine, a Nairobi businessman and former member of Kenya's Legislative Council, expressed shock and paid tribute to Mr. Pinto's fine athletic and sprinting prowess.

"He was a great friend of mine and a great sprinter. I knew him since 1952, when he helped us to participate in the Indian Ocean Games at Madagascar."

Mr. John L. Porter, also a former Legislative Council member, said: "He was a very sincere politician and one of the men who working hard to implement African socialism.

"I admired his courage and ability."

Mr. W. W. W. Awori, a former member of Legislative Council and the Editor of the Sentz Hanserd, said he was deeply shocked "at the assassination of my friend," adding:

Unity

"I have known him for some time as a freedom fighter and it now comes as a great shock that this man should face death at the hands of a gunman. I believe he will ever be remembered although he is dead."

The president of the Kenya Young Christian Workers, **Mr. Peter Abwajo,** said he had learned with profound shock of the death "of this leading nationalist and leading politician."

He added: "Having suffered considerably in the cause of independence for Kenya his reward should not have been murder.

"His is a great loss for his service to Kenya brought about the Afro-Asian unity which the two races now enjoy. To all races in Kenya, Pinto has been more of a real brother than just a Kenya citizen."

The Kenya African Workers Congress had learned with "great shock and sorrow" of the assassination of Mr. Pinto. Its secretary-general, Mr. O. O. Mak'Anyengo, and its deputy secretary - general, Mr. V. G.

Wachira, said in a joint statement.

"As a freedom fighter and true progressive nationalist, his death is a great loss to Kenya and Africa as a whole."

They added: "Everyone who knew this devoted young man saw in him sacrifice and perseverance during his life as a freedom fighter.

The Secretary - General of Kanu, **Mr. Tom Mboya,** said in a statement that the murder has come as a great shock to the nation. He added: "Its was a young man whose name had been associated for many years with the struggle for Kenya's freedom. He had suffered under the colonialists for the part he took in the struggle for independence, not being an African himself.

"Since independence and his return from many years of detention, he had completely associated himself with the struggle of nation-building and had become an active member of the Kanu party and the Parliamentary Group.

"It is not possible to understand who a man such as this should die at the hands of his fellow countrymen. This is a most revolting crime for which there can be no sane explanation. His death is a great loss to the country and to our Parliament. It must be hoped that the police will quickly be able to bring the culprits to justice."

PRESIDENT IN THE HOUSE

THE attention of the Speaker of the House of Representatives has been drawn to the report in your issue of Wednesday, 17th February of proceedings in the House the previous day, in which it is stated that "The President'... came into the House... when Mr. Slade was "reading his communication."

Mr. Speaker directs me to record that this report is incorrect, and implies a discourtesy on the part of His Excellency the President which would be quite foreign to his nature.

In fact, His Excellency carefully timed his entry into the Chamber, so as to take his seat immediately before Mr. Speaker began his Communication from the Chair.

J. K. Githenge, for Clerk of the House of Representatives.

WASHING SINS AWAY

PERHAPS you and your readers are aware of the recent news that 3,000,000 Hindus were "washing away sins" by bathing or plunging themselves in "the sacred Ganges at the Kumbh Mela."

YOU WRITE

The DAILY NATION, P.O. Box 1016, Nairobi.

This was followed by further comments t h a t dishonesty, blackmarket and corruption have increased to such a great extent in India that the Government measures of control or prevention are ineffective.

India is mostly religious and it is religion that seems to encourage everyone to commit sins or acts of dishonesty in the religious belief that all sins can safely be accumulated to be washed away one day by a mere washing of the body in the River Ganges. It is religion that inspires the belief of immunity or salvation.

We Punjabis have a maxim SAU CHUA KHA KAY BILLI HAJ NU CHALLI, which means having eaten a hundred mice the cat goes to pilgrimage. The Indian Community is full of religious persons of this type.

Atan Singh Virdi, Nairobi.

● Flashback to last July. His colleagues in Parliament hold him shoulder-high after he was elected a Specially Elected Member of the House of Representatives.

---

11. *Houses of Parliament pay tribute: Daily Nation (25-02-1965)*

Pio Gama Pinto, Kenya's Unsung Martyr

An Enemy of Neo-colonialism

It is necessary to see the wider political reasons behind the assassination of Pinto as well as the immediate cause and events that led to his assassination. In essence, Pinto was the victim of the regressive, conservative forces, backed by imperialism, who came to power at independence. They immediately set about consolidating their position and eliminating all forces that did or could threaten their rule. The ground had been well prepared for them by the departing colonial power which ensured that Jomo Kenyatta, their favourite to maintain Kenya within the imperialist orbit, got maximum power and support. The constitution gave extraordinary power to the post of the President; the legal system created in the last years under colonialism ensured that the status quo was maintained - with some superficial changes. Capitalism and its policies, however, remained intact and were, in fact, strengthened.

The neo-colonial independence settlement in Kenya addressed a number of key aspects which could have destabilised the Kenyatta regime. First, the return of stolen land had been a key demand of Kenya's war of independence. Under colonial guidance, the policy of "willing buyer-willing seller" was established. This gave the impression of restoring justice to land rights, but in effect it disinherited the real owners of land and maintained the settler and corporate grip on land. This had another advantage from the neo-colonial point of view: besides "solving" the land question, it bought the loyalty of Kenyatta by allowing him to amass vast tracts of land for himself and his family. He was also able to buy out political opposition with land "gifts" to win their loyalty. Thus was created the second great land theft in Kenya's history, the first under colonialism, this one under neo-colonialism. It also entrenched the culture of corruption and impunity in Kenya.

The second aspect of the neo-colonial settlement was linked to the creating of a vested middle class that would be dependent on the local elite and foreign interests for survival and to flourish. It also facilitated the consolidation of capitalism in Kenya. Laws, international treaties and agreements and the legal systems were used to marketise and privatise state owned properties and industries. This enabled foreign corporations to gain greater control over Kenyan resources and, at the same time, allowed the homeguards to ease themselves into positions of industrial and commercial power. Kenyatta and his trusted supporters had been given the power to oversee this process of "neocolonising" the country, in the true homeguard tradition.

But Kenyatta and his government were given additional tools, besides power, land, and laws, to run things for imperialism and to eliminate the threat posed by the KANU left-wing. This was military power to consolidate his imperial rule. He used these military tools to kill those Mau Mau leaders who had refused to surrender and had continued the struggle for land and freedom after independence. The Kenyan military, in addition, was essentially under the "guidance" of British, USA and later Israeli direction. Their finances, training, equipment and policies were all controlled from London and Washington and their loyalty to the people of Kenya thus diminished. But as the mutinies and a coup attempt later were to show, the real power for military activities was guaranteed by the presence of British troops in Kenya. Ostensibly in Kenya for "military training and exercise," these forces in effect guaranteed power to Kenyatta to rule on behalf of imperialism. Secret treaties with USA and Britain made the port of Mombasa a crucial centre for imperialist espionage in the Indian Ocean region. Kenya, the land of Mau Mau, was turned into the preferred headquarters of CIA activities in Africa.

Imperialism needed total control over some other aspects of social life to ensure total control by Kenyatta and imperialism over Kenya. One was to make the capitalism accepted by all. The state needed to ensure the "free" flow of only capitalist thought and news while discrediting socialism, Soviet Union and China. These channels were controlled in various ways, ranging from control over books, newspapers, libraries, press, mass media, education system as well as scholarships for young people to Britain and USA where capitalism was the only system they saw and learnt and propaganda against communism was broadcast world-wide by the "independent" BBC (British Broadcasting Corporation) and VOA (Voice of America).

However, one huge source of irritation continued to rattle both Kenyatta and his imperialist backers: Activism by radicals based on their commitment to socialism. To eliminate this hurdle, trade union activities were curbed, and a pro-Western trade union movement was created under the capable hands of Tom Mboya, carefully guided by Western experts. Makhan Singh was safely removed by imprisonment from doing further damage on the industrial front. Other progressive trade unionists were side-lined and rendered powerless. And yet the militant wing of KANU refused to die. Instrumental in its survival and growth was Pio Gama Pinto. In addition to his tireless work for the progressive cause, he came up with ideas of socialism not only for Kenya but for other African countries still under colonialism. The damage that this young man could do to imperialism was incalculable. In addition, not only was he well known, loved and connected with the working class and progressive people in Kenya, he had links with progressive people in India, Britain and other countries. Imperialism's only solution to deal with the "Pinto problem" was to eliminate him in such a way that Kenya government, as well as its foreign backers, could claim to be innocent of spilling his blood. At one stroke, his elimination from the scene would solve the problem of the radical wing within KANU and remove international concerns about the situation in Kenya. His assassination would also give a clear warning to those seeking a socialist path in Kenya that they would face the same fate as Pinto's if they refused to toe the Kenyatta line and follow his *nyayos*.[31]

There was thus no alternative for imperialism except the elimination of Pinto.

Rosario de Gama Pinto's Struggle for Truth

There is no doubt that Pinto was admired and held in high regard by many politicians, community leaders, workers and peasants. There was a great display of sorrow and grief at his assassination and many politicians, trade unionist and other prominent people paid glowing tributes to him. Yet it remains true that there were few voices asking for an independent public inquiry into his assassination to establish the truth about who was behind

31   Kiswahili for footsteps. Moi used this term to indicate that he was following Kenyatta's footsteps into the capitalist, imperialist camp and expected the country to follow him on pain of death.

the assassination and why. Politicians who had much to be grateful to Pinto for the support he gave them and their families over many years were tight-lipped; trade unionists were silent; civic society had no voice to raise its concerns. As Fernandes (2016b:139) says:

> After the assassination no one really spoke out or pointed a finger in public at the 'prominent politicians' or 'the powers that be'. Murumbi knew but said nothing…Odinga knew but said nothing. Neither did fellow independence hero Achieng' Oneko or any of Pinto's Goan confidantes, except Fitz de Sousa. He at least voiced the war of words between Pinto and Kenyatta.

It was Pinto's brother, Rosario De Gama Pinto who was a prominent person in his own right, who called for a public enquiry into his assassination. History records, albeit inadequately, Pinto's work but remains almost silent about Rosario who took up the struggle for truth about Pinto's assassination. He also gave up his political career by withdrawing from KANU elections on which Joseph Murumbi commented:

> I am glad to know that you have withdrawn your candidature as this would have been very embarrassing to the Party (Letter from J. Murumbi to R. De Gama Pinto, 24-03-1965. KNA, Assassination Correspondence).

Murumbi was concerned for Rosario, and merely showed how those in power in Kenya would react were Rosario to stand for any post. There were clear risks for anyone raising their voice at the time about who the assassins were, as they themselves would have faced a fate similar to Pinto's. That itself is an indication of the state of Kenya at the time and indicated the grip over power that the comprador government had already established within a few years of independence. What is perhaps more surprising is that those active at the time, those who were in the know, have remained silent to this day.

Rosario was so affected by the assassination that he commented: "Since Pio's death, I haven't slept a night without thinking for hours about the tragedy".[32] Rosario De Gama Pinto wrote to the President, to various KANU officials and to the KANU Parliamentary Group to seek an independent enquiry to establish the truth about Pinto's assassination - some of these are reproduced in the following pages. All these attempts failed, and Rosario became the next possible victim of those behind Pinto's assassination. He was forced into exile as he faced the same threat of death as his brother. Fernandes (2016b) quotes a "former work mate":

> After Pinto was assassinated, Rosario was told by a friend who was in the CID to leave Kenya quickly because he was earmarked and would be next. Rosario worked at the same office as I did and he quickly left the country telling everyone he was going to Brazil on vacation. He never came back.

This indicates the seriousness with which the conservative wing of KANU's ruling class, which instigated the assassination of Pinto, viewed any disclosure or discussion about Pinto's assassination. The ruling class, even after Kenyatta's death and when Moi was the President, showed a similar intolerance to debate on Pinto. As late as 1984, under Daniel Moi, the present author was forced into exile for writing articles on Pinto in the *Standard* in September 1984. Interrogation by the Special Branch after the publication of the article[33] included the following questions:

> Do you not know that his [Pinto's] was a political murder? What you have written touches on the security of the state. Very high people in government have been affected by your article and they are very concerned.[34]

Given this level of hostility to the very memory of Pinto from the ruling

---

32   Letter, R. De Gama Pinto to J. Murumbi, Minister of External affairs, on 20-07-1965, (KNA).
33   The articles appeared in The *Standard*, September 17-18, 1984. The questions are reproduced in this book (see List of Illustrations).
34   Some questions asked by the Special Branch are reproduced in this book. They were written once the author landed in London in September 1984 while the questions were still fresh in his mind.

classes even to this day, it is not surprising that Pinto could not escape the clutches of those who saw him as the greatest threat to their continued rule. Nor would Rosario have been spared had he not decided to leave Kenya.

Needless to say, no public enquiry on Pinto's assassination has taken place.

PERSONAL & CONFIDENTIAL.

R.da Gama Pinto,
P.O.Box 5568,
NAIROBI.
20th July,1965.

The Hon. Joseph Murumbi,M.P.,
Minister for External Affairs,
NAIROBI.

My dear Joe,

   I enclose a copy of an appeal, of even date, addressed to the President which is self explanatoyy. I know you might consider this move as foolksh but since Pio's death, I haven't slept a night without thinking for hours about the tragedy. Hence I have taken this step in the hope that some justice will prevail.

   I would like to talk to you a number of projects which will be of interest to you and of the country, may be you will be kind enough to give me an appointment at your earliest convenience.

   With best regards,

         Sincerely yours,

---

12. *Rosario Da Gama Pinto to Kenyatta (20-07-1965)*

KNA Miscellaneous Correspondence 1952-1972: Assassination

Correspondence

Tel. 21448.
By hand.

P.O.Box 5568,
NAIROBI: Kenya.
20th July, 1965.

H. E.The Hon. Mzee Jomo Kenyatta, M.P.,
President of Kenya,
President's Office,
Harambee House,
NAIROBI.

Dear Mr. President,

As the only brother of the late Pio da Gama Pinto who was murdered for political reasons on February 24,1965, I beg to appeal to you for the holding of a public enquiry in addition to the Trial which took place and is now a closed chapter.

Despite sleepless nights, worries and illhealth, I refrained from writing you earlier in this matter pending relevations from Court proceedings but since no motives were indicated thereat for this gastly crime, it would be apparent that the case has not been thoroughly investigated by the Government or hampered by interested parties. Even if you are assured that this has not been the case by the Departments concerned, it has cut a very poor picture both at home and internationally.

I am not at all happy with the outcome of the trial which casts aspersions on the country and the people ans as a whole and in view of your statement that you will leave no stone unturned to bring this matter to light, I sincerely hope that you will kindly consider this appeal with a view to remedying this unhappy situation which might encourage similar assissinations and outrages against the persons and families of public spirited individuals who are really dedicated to the implementation of African Socialism.

There is no need for me to eulogise my Brother's contribution towards your present exalted Office sufficient to say that he, supported by a band of loyal and sincere personalities, managed to keep away many contenders from your chair during the time of your restriction thereby incurring their enimity and intrigues for life. If for no other reason but this and his contribution in many fields towards the attainment of Independence, this tragedy should warrant an impartial enquiry, free from any interference, to clear his name as a fighter for freedom heedless of any honours and personal gains attained or which might be forthcoming which are of a poor solace to his widow, 3 little children and myself.

I appeal to you in the good name of Kenya, justice and of humanity to bring your personal weight to bear in this matter.

In addition to the foregoing, I would request your protection for personal safety for obvious reasons.

Thanking you in anticipation,

Yours respectfully,

(R.da Gama Pinto)

13. Rosario Da Gama Pinto to Murumbi (20-07-1965)

Pio Gama Pinto, Kenya's Unsung Martyr

By hand.

R.da Gama Pinto,
P.O.Box 5568,
NAIROBI:Kenya.
8th October 1965.

The Secretary General of K.A.N.U.,
KANU Headquarters,
Jeevanjee Street,
NAIROBI.

For the att. of T. J. Mboya Esq., M.P.

My dear Tom,

Re: Assassination of Pio Gama Pinto.

As a Member of KANU, I appeal to you for redress!

I enclose a copy of my appeal dated Sept.9,1965, addressed to Mr. Ngala, which is self explanatory.

I am much dis-satisfied with the manner in which this matter has been conducted from the outset in spite of loud assurances of justice being meted. The trial was, in my humble opinion, and knowing some facts, a farse and the outcome was as expected.

I knew I cannot get Pie back into this world but, on a matter of principles, I very strongly protest to the violent methods used to liquidate true nationalists after the achievement of independence. This is unparallelled with events in our neighbouring States. In fact it is yet unbelieveable and disgusting to say the least. I am sure you will appreciate, even though it has not been expressed in public for fear of victimisation, that numerous citizens are justifiably upset and shaken with this brutality and this has resulted in a general loss of faith.

It is my intention as a citizen to make representations through all legitimate quarters in the first instance, for justice, before going to the press or taking any other line of action in order to avoid embarrassment to the Party, the Government and the peoples of the country. I am sure you will agree that I have served the country as best as I could during the past 14 years and have exercised great patience over this matter and would have been the last to revive this unhappy incident but for the fact that the reasons for the murder are unknown to me nor have the real culprits been brought before the law.

I shall be most grateful if you will kindly discuss this petition with the Executive of the Party and influence an enquiry to be held, free from interference, or pressure, and high powered.

It is my intention to copy this letter also to the Branch Chairmen of KANU throughout the country for your information and action.

Thanking you in anticipation and with best regards,

Yours sincerely,

Encl: 1.

c.c.The Executive Officer, KANU Headquarters, Nairobi.
The Branch Chairman, KANU, Nairobi, Mombasa, Nakuru,
Kisumu, Thika, Nyeri, Fort Hall, Eldoret, Kitale,
Kisii, Machakos, Makamega, etc.

14. *Rosario Da Gama Pinto to KANU Secretary General (08-10-1965)*

KNA 3 Miscellaneous Correspondence 1952-1972. Assassination Correspondence

well known, respected and admired for his sincerity, work and dedication
to Kenya and the peoples of Africa.

I am copying this appeal to my other friends in Parliament
in order to acquaint them that I have addressed this Appeal to you and
that you, as Chairman of the Parliamentary Group, will doubtless bring
this matter up for discussion at the meeting.

Should this request be turned down, for whatever reasons
unknown to me, it is my intention to take other steps to clear the fair
name of my Brother and that of the family, which I am proud to say has
contributed to Africa some six generators of public spirited individuals.

Looking forward to hearing from you and with best regards,

Yours sincerely,

c.c.The Hon. T. N. Malinda, M.P.,
    Secretary to the Parliamentary Group,
    Kenya House of Representatives,   (BY EXPRESS POST)
        P.O.Box 1842,
          NAIROBI.

15.   *Rosario Da Gama Pinto to Chair KANU Parl. Group (09-09-1965)*

R.da Gama Pinto,
C/o P.O.Box 5568,
NAIROBI:Kenya.
October 8, 1965.

Pinto

Dear Honourable Member,

As a colleague of my late Brother, Pio Gama Pinto, I am now compelled to bring to your notice the following appeal which I made to Mr. Ngala as Leader of the KANU Parliamentary Group in Parliament, on September 9,1965, which is self explanatory, and to which I have not had a reply.

I shall be grateful for your support and further action to bring this matter to light in the interest of justice and to safeguard the rights of every citizen of Kenya.

Thanking you,

Yours truly,

P. da Gama Pinto

_____
By express post.   COPY.   9th September,1965.
copy delivered by hand & signed for.

The Hon. Ronald G.Ngala, MP.,
Chairman of the Parliamentary Group,
Kenya House of Representativ ,
P.O.Box 1842,
NAIROBI.

Dear Mr. Ngala,

I am today appealing to you in your capacity as Leader of the KANU Parliamentary Group for political equality, social justice and human dignity as embodied in the Constitution and as contained in Page 1, paragraph 4(1),(ii) and (iii) of Sessional Paper No.10 of 1963/1965.

I wish to introduce myself as a staunch member of KANU and an early citizen of Kenya. I have played an active part in the background in this country's social and political life culminating in its independence; have contributed towards similar ideals and goals in the neighbouring territories; assisted freedom fighters from South and South West Africa and other parts of the continent in their dire wants and propagating their ideals, and am still continuing to contribute my mite towards the liberation of Mozambique and other territories still under the shackles of colonialism in a practical manner and in the spirit of Pan Africanism.

The purpose of this appeal is to seek immediate Parliamentary assistance for the setting up of an impartial enquiry, public or otherwise, high-powered, and free from any interference, to uncover the reasons and the persons really responsible for the murder of my only brother, the late Pio da Gama Pinto, assassinated on 24th February 1965, who was a respected Member of K.A.N.U., a Specially Elected Member of Kenya's Parliament, its Representative on the East Africa Central Legislative Assembly and who also held other high offices in public life.

It is obvious to me and to the public, whose silence must not be misunderstood, that the murder was a political one and that those brought before the Court were merely hirelings. In fact, the one who has been found guilty by the Court is less culpable than its real perpetrators, who are in the background, in the eyes of both men and God.

This ghastly incident has cast aspersions and serious doubts on the country and the people of Kenya as a whole and it is more your duty and that of fellow Parliamentarians, to look carefully into this matter irrespective of whether or not my late Brother had any differences of opinion on matters of policy which is not unusual in any truly democratic National Assembly. The method adopted of silencing a dedicated nationalist of the calibre of my late Brother is not only degrading, disgusting and horrifying but is beyond expressions or imagination.

Bearing in mind the great damage done, it is all the more in the interest of Parliament itself for the setting up of an enquiry etc.,as a precedence such as has occurred, is likely to spark and encourage similar outbreaks against persons and families of such public spirited individuals who are really dedicated to the implementation of African Socialism. Should this matter be left unturned, at some future date, it would spell disaster to Parliament and the country as a whole.

I trust you will discuss this letter and appeal at your forthcoming Parliamentary Group Meeting on the 10th instant and come to some satisfactory decision.

I, on my part, will leave no stone unturned to erase the ugly and horrifying picture of an unsolved murder, the circumstances of which are reminescent of those attending the death of the Great Patrice Lumumba, to many of us in this country and in many parts of the world where my late Brother was

P.T.O.

KNA 3.   Miscellaneous Correspondence 1952-1972. Assassination Correspondence

Pio Gama Pinto, Kenya's Unsung Martyr

R.da Gama pinto
P.O.Box 9568,
NAIROBI.
Nov.24,1965.

The Hon. T. R. Malinda, M.P.
Secretary,
KANU Parliamentary Group,
National Assembly,
Parliament Buildings,
Parliament Square,
NAIROBI.

Dear Mr. Malinda,

Re: The Late Hon.Pio GAMA PINTO.

I refer to the courtesy of your kind letter of Nov.10, 1965 sending me a copy of Minute No.63/65 of the Parliamentary Group Meeting held on October 26, 1965, and to my letter of Nov.12,1965.

Now that the matter has been dealt with by the Appeal Court, I sincerely trust that you will be good enough to place this matter once more on the Agenda of the Meeting of the Parliamentary Group to be held on the 30th instant.

As stated before, principles are involved and morals affected. As mentioned before, I refuse to accept the contention that just because the Courts have dealt with this ghastly crime, as a result of the evidence before it, Parliament cannot go into this affair once again with a view to instituting an impartial and high level enquiry and carrying out further investigations particularly as a Member of Parliament was murdered and the motives definitely political. I also repeat that this Enquiry is more in the interest of the present Parliamentarians than a post-mortum which is a poor consolation to his family.

In this connection I also enclose a copy of an appeal addressed to the Secretary General of KANU dated Nov.8,1965, wherein I have raised matters of principles which, I feel, in the interest of all Kenyans, serious heed should be taken.

Looking forward to hearing from you and with best wishes,

Yours sincerely,

Encl: 1.
c.c.The Hon.Ajuma Oginga Odinga,M.P.,Box 30520,Nairobi.
    The Hon. Joseph Murumbi, M.P.;
    The Hon.T.J. Mboya, M.P.Box 30561;
    The Hon. Paul J.Ngei, M.P., Box 30547.
    The Hon. Laurence Sagini, Box 30004;
    The Hon.T. Okelo Odongo, C/o The Treasury.
    The Hon. B. M. Kaggia, M.P.
    The Hon. J. D. Kali, M.P.
    The Hon. Ngala Obok, M.P.

16.   *Rosario Da Gama Pinto to KANU Parl. Group (24-11-1965)*

COPY.

NATIONAL ASSEMBLY,
PARLIAMENT BUILDINGS,
P.O.BOX 1842,
NAIROBI.
10th Nov.1965.

R.Pinto Esq.,
P.O.Box 5568,
NAIROBI.

Dear Mr. Pinto,

re: LATE HON. GAMA PINTO.

I refer to correspondence between you and me on the above subject culminating with my undertaking to put this matter before the Parliamentary Group Meeting which took place on the 26th of October 1965.   I enclose herewith a copy of Minute 63/65 of the meeting which is self-explanatory.

In view of the fact above, therefore, I do not think that there is any further action on my part to take in the matter. I am sorry for not being much of assistance to you in this regard.

Yours sincerely,

sgd. T.N. Malinda,
Secretary,
PARLIAMENTARY GROUP.

Encl:

EXTRACT OF MINUTE NO 63/65. LATE PINTO BROTHER'S LETTER.

" Reference was made to a letter received from the brother of the late Mr.Pinto relating to circumstances surrounding the death of his brother.   The President explained that the letter was understandably emotional, but said that the matter had been dealt with in Court and that constitutionally the Government could not interfere. In view of the fact that the case was pending hearing in the Appeal Court, the matter was sub-judice and could not be discussed further. If, however, Mr.Pinto's brother or anybody else had any material evidence, he was at liberty to submit such evidence to the Attorney General ... "

Not the End

Pinto's lifelong struggle was to achieve social justice for people of Kenya. That struggle earned him powerful enemies. The final straw that got Pinto murdered was his opposition to the theft of funds from overseas which were meant to help ex-freedom fighters and ex-detainees. Instead, "a few powerful persons pocketed it" (Nowrojee (2007:56). Pinto was to raise these "betrayals of the freedom struggle" in Parliament. As Nowrojee (2007:56) says, "The powerful persons saw such an exposure as a threat to their wealth and their positions. They decided to get rid of Pio".

On February 24, 1965, Pio Gama Pinto was shot outside his house by three men. He died instantly.

Those who murdered Pio Gama Pinto did so in order to defeat the vision and values that he represented and to stop him from achieving his goals. The path that Kenyan neo-colonial regime had taken after independence, with the active support of the USA and British imperialist powers, was in stark opposition to the values and principles that Pinto advocated. Pinto stood for socialism and anti-imperialism. His enemies, who were enemies of the working people in Kenya and who had fought colonialism and imperialism over many generations, shuddered to think what socialism and anti-imperialism would do for their personal and class interests. Joseph Murumbi (1966:9) expresses the indignation of Kenyan working people:

> Pio was accused by his enemies of being a communist. Even if he were, surely in a democratic Kenya, it is not a crime warranting death to follow any political persuasion. To me Pinto was a SOCIALIST.[35] He lived by his Socialist beliefs in thought and deed. What he possessed belonged to those in need even to the extent that he deprived himself and his family of many of the simple comforts which we all enjoy... Politically his views were beyond many of us in his depth of political understanding and social consciousness. To him Socialism meant its true application.

---

35   Capitalisation in the original.

Kaggia (1966:14) was entirely correct when he said: "... what he stood for, his beliefs, principles and the teachings of his actual life will live forever".

Tettegah (1966:25) who sums up Pinto's life, achievements and the best way to pay homage to the great man:

> Pio Pinto fell on the battlefield in our common war against neo-colonialism. He is not the first person to die for the cause of emancipating Africa. He will not be the last to pay the price for the path we have chosen. Along with the immortal Patrice Lumumba, Reuben Um Nyobo, and Felix Moumie, he has joined the ranks of our martyrs whose blood must be avenged. In such honourable company, his death — like theirs — will recruit new armies of Pintos to continue the fight in which he died, the effort to create a united socialist Africa. That achievement alone can repay the honesty, the sincerity, sacrifice and love of justice that characterised the man Pio Pinto. That alone can embody the essence of his life, through the freeing of subject peoples. To me his death was noble. It was symbolic. He died a true revolutionary socialist.

Pio Gama Pinto is no longer with us. But the struggle in which he gave his life continues. His enemies will forever be looking behind them to see what the successors of Pinto have in store for them. His legacy of struggle for socialism, equality and justice cannot be ended with bullets. So long as people lack the basic means of survival, lack equality and justice, the struggle that Pinto waged will continue to inspire those who took the baton from him.

Be vigilant

> Every time we talked, Pio spoke of the need to be vigilant against the imperialists. Yes, he would say, we are marching forward, more and more countries are becoming independent, but be vigilant, for the imperialists have not been liquidated - they are here, striving to come back, to divide us. - Romesh

Chandra, a journalist for the Delhi paper New Age [36].

More than 50 years have passed since Pinto was assassinated. It is high time we assessed the impact of Pio Gama Pinto's work, life and death. Kenya remains in the grip of a ruthless comprador regime and is nowhere near the vision that Pinto - in common with those who fought for uhuru - had for an independent Kenya. Imperialism still controls the land, resources and lives of people - just as it did under colonialism. The facade has changed but the substance of exploitation, inequality and oppression remains. Corruption and looting among the ruling classes are endemic. Pinto's fear that we will have achieved very little if after independence we will have "black Lord Delameres instead of white Lord Delameres," has come to pass. The cause for which Pinto gave his life remains to be achieved.

Imperialism and their comprador agents around the world have used a number of methods to defeat forces of organised resistance to capitalism and imperialism. Regime change, the misuse of non-governmental organisations (NGOs), financial and economic strangulation, the use of the World Bank, IMF and WTO as agents of imperialism, the control over mass media to create, misinform and spread imperialist propaganda and creation of artificial "contra" opposition groups are some of these methods. When all these methods fail to deliver a clear avenue for imperialist control, their ultimate weapon remains political assassinations. The methods used for such assassinations vary too, but the aim is always to eliminate leaders who are most likely to succeed in creating a society free from capitalism and imperialism. New technologies of oppression are being invented and used daily. These include drones to kill leaders and people via remote control. President Barak Obama used to hold weekly sessions on Tuesdays to decide on the victims of that week's drone assassinations around the world. Eliminating key leaders has another advantage for imperialism: it destabilises resistance organisations. This, in turn, ensures imperialist and comprador control over peoples and countries until the next generation of revolutionary leadership emerges.

Such was the case in Kenya too, with murders and assassinations initially

---

36   Pio Gama Pinto (1966).

Pio Gama Pinto, Kenya's Unsung Martyr

carried out by the British colonial power, later by their comprador regimes. The murder of resistance leaders and activists was the norm for the British colonial administration. They refined their murders by using the latest technology of the time - mobile gallows which went around the country, leaving behind hundreds of dead bodies, fear and threats in its wake. Kimathi's abominable murder after a pretend-trial was the culmination of this fine-tuned attack on people's forces.

The comprador regime was then handed over all the colonial laws and extra-judicial powers to carry on the slaughter of activists and populations. Pio Gama Pinto was among the first victims of the comprador regime to be assassinated, others included many Mau Mau activists and leaders who refused to buy into the imperialist independence settlement. At a national level, Tom Mboya and J. M. Kariuki were among many others assassinated by the regime using "remote control" assassinations so they could emerge in public with bloodless hands. At an organisational level, the regime attacked leaders of the underground movements to eliminate the threats they posed.

It was as a result of the imperialist methods of eliminating leadership that resistance such as the December Twelve Movement worked underground or in overseas centres. But even this did not prevent the regime from forcing its leadership into detention, exile and finally resorting to murder. The killing of Karimi Nduthu[37] in 1996 marked yet another milestone in the regime's attempts to eliminate all opposition to its rule for the 1% against the 99%.

While it is true that the ideas and work of Dedan Kimathi, Pio Gama Pinto, Karimi Nduthu and other activists assassinated or murdered by agents of imperialism will live on in different ways, it is also true that such assassinations destabilise their organisations and create a climate of fear among its actual and potential supporters. Imperialism has thus ensured that the left in Kenya has not been able to organise in a continuous and consistent manner and provide the alternative to capitalism and comprador rule that is desperately needed by the working people.

---

37   For details on Karimi Nduthu, see *Karimi Nduthu, A Life in the Struggle.* (1998).

Lessons from the assassination of Pinto and others have to be learnt by those seeking a socialist solution in Kenya. New methods of surviving imperialist assaults and of sustaining progressive movements must be found. Latin America has seen a similar elimination of progressive politicians and trade unionists. Nonetheless, many popular, progressive movements have emerged and taken over power there. Cuba and North Korea (PDRK) have managed to survive a constant barrage of imperialist attacks.

It is perhaps time to reassess the situation in Kenya and to seek out a socially just resolution to the comprador-imposed order. Newer generations will find a way out, perhaps learning from the experience of an earlier generation many of whose leaders, such as Pinto and hundreds of Mau Mau activists, gave their lives for liberation. Creating monuments to fallen leaders is necessary but needs to be followed up with progressive ideas and action. On this, Pinto's (Pinto, P. G. 1964). words can be a guide:

> I shall endeavour to exert my efforts towards building of a society based on social and economic justice and political democracy. I believe that every effort must be made, not only towards the eradication of the "imbalances" created by colonialism, but equally to ensure that the solutions applied conform to the needs of the masses of Kenya; that they do not produce other kinds of "imbalances" contrary to the need to develop national unity; and finally, that our efforts are directed towards the creation of a national consciousness dedicated to the realisation of inter-territorial and Pan African unity, and the liquidation of colonialism in all its forms.

Activists in 1960s charted the way forward in the following way (Barnett, 1972:9):

> Let us then fashion an ideology which will unify the vast majority of our people by articulating their needs and by advancing a program of socialist development in agriculture and industry which promises to eradicate poverty, disease

and illiteracy, a program which will draw out the creative talents and energies of our people, giving them that personal dignity and pride which comes from socially constructive and productive activity.

Let us, in short, provide our people with the ideological and organisational tools necessary for the achievement of genuine independence and development.

Let us not sell them cheaply down the glittering path of neo-colonialism and social, economic and cultural stagnation.

Following this path is the best way to honour the principles for which Pinto lived and for which he died.

References and Bibliography

Aiyar, Sana (2015): Indians in Kenya: The Politics of Diaspora. Cambridge, Mass.: Harvard University Press.

Akumu, J. Dennis. (1966): "Trade union" in: "Pio Gama Pinto, Independent Kenya's first martyr - socialist and freedom fighter".

Atwood, William (1967): The Reds and the Blacks: A personal Adventure. London: Hutchinson.

Barnett, Donald L. (1972): Kenya: Two Paths Ahead. Introduction to Muchai, K.: "Hardcore: the story of Karigo Muchai" (1973). Richmond, B.C., Canada: LSM Information Centre.

Branch, Daniel (2011): Kenya: Between Hope and Despair, 1963-2011. London: Yale University Press.

Brockway, Fenner (1953): Letter to Douglas Rogers, 22-01-1953. Kenya National Archives. Pinto Pio da Gama, 1927-1965. Miscellaneous Correspondence, 1952-1972. MAC/KEN/71/3.

Chandra, Romesh (1966): Son of Africa. in: *Pio Gama Pinto, Independent Kenya's first martyr - socialist and freedom fighter* (1966). Reproduced from New Age, Delhi.

Chokwe, Muinga Chitari. (1966): "Early days". in: *Pio Gama Pinto, Independent Kenya's first martyr - socialist and freedom fighter*.

De Souza, F. R. S. (1966): "Goa's liberation". in: *Pio Gama Pinto, Independent Kenya's first martyr - socialist and freedom fighter*.

De Souza, Fitz de. (2014): Interview with Fitz De Souza by Alan Donovan, August 2014. in: Murumbi, Joseph (2015): A Path Not Taken: The Story of Joseph Murumbi. From interviews by Anne Thurston. Book design and Notes by Alan Donovan. Nairobi: The Murumbi Trust. p. 401.

De Souza (2015): Interview by Alan Donovan. *in*: Murumbi, Joseph (2015): A Path Not Taken: The Story of Joseph Murumbi. From interviews by Anne Thurston. Book Design and Notes by Alan Donovan. Nairobi: The Murumbi Trust.

Drum (1965): Africa Mourns a Brother. May 1966. Available at: https://books.google.co.uk/books?id= B3ch2Vefs5YC&pg= PA158&lpg= PA158&dq=drum+ africa+mourns+a+brother&source = bl&ots=laVOu-JgjH&sig= aeJt8lIr5NG378m6RP8KAFAs3NU&hl= en&sa=X&ved=2ahUKEwjXpsS__IzdAhWFDs AKHbvnD00Q6AEwBnoECBMQAQ#v= onepage&q= drum%20 africa%20mourns%20a%20brother&f=false [Accessed: 27-08-2018].

Durrani, Nazmi (2017): Pio Gama Pinto (1927-1965) *in* Durrani, Nazmi, Naila Durrani and Benegal Pereira, (2017): Liberating Minds, Restoring Kenyan History: Anti-Imperialist Resistance by Progressive South Asian Kenyans, 1884-196. Nairobi: Vita Books. Initially published in Gujarati in Alakmalak (Nairobi) December 1985. Biographies of Patriotic Kenyan Asians (Series). This article has also been used in preparing the article on Pinto.

Durrani, Nazmi, Naila Durrani and Benegal Pereira, (2017): Liberating Minds, Restoring Kenyan History: Anti-Imperialist Resistance by Progressive South Asian Kenyans, 1884-196. Nairobi: Vita Books.

Durrani, Shiraz (1984): Pio Gama Pinto: Some Facts About the Life of a Great Leader and a Patriotic Journalist. Sauti ya Kamukunji (Nairobi) Vol.1 No.8 (June 1984). Also published in The Standard (Nairobi) in two parts: (a) Gama Pinto: A Kenyan Freedom Fighter. September 17, 1984. p.7. (b) Pinto Backed Nationalism. September 18, 1984. pp.10-11.

Durrani, Shiraz (2003): Submission to the Task Force on Truth, Justice and Reconciliation Commission. Available at:http://vitabooks.co.uk/wp-content/uploads/sites/6/2014/11/Submission-on-Pinto-to-Task-Force-on-Truth-Aug03-.pdf [Accessed: 10-03-16].

Durrani, Shiraz (2006): Never Be Silent: Publishing and Imperialism in

Kenya, 1884-1963. London: Vita Books.

Durrani, Shiraz (2013): Mau Mau: the Revolutionary Force from Kenya. *Communist Review*. Nos. 67-69. Available at: .http://www.communist-party.org.uk/communications/cr/1871-communist-review-no-67-spring-2013.html [Accessed: 05-03-16].

Durrani, Shiraz (2018): Kenya's War of Independence: Mau Mau and its Legacy of Resistance to Colonialism and Imperialism, 1948-1990. Nairobi: Vita Books.

Fernandes, Cyprian (2015): Emma Pinto: They killed my husband too soon. *Daily Nation*, 14-02-2015. Available at:http://www.nation.co.ke/lifestyle/women/They-killed-my-husband-too-soon/-/1950830/2623828/-/g5u6koz/-/index.html [Accessed: 05-03-16].

Fernandes, Cyprian (2016a): Remembering Pinto: He was Killed for Speaking Truth to Power. *Pambazuka News*. 01-03-2016. *Available at:* http://allafrica.com/stories/201603041529.html. [Accessed: 09-06-2018].

Fernandes, Cyprian (2016b) Yesterday in Paradise, 1950-1974. Bloomington, IN, USA: Balboa Press.

Gregory, Dick (2016): Malcolm X's Assassination. https://www.youtube.com/watch?v=y7i3XTHrUxo [Accessed: 19-06-2016]. Published May 28, 2016. [Accessed: 09-06-2018].

Hechio, Steve (2018): Miguna links former presidents to murder of key opposition figures. *Hivisasa*. ["A local news website in Kenya"]. Available at: https://hivisasa.com/posts/837-miguna-throws-another-bombshell-that-might-land-him-to-trouble [Accessed: 13-07-18].

Hornsby, Charles (2012): Kenya: A History Since Independence. London: Tauris.

Independent Kenya (1982). London: Zed Press.

Jabbal-Gill, Inderjit (2015): Makhan Singh, the Family Man. in: Durrani, Shiraz (2015): Makhan Singh, A Revolutionary Kenyan Trade Unionist. London: Vita Books.

Jukwaa: Kenya Discussion Platform (2005): Pio Gama Pinto - Independent Kenya's First Marytr. Available at: http://jukwaa.proboards.com/thread/177 [Accessed on 29-03-16].

Kaggia, Bildad. (1966): "A friend". in: "Pio Gama Pinto, Independent Kenya's first martyr - socialist and freedom fighter".

Kaggia, Bildad (1975): Roots of Freedom, 1921-1963; the Autobiography of Bildad Kaggia. Nairobi: East African Publishing House.

Kaggia, Bildad M, W. de Leeuw and M. Kaggia (2012): The Struggle for Freedom and Justice: The Life and Times of the Freedom Fighter and Politician Bildad M. Kaggia (1921-2005). Nairobi: Transafrica Press.

Kali, J. D. (1966): "In Parliament". in: "Pio Gama Pinto, independent Kenya's first martyr - socialist and freedom fighter".

Karimi Nduthu, A Life in the Struggle (1998). London: Vita Books.

Kenya National Archives, Pio Gama Pinto: Miscellaneous Correspondence, 1952-72. Kenya Indian Congress Letter to Fenner - 12th January 1953.

Kimena, N. (1970): In Kenya Now. *The African Communist.* No. 42, pp. 17-34. Available at: http://psimg.jstor.org/fsi/img/pdf/t0/10.5555/al.sff.document.0001.9976.000.042.1970_final.pdf [Accessed: 27-08-2018].

Kinyatti, Maina wa (2008): History of Resistance in Kenya, 1884-2002. Nairobi: Mau Mau Research Centre.

MacDonald, Malcolm (1976a): MacDonald Papers, University of Durham. Correspondence re Kenya 1969-1981. 76/7/44.

MacDonald, Malcolm (1976b): Interview given on April 24, 1976 by the Rt. Hon. Malcolm MacDonald to Arnold Raphael and Celia Curtis.

MacDonald Papers, University of Durham. Correspondence re Kenya 1969-1981. 76/7/44.

MacDonald, Malcolm (1976c): Second Interview [by Arnold Raphael and Celia Curtis] with Malcolm MacDonald on 21 May 1976. MacDonald Papers, University of Durham. Correspondence re Kenya 1969-1981. 76/7/1-126. SDMP-LIBPG-9.

Manji, Firoze (2015): Memorials are more about the future than about the past: tribute to Pio Gama Pinto. Presentation at the Commemoration of the 50th Anniversary of the Assassination of Shujaa Pio Gama Pinto, Mazingira Institute, Nairobi, 7 March 2015. Revised version of the paper is reproduced in the present book.

Murray-Brown, Jeremy (1972): Kenyatta. London: Fontana.

Murumbi, Joseph (1966): An Appreciation. in: Pio Gama Pinto, Independent Kenya's First Martyr: Socialist and Freedom Fighter. (1966). Nairobi: Pan African Press.

Murumbi, Joseph (2015): A Path Not Taken: The Story of Joseph Murumbi. From interviews by Anne Thurston. Book Design and Notes by Alan Donovan. Nairobi: The Murumbi Trust.

Mwakenya (1987): Draft Minimum Programme. Nairobi: Mwakenya.

Mwenda, David (2017): Does Moi owe the Kenyattas? *The Star* (Nairobi). 21-02-2017. Available at: https://www.the-star.co.ke/news/2017/02/21/does-moi-owe-the-kenyattas_c1509679 [Accessed: 26-05-2018].

Nazareth, J. M. (2014): Brown Man, Black Country: On the Foothilla of Uhuru. Edited by Jeanne Maxine Hromnik. (Kindle Locations 2364-2371). Goa,1556. Kindle Edition.

Nabwera, Burundi (1966): A Nationalist and Socialist. in: Pio Gama Pinto, Independent Kenya's First Martyr: Socialist and Freedom Fighter. (1966). Nairobi: Pan African Press.

Ness, Immanuel (ed, 2009): Pinto, Pio Gama (1927–1965). International Encyclopedia of Revolution and Protest. Blackwell Publishing, 2009. Blackwell Reference Online. Accessed; 10-03 2016 <http://www. blackwellreference.com/public/book.html?id=g9781405184649_ yr2012_9781405184649>

Ng'otho, Kamau (2008): Secret land deal that made Kenyatta first president. Daily Nation. 20-09-2008. Available at: http://www.nation.co.ke/news/-/1056/473158/-/5gb13cz/-/index.html [Accessed: 02-07-2016].

Ngunyi, Gitahi (2015): Pinto's Daughter Speaks of Values Dad Wanted for Kenya. *People Daily*. 25-02-15.

Ng'weno, Hillary: Pio Gama Pinto. DVD. Makers of a Nation Series. Nairobi: NTV and Kenya History & Biographies. 28 mins.

Nkrumah, Kwame (1966): Foreword to Odinga (1968), pp. xiii-xv.

Noronha, Frederick (2000): Pio's Total Focus was to Work to Fight Colonialism. Interview with Emma Gama Pinto. News Feature sent to goa-research-net@goacom.com 13-08-2000. Posted on the Namaskar Forum by B.D. Pereira, 14-08-2000.

Noronha, Subhash. (1987): A true son of Kenya. The Standard (Nairobi). June 22.

Nowrojee, Pheroze (2007): Pio Gama Pinto: Patriot for Socialist Justice. Nairobi: Sasa Sema.

Nowrojee, Pheroze (2014): Pio Gama Pinto Commemorated. Asian African Heritage [On-line] News. Available at: http://www.asianafricanheritage.com/news-2012-06-06.htm [Accessed: 27-08-2018].

Odinga, Oginga (1967): Not Yet Uhuru, An Autobiography of Oginga Odinga. Nairobi: Heinemann Educational Books.

Okoth, Dann (2013): High Profile Assassinations a Stain on our Political

History. Standard Digital, 13-12-2013. available at: www.standardmedia. co.ke/article/2000100033/high-profile-assassinations-a-stain-on-our- political-history/?pageNo=1 [Accessed: 20-06-16].

Oneko, Ramogi Aching (1966): in: Pio Gama Pinto, Independent Kenya's First Martyr: Socialist and Freedom Fighter. (1966). Nairobi: Pan African Press.

Pan Africa (Nairobi). 12-12-1963.

Pant, Apa. (1987): "Undiplomatic incidents". Hyderabad: Sangam Books.

Patel, Ambu H. (comp) 1963: Struggle for Release Jomo and his Colleagues. Nairobi: New Kenya Publishers.

Patel, Ambu (1966): Letter from Ambu Patel to Hon. J. Murumbi, M.P. dated January 03, 1966. Kenya National Archives.

Patel, Zarina (2006): Unquiet, the Life & Times of Makhan Singh. Nairobi: Zand Graphics.

Pinto, Emma Gama (1972): Communication with Pan Africa Press. June 22, 1972.

Pinto, Emma Gama (2000): Emma Gama Pinto interviewed by Frederick Noronha. Reproduced in News Feature, Pio's Total Focus was to Work to Fight Colonialism. Sent to goa-research-net@goacom.com on 13-08- 2000. Circulated by Benegal Pereira.

Pinto, Pio Gama (1952a): Letter to Fenner Brockway, March 10. Kenya National Archives. Pinto Pio da Gama, 1927-1965. Miscellaneous Correspondence, 1952-1972. MAC/KEN/71/3.

Pinto, Pio Gama (1952b): Letter to Fenner Brockway, April 8, 1952. Kenya National Archives. Pinto Pio da Gama, 1927-1965. Miscellaneous Correspondence, 1952-1972. MAC/KEN/71/3. [Listed in KNA as "Misplaced page"].

Pio Gama Pinto, Kenya's Unsung Martyr

Pinto, Pio Gama (1953): Letter to Fenner Brockway, 28-01-1953. Kenya National Archives. Pinto Pio da Gama, 1927-1965. Miscellaneous Correspondence, 1952-1972. MAC/KEN/71/3,

Pio Gama Pinto (1961): Letter to Joseph Murumbi, London. 07-01-1961. Kenya National Archives. Pinto Pio da Gama, 1927-1965. Miscellaneous Correspondence, 1952-1972. MAC/KEN/71/3.

Pinto, Pio Gama (1963a): A Brief Biographical Note. Introductory Note written on May 29, 1963 to "All KANU Members of the House of Representatives". Kenya National Archives. Miscellaneous Election Communications. May 29, 1963.

Pinto, Pio Gama (1963b): A Detainee's Life Story (by himself). in Patel, Ambu H. (comp) 1963. pp. 155-157.

Pinto, Pio Gama (1963c): Glimpses of Kenya's Nationalist Struggle. Pan Africa. 12-12-1963. Also published as a monograph: Nowrojee, Viloo and Edward Miller (Editors, 2014): Glimpses of Kenya's Nationalist Struggle by Pio Gama Pinto. Nairobi: Asian African Heritage Trust. Reproduced in this book.

Pinto, Pio Gama (1964): Statement to all KANU Members of Parliament setting out why he wanted to be elected as a Specially Elected Member of Parliament.

Pio Gama Pinto, Independent Kenya's First Martyr: Socialist and Freedom Fighter. (1966). Nairobi: Pan African Press. [Edited by Ambu Patel]. Reproduced in this book.

Red Star (2013): The Land of the 10 Millionaires and 10 Million Beggars. Available at: http://www.cpiml.in/home/index. php?view=article&id=701:the-land-of-the-10-millionaires-and-10-million-beggars&Itemid=112&option=com_content [Accessed: 27-02-16].

Rothmyer, Karen (2018): Joseph Murumbi: A Legacy of Integrity. Nairobi:

Zand Graphics.

Seidenberg, Dana April (1983): Uhuru and the Kenya Indians: The role of a minority community in Kenya politics. New Delhi: Vikas.

Shivji, Issa G. (1988?): Is Might a Right in International Human Rights? Notes on the Imperialist Assault on the Rights of People to Self-Determination. 40th Anniversary Human Rights Seminar. University of Dar es Salaam, Faculty of Law. Available at: http://repository.udsm.ac.tz:8080/xmlui/bitstream/handle/20.500.11810/2039/Is_Might_a_Right_in_Human_Rights.pdf?sequence=1&isAllowed=y [Accessed: 27-08-2018].

Sicherman, Carol (1990): Ngugi wa Thiong'o: The Making of a Rebel, a Source Book in Kenyan Literature and Resistance. London: Hans Zell.

Singh, Makhan (1969): History of Kenya's Trade Union Movement to 1952. Nairobi. East African Publishing House.

South African History Online (1965): Notes on Current Events: Kenya. Available at: http://www.sahistory.org.za/sites/default/files/DC/Acn2065.0001.9976.000.020.Jan1965.10/Acn2065.0001.9976.000.020.Jan1965.10.pdf

Spencer, James (1983): James Beauttah: Freedom Fighter. Nairobi: Stellascope.

Truth Justice and Reconciliation Commission of Kenya (2013) [TJRC] Final Report. Available at http://digitalcommons.law.seattleu.edu/tjrc/ [Accessed: 08-04-17]. Vol.IIA.

Umoja (Umoja wa Kupagania Demokrasia Kenya/United Movement for Democracy in Kenya) 1989: Moi's Reign of Terror: a Decade of Nyayo Crimes Against the People of Kenya. Background Document No. 2. London: Umoja.

Willy Mutunga (2018): Celebrating Pio Gama Pinto[38]

At Mazingira Institute on March 07, 2015 we celebrated Pio Gama Pinto on the 50th anniversary of his political assassination. On that occasion, I drew the attention of the audience to the following facts about Pinto:

o   Pheroze Nowrojee had published a brilliant book on Pinto;

o   *Awaaz* in its Issue 1, 2005 had carried an Exclusive coverage of Pinto on the 40th Anniversary of his political assassination under the title "Pio Gama Pinto: Independent Kenya's First Martyr, 1927-1965." [In their Volume 12, Issue 1, 2015 *Awaaz* had Pinto's 50th Anniversary feature];

o   I myself had glorified Pinto by using his name as part of a pen-name in my column in the Saturday edition of the Nation. During the period 2006-2011, under the pen-name *Cabral Pinto*, I authored articles glorifying resistance struggles in Kenya. The collection of these articles, edited by Charles Onyango Obbo & Murithi Mutiga, will be published this year; and

o   William Attwood, the first American ambassador to Kenya in his book *The Reds and the Blacks* writes about Pinto. He calls him a brilliant strategist and comments on how his death was a blessing to anti-Odinga forces. The possession of this book was banned by the Kenyan government since its publication in 1965. Its ban, along with other publications (all publications by Beijing Foreign Languages Press, Playboy and other Magazines) was only lifted after the promulgation of the 2010 Constitution. Glorification of a patriot by his enemies means a lot to his patriotic legacy.

Today, I have one further reflection. I wanted to draw a parallel between Pinto, Lumumba, Chris Hani, Tongarara, Thomas Sankara, and Amilcar

---

38   Celebrating Dedan Kimathi and Pio Gama Pinto on the launch of Shiraz Durrani's book, *Kenya's War of Independence*. National Theatre Kenya, February 21, 2018. Dr. Willy Mutunga, D.Jur,SC,EGH. is the former Chief Justice/President, Supreme Court of Kenya.

Cabral to bring home one lesson about revolutions and counterrevolutions. Pinto, like the other five, struggled to end foreign domination, exploitation, and oppression. Like Hani, Tongarara, and Cabral he was involved in the armed struggle against colonial power. Except for Hani and Tongarara all the others served in post-colonial parliaments or governments. All six of them were murdered by counterrevolutionaries at the behest of their imperialist masters. The lesson here is that we need to study the many examples of counterrevolutions that bring about NOT YET UHURU in African countries, and others in the Global South. Revolutions and counterrevolutions are nurtured in the same wombs of wars of independence or liberation, both are twins of the same struggle, but are deadly opponents. Our revolutionary role is to abort the counterrevolutions before birth. Such a task requires great organization, leadership, criticism, and robust vigilance as the struggle continues.

In the case of Pinto, he played a great role in the Mau Mau War of independence. He was detained by the British. He ended up in Parliament. He, and others including Kaggia, Murumbi, and Odinga, decried the continuation of colonial policies by the first independence government. As a lawyer I can understand their legal and political arguments on the law and policy that allowed the British settlers to sell land to Kenyans. The British stole that land from the Kenyans. Under their law, thieves do not pass good title to anybody because they do not have the title to the property in the first place. So our stolen land that the British state and settlers used for 70 years was sold back to us without considering the historical costs. Pinto was the leading ideologue of this opposition to the policy of "willing buyer willing seller." He was assassinated on February 24, 1965.

Angelo Faria[39] Remembers Pinto (2018)[40]

As for Pio Gama Pinto, we are distantly related through my maternal grandmother. I first met him in 1948 in Mombasa when he competed in the Easter athletics meet of the Goan Institute. So, it would be natural that I had some inkling of his goings on; as such, and because I was boarding with Goan family friends on 5th Avenue Parklands (High Ridge) during 1953-54, this led to my attending his wedding to Emma in January 1954.

My connection with Pio deepened after 1960 when I moved to Nairobi to be employed by the East African. High Commission (Income Tax Department), and I visited them on numerous occasions, initially at their Nairobi West home and subsequently when they moved to their last home behind the Sarit Center in Westlands.

I had several off-the cuff conversations with an indulgent Pio, and even wrote him an extended note at his request on the nature and operation of a national cooperative structure for Kenya. I never heard any more about it; although Pio said he liked it, said that it would be used "productively at the appropriate time", and reminded me that one should regard this as a communal not individual outcome.

I had discussed my own (and Asians') situations and experiences [with Pinto] in this narrow period of a false dawn [post-independence] on several occasions as a way of better understanding where he was coming from himself. While I got some sympathy from Pio, his constant, if gentle refrain (no raising of his voice in counter argument!) was that one should consider oneself honestly lucky that one is so much better off in life with more than adequate income and a roof above one's head, no less! He constantly urged me not to dwell negatively (racial aspects personally experienced) on the evolving nationhood and political/tribal squabbles but rather to look ahead positively with altruism and hope. For him, the battle worth fighting to one's last breath was the unyielding expectation for much better prospects

---

39   Angelo Faria was born to Goan parents in Mombasa and attained degrees in economics from the London School of Economics (UK) and the University of Wisconsin (Madison). He currently resides in Washington DC. USA. (Kindly supplied by Awaaz Magazine).

40   Personal communications (email) 09-08-2018 from Angelo Faria, Bethesda, MD. USA.

for all, in particular the poor and the working class; an outlook for which he lived and ultimately gave his life, only to be forgotten if not brutally rejected by those who should have known so much better!

On one occasion, I arrived at his house just as he was leaving to drive to the Lumumba Institute, and he invited me along for the ride in his ill-fated Saab – the same Saab in which he was subsequently shot. I recall being surprised why we had not taken the most direct route past City Park Stadium and Muthaiga to the Thika Road next to the Drive-In cinema but chose rather to go through Grogan Road and Kariakor, but he did not respond. He merely kept talking and looking continuously at his rear-view mirror as if he suspected that he was being followed, saying merely "one cannot be too careful"!

By a strange twist of fate, however, my most striking and tragic experience with Pio came during the period I had been transferred to tax office in Arusha in 1964-66. I came with a friend from there, who was visiting Nairobi for a coffee auction session. We made the 3-hour trip by late morning. He then gave me his car to go around and asked that I come back to pick him up at 4pm to drive back. I went directly to Fitz de Souza's office at (then) BMC House, just up from Channi's Pharmacy and the Copper Kettle restaurant on (then) Government Road in the city center. The three of us – Pinto, de Souza and I - conversed for a while and I then invited them to lunch at the restaurant. After lunch, they said they were going to walk to Parliament for the start of afternoon session but accepted my offer to drop them there at the gate. I recall my saying to Pio something to the effect that I had spoken to a few friends who said that Pio was in some sort of political danger. I even suggested that he consider leaving town, if not Kenya, temporarily until matters had cooled down. He stuck his head into the passenger side, smiled unaffectedly and said something about perhaps visiting Mozambique, and even possibly Tanzania (Arusha) to visit with me, so I should be prepared at short notice. I heartily encouraged him to do so at the earliest feasible time. Imagine my horror when the next day, like a bolt from the blue on the radio news from Nairobi, I heard that he had been shot dead at his home gate with his youngest daughter in the Saab car and that, despite differing oral accounts, no suspects had been identified!

Pio Gama Pinto, Kenya's Unsung Martyr

Rosario Da Gama Pinto (2015): Pio, My Brother[41]

'Let us hear from Pinto's own brother, the late Rosario Da Gama Pinto, who was also a political activist in his own right. Rosario endeavoured to chronicle his sibling's historical achievements. After his death, his daughter, Audrey Da Gama Pinto, took pains to type up his notes. As the copyright holder, she gave Cyprian Fernandes permission to post 'Pio, My Brother' on his blog cyprianfernandes. blogspot.com (February 8, 2015), a veritable and valuable trove of information.' – Onyango Oloo (quoted by Audrey da Gama Pinto, 15-07-2018, personal communications with the Editor).

Although it is unusual for a brother to pay public tribute to another, I am doing so in view of our rather close political relationship for the better part of 20 years and also to highlight some important aspects of Pio's life, which would otherwise have passed unnoticed. Pio's participation in anti-colonialism stemmed from the treatment accorded to his father who served in the pre-independent Kenya Administration Services and from his own personal experiences in European schools in British India.

While for generations the Pintos, Da Gamas and the merger of Da Gama Pintos have contributed towards producing men of letters, clergy, administrators, we have also over the years produced a number of dedicated nationalists. These include our late uncle Mathias Da Gama Pinto in Brazil and our sister, Mrs Sevigne Athaide. However, Pio has undoubtedly left a more distinguished mark in modern day history undistorted by colonial historians.

In the mid 1940s, Pio had his first baptism in politics in Dharwar (Karnataka), where he joined both in the hartal movement by peaceful agitation and even violent protest at a time when Gandhi, Pandit Nehru and others were languishing in prison. He later followed up the campaign and gained experience in the trade union movement, as also co-operatives in Bombay and participated in the civil disobedience campaign following the Indian Naval Mutiny, which culminated with India's independence. Simultaneously, he

---

41   Pio, My Brother by Rosario Da Gama Pinto © Audrey Da Gama Pinto 2015. .

participated in the Goan liberation movement, led by Dr Juliao Menezes, and established friendships with many Goan patriots who are prominent in Goa today.

In the interim, I decided to return to Kenya in early 1948, but being under-age, my father (who had prematurely retired from the Civil Service in 1941) was compelled to accompany me. At this juncture, it was necessary for Pio to return to Goa to look after our mother who was unwell and oversee the running of the family estate. He took the opportunity to build an underground movement for the liberation of Goa, along with many other colleagues. Portuguese Intelligence soon became aware of his activities and kept a close watch on him. If it had not been for family connections and influence, he would have been arrested and deported to an overseas colony, like most of his colleagues. It was at this time that Pio felt that East Africa would be his next target to put his ideals into practice and carry out the anti-colonial campaign based on Gandhi's principles. When he reached Kenya in 1949, he threw himself into reading material on Kenya, East Africa, the various tribes, customs and culture and different patterns of colonial administration in these territories. To avoid interruptions and temptations of city life, he took up a job with the Magadi Soda Company, (a subsidiary of I.C.I.) and only returned to Nairobi several years later. By this time, he was well read, knowledgeable and au fait with the conditions prevailing in East Africa vis-à-vis the injustices suffered and the anguish of the sons of the soil.

Pio took up employment as a paid Secretary to the East African and subsequently Kenya India Congress, the only forceful political forum of the Asian community where he felt he could establish closer contact with the more progressive elements of the Asian community. He held this position for a few years until he branched out into journalism. His position allowed him to influence a joint meeting between the Congress Executive and the Kenya African Union Executive, which was considered an impossible task, bearing in mind the privileges enjoyed by a large number of the Asian community. The agreement reached was for the Asian members of the Legislative Council to press for increased elected African representation on the Legislative Council and other bodies which, in the past, were represented

Pio Gama Pinto, Kenya's Unsung Martyr

by a European as a Chief Native Commissioner and later by nominated and hand-picked puppets as African Nominated Members, whereas the other communities were free to elect their own representatives on a communal basis.

Pio then joined *The Daily Chronicle*, an English/Gujarati daily newspaper, as its editor and simultaneously co-operated with the late D. K. Sharda, in printing and publishing *The Tribune*, later banned by the Government.

Pio made his mark in journalism by highlighting the African cause, the racism and glaring injustices that prevailed, the awful slums around Nairobi, the terrible living conditions and lack of educational facilities for those living on the African Reserves, the absence of employment opportunities for educated Africans (even when they were better qualified!), the enormous amount of money spent on European education compared with that allocated for Asians and Africans. His articles and editorials were a source of annoyance and embarrassment to the authorities. He was often subjected to threats and other forms of intimidation, but he was strong enough to withstand these and much more!

Pio, together with another Goan journalist, Mike Fernandes, started a Goan paper, the *Usvad*[42] (*Torch*) a Konkani weekly, to highlight the Goan liberation struggle, but this was quickly sabotaged by the Portuguese authorities who intimidated the readers and printers and also made representations to the British authorities who were their allies.

Pio was also the writer of the *Goan Newsletter*, which was broadcast over All India Radio Service New Delhi to Africa until his detention and subsequently by Michael Fernandes. Pio was also the Press Trust of India Representative in Kenya, which allowed the press and Parliament in New Delhi to raise protests over events in East Africa. Realising the importance of the press and the overwhelming power of the authorities to suppress licences for the printing of newspapers, Pio used to churn cyclostyled newsletters in various African languages and sell them at cost,

---

42   Referred to as *Uzwod* in other places. This is the correct spelling, according to Audrey Da Gama Pinto – Editor.

often making a loss. At this time, Pio and W.W.W. Awori, a progressive nominated Member of the Legislative Council (Legco), decided to buy a press, but this did not eventuate. In the interim Pio was detained under the Emergency Regulations.

Pio married Emma Dias in 1954. She understood his aspirations.

Pio had, in the interim, established contact with M.P.s in England and other Ministers in India and acquainted them with the state of affairs, submitting memoranda and notes, as also contributing material to the local press (owned by the European community) and the English press, both under his own name and a nom de plume. Pio's network has grown immensely. Africans from Madagascar even sought his assistance and advice. Pio's opinions and advice were also sought by Executive Members of the Kenya African Union (KAU). He managed to get the KAU Executive to pass a resolution to accept that the only way to achieve independence was by non-cooperation, protest meetings, boycotts and other non-violent means. He was fully aware that the European settlers were only waiting for a chance to use violence. They were well equipped and backed by the British Government. It was only a matter of time before there was a blood bath.

As the situation for Africans in Kenya grew worse, the European settlers managed to convince the British Government that subversion had set in. As a result, Jomo Kenyatta, Ramogi Achieng Oneko, Paul Ngei and hundreds of others were arrested under Operation Anvil. Pio got much international aid, financial and legal assistance to fight their cases. Pio also managed to arrange for hundreds of others to be represented in virtual mock trials under the Emergency Regulations, and their businesses and other interests safeguarded by progressive Indian lawyers like Achhroo Ram Kapila, Fitz de Souza, Hirabhai Patel, Bill Inamdar, etc. However, this was a drop in the ocean considering the numbers involved. Pio, both in the press and otherwise, had opposed Asian participation in the establishment of the Asian Manpower Unit to quell the Mau Mau rebellion. This made him a candidate for detention. In fact, the Mau Maus ('Forest Fighters') had vowed as a retaliatory measure to cut down the Asian traders in the African Reserves and small towns. However, Pio managed to dissuade them from

Pio Gama Pinto, Kenya's Unsung Martyr

this course of action. He argued that these poor Asian traders should not bear the brunt of the attack as their misguided leaders (some British stooges) were to blame. Not only did Pio obtain and channel help to the families of the victims, but he even paid for their children's schooling, food and clothing, as far as was possible, out of his own pocket.

When the freedom fighters found that they could not hold out indefinitely against the well-equipped army, they fled into the forests and used Pio as a go-between to request a ceasefire. Knowing that the settlers would crush the rebellion, Pio approached the Government of India via its Acting High Commissioner (R. K. Tandau) and asked that the question of negotiations be taken up at the highest level with the Colonial Office. The British Government's attitude was favourable and the then Commander-in-Chief, General Erskine, and other officials were asked to meet with the Forest Fighters. However, this meeting was sabotaged by the local settlers who held high posts. The security forces opened fire on the representatives of the Forest Fighters. The local government wanted a scapegoat to take the blame for the failure of the meeting, so they detained Pio under the Emergency Regulations. He was not allowed a proper trial or hearing; he was also denied legal aid. He was held incommunicado and after a few days in Nairobi sent to Mombasa under heavy police escort. He was later moved to Lamu Island and then Manda Island where thousands of hard core Mau Maus were exiled for years under terrible conditions. Pio was offered better facilities but decline them on principle. He lived like the rest of his comrades on maize-meal flour, rice, fish etc. Our family sent him 1.50 shillings a month for cigarettes etc. However, he preferred to share the money with the needy. He was interrogated by the Special Security teams on several occasions. They promised him an early release if he would confess. He refused to give into their threats even at the threat of deportation. He was offered a one-way ticket to India which he again declined as he wanted a fair trial. His time in the detention camp has been covered in various publications.

While in detention, Pio was not allowed to see his dying father, Anton Filipe. Ironically, they are both buried in the same grave at the City Park Cemetery in Nairobi. I was not allowed to see him in detention because of my political associations and involvement. Years later, Pio was exiled to an isolated district called Kabarnet where he worked as an administrator in the District Commissioner's office. (While he was in Kabarnet, he met Daniel arap Moi and guided him into politics, which resulted in the formation of the [an opposition] political party. Pio's new job allowed him more freedom to read newspapers. Emma was eventually able to join him. He was even allowed to visit Nairobi for Emma's confinement. He stayed with me, under a friend's supervision. Although Pio met up with political figures, he was given a good report, which expedited the rescinding of the Restriction Order a few months later.

On the pretext of being rehabilitated, Pio was allowed a transfer to the Education Department in Nairobi and served eight months. He then resigned and worked full time for Kenya African National Union (KANU), formed by Mboya, Odinga, Gichuru, Kiano etc. The first aim was to seek more representation in Parliament, the immediate release of Jomo Kenyatta and other detainees, without which there would be no cooperation with the Government or further talks on constitutional advancement. Pio drafted many documents and speeches for political figures. He felt the time had come to form a more progressive Asian political party, as compared with the Kenya India Congress, and formed the Kenya Freedom Party lead by Chanan Singh and other progressive Indians from all over Kenya. This body was more forceful and articulate in voicing nationalist sentiment. Pio also had a hand in the formation of the East Africa Goan League under Dr Alex da Costa, which in addition to identifying itself with the problems in Kenya and neighbouring territories, also championed the cause of liberation for Goa and the other Portuguese colonies in Africa.

Pio organised social functions and other fundraising events to meet the cost of political expenses ie sending delegations overseas.

Pio worked tirelessly for Jomo Kenyatta's release and even antagonised former friends who went on to become ministers in Kenyatta's Government. They did not want Kenyatta released from detention. Pio did his best to provide for Kenyatta's and Koinange-wa-Mbiyu's families. In fact, Chief Koinange died in his arms while they were detained in Kabarnet. Pio used

including his own as it turned out.

Pio, knowing that his life was in danger, had expected me to keep out of politics. I obeyed him until his detention when I felt a strong urge to take up the cause despite the negative impact it was to have on my health, family and finances.

Pio was murdered to silence him and put an end to his dream to implement socialism, the ideals for which the people had formed the Government. Now that independence had been gained, and the armed forces' loyalty had been bought, those in power considered it a convenient time to assassinate Pio as a warning to other dedicated nationalists.

He never wanted to occupy any high posts, preferring to assign them to his trusted and talented friends like Joseph Murumbi, Pran Lal Seth etc. Initially, he felt he could achieve more behind the scenes; but then changed his mind. He felt that the only way to achieve his goals and ideals was to be elected to Parliament.

Pio's sincerity and dedication to the African independence cause was greatly admired by representatives of many governments. He was invited to visit Egypt, India, Algeria and Czechoslovakia.

Firoze Manji[43] (2015): Tribute to Pio Gama Pinto

Firoze Manji: Tribute to Pio Gama Pinto: Memorials are more about the future than about the past[44]

A few years ago, I visited Guinea-Bissau. While there, I wanted to pay my respects to one of the greatest intellectuals and revolutionaries of Africa, Amilcar Cabral. It took weeks to arrange a visit to the mausoleum located with the military headquarters in Bissau. I had to apply in writing in advance for permission from the military. When we eventually got a formal letter of permission stating that on a given day at a given time we would be allowed to visit, it took another 30 minutes of negotiations to be allowed in. And even then, we weren't allowed to proceed until we had bought flowers from the shop across the road (which I guess was owned by the military). Some $80 later, senior officers accompanied us to the back of the barracks where we were able to pay our respects and lay our wreath.

As we walked away, I asked the senior military personnel why the mausoleum was in the barracks instead of a place where citizens could have access. The officer insisted to me that anyone could visit the mausoleum any time.

It struck me that the military, descendants of Cabral's assassins, feared him in death as they did in life. They clearly realized that memorials are more about the future than they are about the past.

Which is why the military, who effectively control a state and economy that depends on the illicit drugs trade, have established their headquarters around the mausoleum of Amilcar Cabral.

The erasure of memory is effected through the construction of what symbolizes power today.

What memorials have we built for our Pio Gama Pinto, freedom fighter, nationalist, socialist and internationalist? What have we done for the man who gave sustenance and arms to the Land and Freedom Movement (the so-

43 Firoze Manji is publisher of Daraja Press https://darajapress.com
44 This paper is a revised version of a presentation at the Commemoration of the 50th Anniversary of the Assassination of Shujaa Pio Gama Pinto, Mazingira Institute, Nairobi, 7 March 2015.

called Mau Mau) and who supported the movements for freedom in South Africa, Mozambique, Angola, Goa and elsewhere?

It is singularly apposite, if also depressing, that the place where Pio lived and where he was assassinated has not only been grabbed and its history erased, but we have allowed to be built in its place a large shopping centre that epitomizes Kenya today, a temple to commodity fetishism and to conspicuous consumption, where imported goods are sold, goods that have largely killed off indigenous production in Kenya, a temple designed to satisfy the needs of a parasitic and unproductive local capitalist class that is the product of the policies that Pio so vehemently opposed and for which he gave his life.

The polarization between the KANU and Pio, exacerbated by revelations of misappropriation of funds by the Kenyatta regime, erupted around *Sessional Paper Number Ten of 1965: African Socialism and its Implications for Planning in Kenya*. Authorship of this paper is usually attributed to Tom Mboya. In fact, the key architect of the paper was an American political economist Edgar O. Edwards, who was attached to the Ministry of Planning. Edwards was part of a team of Americans who had *bona fide* credentials at the US Embassy in the 1960s. This team was put at Tom Mboya's disposal by Ambassador Atwood, to help him write economic blueprints as well as to outwit his adversaries. The paper, despite its claims of 'socialism' was a perfect articulation of the prevailing views of how a subservient capitalism would be developed in the post-independence period. It was in opposition to this text that Pio wrote a counter proposal which, had he not been assassinated, could very well have led, some believe, to the removal of Kenyatta as president through a vote of no confidence and the emergence of Jaramogi Odinga as the new president.

The Sessional Paper was to give rise to precisely that class that Frantz Fanon predicted in *Wretched of the Earth*:

> The national bourgeoisie discovers its historical mission as intermediary.
> ... its vocation is not to transform the nation but prosaically serve as
> a conveyor belt for capitalism, forced to camouflage itself behind the

mask of neocolonialism. The national bourgeoisie, with no misgivings and with great pride, revels in the role of agent in its dealings with the Western bourgeoisie. This lucrative role, this function as small-time racketeer, this narrow-mindedness and lack of ambition are symptomatic of the incapacity of the national bourgeoisie to fulfil its historical role as a bourgeoisie.

Over the past 50 years, these small-time racketeers have amassed great wealth gained from handouts, land grabs and other forms of unproductive economic activities. They are managers on behalf of transnational corporations of a rentier economy. Changes in presidencies and the establishment of a new constitution have failed to curtail the parasitic accumulation of this class. Fundamentally, their power has gone unchallenged. Popular movements and organizations that have emerged in Kenya over the last two decades have voiced strong concern at the behavior of this class and have proposed policies that might curtail the more extreme forms of racketeering. But they have hitherto failed to challenge the power of that class.

The challenge of building movements and political organizations that can engage in struggles for real, for freedom and emancipation, remains. Struggle is needed to give rise to the new human being: before we were Africans, Amilcar Cabral reminded us, we were humans. How do we reclaim, nay, invent that humanity that the colonial and neocolonial eras have so cruelly damaged in our people? How do we fulfil such ambitions that I believe Pio so desired?

I would like to offer some thoughts on two areas that I believe we have not sufficiently reflected upon in the past.

First, in contrast to the political trajectory taken by Kenya's Land and Freedom Army, PAIGC and other movements such as those led by Thomas Sankara, most political movements in Kenya – as in much of Africa – have sought only a limited form of freedom, what I would call *licensed or concessionary freedoms*. Licensed freedoms are those whose parameters are set by constraints imposed by others rather than those who seek their own freedom. Those seeking licensed freedoms accept the authority of those who set the limits. Cattle, for example, have the freedom to roam around

Pio Gama Pinto, Kenya's Unsung Martyr

the field to their hearts' content: but the fence around the field delimits that freedom. There is no question of breaching the fence or of contesting the right of the farmer to decide on the limits of the freedom granted within the field. In other words, the power of those who rule is not fundamentally challenged.

In contrast, we need to consider the alternative: that is, *emancipatory freedoms*. Emancipatory freedoms are the fruit of the struggles of a people to invent, assert, release, and ultimately realize their full potential as humans. And being human, realizing their full potential as *social beings*. Emancipatory freedoms imply the collective power of peoples to determine their own destiny. These are an expression of what Lewis Gordon characterizes as an historical aspiration, one that continues to exist and transcends the constraints that might have been wrung in any given historical period. Emancipatory freedom implies, therefore, an assertion of dignity, of self-worth, a commitment to a project that transcends frequently even the threat or possibility of death, a proclamation and assertion of, and an insistence upon, a claim to be part of humanity.

This is not just a rehash of the old debates about 'reform vs revolution'. We have to fight for each and every gain that we can get under the present conditions, and we must protect whatever gains we may have made in the past. But that does not mean that we should lose sight of the freedoms that allow us to reassert our dignity as humans. As Sankara put it, we must have the courage to invent the future.

The second dimension upon which we need to reflect is what kind of state is necessary if we are to achieve real freedom. On coming to power, most of the nationalist governments (oft supported by the left) believed that all that was required was to take control of the state. But what they ignored was that the state that they sought to occupy was (and remains) a *colonial state*, one that was set up to serve, protect and advance the interests of capital, of imperial power and its entourage of corporations and banks. That state has a monopoly over the use of violence. It has police forces, armies and secret police, and a judiciary whose specific task is to protect the interests of the way in which capitalism operates in the peripheries.

Having occupied the state, independence governments essentially sought to make modest reforms consisting primarily of deracializing the state - the so-called 'Africanisation' programme – and modernizing it so that the economy could be more fully integrated with the new emerging international order that the US, Europe and Japan were busy creating in the post-World War II period. The structures of state control, the police, army, secret services, the judiciary, even the structures and powers of native authority established under colonialism, all these were left fundamentally intact, albeit now dressed up in the colours of the national flag. It is hardly surprising, therefore, that extrajudicial killings, incarceration without trial, excessive use of force against citizen protests and workers strikes, torture and other forms of abuse are as common today as they were under colonial rule. And under conditions of the hegemony of neoliberalism, the interests of financialised capital, of the transnational corporations that grab our land and amputate our natural resources are vehemently protected by the neocolonial state. The minority elites have become filthy rich, while the majority are poorer today than ever.

While many protest at government policies and even sometimes come forward with alternatives, the nature of the state is rarely challenged – indeed, in everyday usage, there is rarely a distinction made between 'government' and 'state'.

Cabral was emphatic: "It is our opinion that it is necessary to totally destroy, to break, to reduce to ash all aspects of the colonial state in our country in order to make everything possible for our people." It wasn't, in his opinion, the colour of the administrator that was the problem, but rather that there was an administrator!

Perhaps Pio Pinto never had time to expressly articulate such ideas, but it is clear through his praxis, for the causes for which he fought, that these are some of the ideas that he had had to consider during his short life.

The challenge that we face is to construct a memorial to Pio Pinto that truly represents not only such aspirations, but that also lays the foundation for our own liberation, a memorial that is as much about the future as about the past.

Pio Gama Pinto, 1926-1965 (2005) - Compiled by Awaaz Magazine

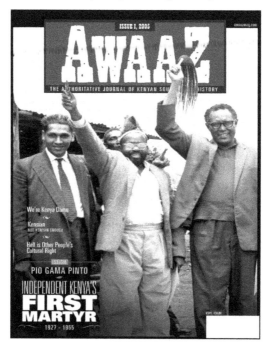

8. Awaaz Magazine, No. 1 (2005)

The following article, compiled by Awaaz magazine, is based on a number of sources: Nazmi Durrani's 1985 article on Pinto[45], the Pan African Press, Shiraz Durrani, Daily Nation (Special Report, June 2000) and personal interviews. It was published in the the special issue of Awaaz Vol. 3 (1), 2005. The Editor would like to thank Awaaz for making the article and photos on Pinto available for this book.

Pio Gama Pinto was born in Nairobi, Kenya, on 31 March,1927. He was the eldest son of the late Antonio Filipe da Gama Pinto (ex-Kenya Administrative Service) and Ema Ribeiro da Gama Pinto of Carren, Socorro, Bardez, Goa. His sister was Mrs Sevegno Athaide, MLA JP (Maharashtra), his brother was

---

45   Durrani, Nazmi (1985): Pio Gama Pinto, 1926-1965. It was originally published in the Gujarati magazine *Alakmalak* (Nairobi, December 1985) in the series "Profiles of Kenyan Asian Patriots" also by Nazmi Durrani. It was translated into English by Naila Durrani in 2005 to mark 40th anniversary of Pinto's death. The full version of the article and all the others in the Series are included in Durrani, Nazmi (2017): Liberating Minds, Restoring Kenya's History: Anti-Imperialist Resistance by Progressive South Asian Kenyans, 1884-1965. Nairobi: Vita Books.

Rosario Da Gama Pinto.

At the age of eight he was sent to India for his education at St. Joseph's European High School, Bangalore, and later passed his matric through St. Joseph's High School, Arpora. He studied science for two years at the Karnatak College, Dharwar, before joining the Royal Indian Air Force in 1944 as an apprentice ground engineer. At only 17 years of age, he started agitating against the British Raj in India and for political freedom for Goans. When he took up a job in the Posts and Telegraph office in Bombay, after demobilization, he enthusiastically took part in a general strike and got his first glimpse of mass action and organization. He was a founder member of the Goa National Congress whose aim was to liberate Goa from colonial rule. His activities in Bombay and later in Goa made it imperative for him to leave for Kenya in order to avoid being arrested.

Pio was a top athlete in school and college in Bombay, as well as in East Africa. He won hundreds of trophies in the field of sports which he donated to poor African schools. In addition to being the Asian champion for several years he represented Kenya for the Madagascar Games and won laurels for Kenya in both 100 and 200 yards events. He was an all-rounder but excelled in short distances. He was a keen footballer and tennis player as well. He was compelled to give up sports which involved strenuous training and physical fitness to devote more time to the greater causes to which he was dedicated.

Once in Kenya, Pinto worked initially as a clerk but when he saw the conditions in Kenya under British rule, he was drawn to the struggle for independence. In 1951, Pinto started working for the East African Indian Congress movement which had its offices in the Desai Memorial Building. He formed relationships with the members and leaders of African freedom movements, Kenya African Union (KAU) and workers' organisations and worked towards achieving African-Asian unity. In 1950, when Chege Kibachia, Makhan Singh and Fred Kubai were arrested, Pinto joined hands with workers and helped to continue with the movement's work for independence.
In order to facilitate this political work, Pinto learnt Kiswahili. He believed

that it was essential to learn Kiswahili if he was going to work successfully with African leaders and workers.

To further his goal of overthrowing colonialism, he turned to journalism. With the help of D K Sharda, Haroon Ahmed, Pranlal Sheth, and later Ambu Patel, he participated in the publication of anti-government newsletters. Together with other African and Asian Kenyans, he wrote and published several newspapers and political posters. He distributed these throughout the country and put up the posters in the middle of the night throughout the city. An account of his publishing activities is given in the accompanying article 'Pio Gama Pinto – the patriotic journalist.'

Pinto was actively involved in the trade union and worker movement, hence his close relationship with the struggle for independence. Trade unions played a major part in the struggle for political and economic independence.

Pio married Miss Emma Cristine Dias of Borda, Margao, (educated in Jamshedpur), in Nairobi on 9 January 1954. Just five months later he was detained following the notorious Operation Anvil and spent the next four years in Takwa Detention Camp on Manda Island and then in restriction in Kabarnet from 1958 to 1959. He was released in July 1959. Just prior to his detention he had helped to set up a Mau Mau War Council city headquarters in Mathare and acquired a cache of arms for 1,500 city youths who had joined the freedom fighters in the Nyandarua forest.

While he was still in detention, Pinto's father passed away. From his death bed, Pinto's father requested the colonial government to allow him to see his son for one last time. But the pitiless government which his father had served loyally for 30 years, adamantly denied him this one last wish. The father died without ever seeing his son again. Pio was deeply affected and for the first time broke down and cried.

Pinto worked ceaselessly in the 1961 elections to bring KANU to victory. He joined hands with Asian Kenyans such as Chanan Singh and K P Shah and together they founded the Kenya Freedom Party as a way of marshalling support of Kenyan Asians to the African people and their leaders in the struggle for freedom. In 1963 he was elected as Member of the Central Legislative Assembly and in July of the following year he became a Specially Elected Member of the House of Representatives. In 1964 he worked late hours to establish the Lumumba Institute which was principally to train party cadres. He was a member of the Board of Governors and took a keen interest in its functions. He kept in close touch with African liberation movements and the liberation of Goa from Portuguese rule and worked to 'de-colonise' the Goans of East Africa.

It was his relentless exposure of neo-colonialism and especially his success in establishing (with others) in 1964 the Kenya African Workers' Congress, a trade union organization independent of the US dominated International Confederation of Free Trade Unions (ICFRTU) and aligned to the All Africa Trade Union Federation (AATUF), that alerted the imperialists and their stooges to classify Gama Pinto as 'a man to be watched very closely.' He began to be known as a 'leftist firebrand'.

However, it was the parliamentary coup that Pinto and his radical socialist comrades plotted that was the last straw, or final nail, in Pinto's coffin. The dawn of Uhuru had given rise to a serious ideological rift. As Kenyatta and his clique of Kanu-Kadu rightists moved closer to the neo-colonialists, the socialist group demanded a ceiling on land ownership, a more equitable distribution of wealth and just rewards for the Mau Mau freedom fighters.

A secret conclave, held at the defunct Lumumba Institute, was chaired by Odinga, Pinto was the rapporteur. Others in attendance were Kaggia, Oneko, Akumu, Henry Wariithi, Odongo-Okello, Mak'Anyengo and Kali. The matter for discussion was the controversial Sessional Paper No 10 on African Socialism prepared by Tom Mboya and to be presented by Kenyatta to Parliament on 29 April 1965. Odinga, Pinto and Odongo-Okello had prepared their own blueprint on African Socialism and now planned to launch it on the same day thus rejecting the one of the Kenyatta government. This would have led to a vote of no-confidence, forcing Jomo Kenyatta's government to resign barely four months after he was sworn in as Kenya's first president on December 12, 1964.

Pinto was the master-mind of the coup plot. When in February, 1965 the National Intelligence Service informed Kenyatta that the plot could succeed, Pinto was eliminated. Then began a more concerted drive to destabilize and ultimately silence the Left in Kenya. Pio Gama Pinto was the man who came closest to organizing a real political revolution in Kenya. He was Odinga's foremost tactical adviser and link-man with Eastern embassies. He was the power behind the progressive group which then controlled 98 of the 158 votes in parliament. In May 1964 he had arranged a meeting in Peking between Odinga, Murumbi, himself and the Chinese Prime Minister Chou Enlai. The latter had already stated that 'the revolutionary prospects in Africa are excellent'. Commentators say that after Pinto's murder, Odinga's political strategy floundered and never recovered.

Pio Gama Pinto's death on 24 February 1965 is best described by *Drum* magazine:

On a Wednesday morning last February, a young man drove his wife to work and then hurried home for a quick breakfast and a few minutes' play with his three daughters.

For Tereshka, aged 18 months, her father had a special treat, and one he did not often have time to give her – a drive in his car from the front door to the gateway of their home. The little ritual cost Pio Gama Pinto, one of Kenya's most loved freedom fighters, his life. For as he stopped the car to let Tereshka out, a man stepped out of the bushes near the front gate and a second man approached him from the right of the driveway.

While the little girl crouched in wild-eyed terror in the back seat, Pinto was riddled with bullets from the guns of assassins... Pio Gama Pinto was a man whose activities in Parliament, the Pan African Press, the Lumumba Institute and KANU had made him a stranger to routine. The killers who struck him down must have been determined – even desperate – to have risked assassinating him in broad daylight, in a busy thoroughfare.

It is thought they even followed him as he drove his wife, Emma, to her office – she is personal secretary to the Minister for Information – and back again, seeking any opportunity to kill.

'While police, called to the scene of the murder by horrified neighbours, operated the biggest man-hunt in Kenya's history, the great men of the land mourned one they looked on as a brother.

Pinto's selfless-ness, his caring for the down-trodden, his universality, his desire for justice and freedom not just for himself but for all human beings, his unbounded capacity for work, his crusade against imperialism, his belief in the power of the written word, his incredible generosity (he died a pauper) – all this and much more is captured in the many eulogies written by prominent nationalists and publishing pioneers for a booklet published on the first anniversary of Pinto's death, *Pio Gama Pinto, Independent Kenya's First Martyr Socialist and Freedom Fighter,* published in 1966 by Pan African Press.

Some latter-day reflections

Wang'uhu Ng'ang'a (Narc Council official)

I worked closely with Pinto as I was the deputy principal of the Lumumba Institute 1964-65. Mathew Mutiso was the principal. Pinto served on the Board of Trustees together with Bildad Kaggia (Chairman), Paul Ngei, Koduho Olwande and others. Jomo Kenyatta and Jaramogi Oginga Odinga were the patrons. The Institutewas built just beyond the present-day Safari Park Hotel on land donated by Odinga.

Pinto was a hard worker and though very soft spoken, a fantastic organizer. He was a genuine and dedicated patriot, not an opportunist, and would not have been able to fit into the present political set-up where leaders seem to be concerned only with money and glory . . .. Yes, he has been forgotten . . . those who wiped him out physically cannot be expected to preserve his memory. But now we should try to revive it so that our people can learn from his greatness. At least a road should be named after him and the Asian African exhibition at the National Museum should highlight his work.

Dr Munyua Waiyaki (one-time foreign minister)

Pinto was a first-class schemer and strategist. He outmanoeuvred the security network to secretly secure funding for KANU in the countdown to the May 1963 independence elections. The colonialists were rooting for KADU and keeping tabs on KANU's financial strength. Pinto had pulled a fast one on Intelligence by having funds from his contacts in the communist world channeled through India, re-routed to the Indian High Commission in Dar es Salaam and thence to his friend Appa Saheb Pant, the Indian High Commissioner in Kenya. While Mboya brought in 40,000 pounds from his American friends and Odinga 75,000 pounds from the Russians, Pinto brought in 160,000 pounds. On the whole, Pinto was very instrumental in delivering victory for KANU in the 1963 elections.

For maximum efficiency he chose not to contest any seat. Pinto preferred quiet operations. When most of us were shouting ourselves hoarse in the field, he remained in the office to think and plot. His prowess at scheming also came in handy for various groups working to undercut each other within Kanu. When Kenyatta felt threatened by Mboya's strong trade union base, it is Pinto he turned to in disorganizing Mboya. Using funds directly provided by Kenyatta, Pinto would secretly engineer leadership coups in labour unions allied to Mboya. Similarly, he helped Odinga to counter Mboya's Scholarships programme. Kenyan Intelligence suspected he had a hand in the murders of Chiefs Waruhiu and Hinga, and Mbotela and Ofafa. 'The murders were so professionally executed, a person with military training must have been involved,' the report stated. Pinto had trained as a soldier in the Indian Air Force.

Dennis Akumu (Chairman, Pan African Reparations Movement, Kenya)

Pio Gama Pinto and Bildad Kaggia were two ex-detainees who had a very definite ideology and a clear vision regarding the Kenya they wanted to see. They fought and made great sacrifices, not just for freedom, which was important, but for an improvement in the lives of the Kenyan people and there were two issues they were particularly concerned about: land and workers' rights.

That is why Pinto went into Parliament but refused to join government. Kenyatta tried very hard to get him to serve in the government, but Pinto wanted to influence members of Parliament to legislate on behalf of the wananchi.

Those who planned Pinto's murder and killed him did it for two reasons:
1. They believed that he was organizing a socialist alliance with Jaramogi Oginga Odinga. A group of us worked very closely with Odinga to legislate a limit of 500 acres on land ownership in Kenya. This was even agreed in a committee but never got further. Kaggia had been made an assistant minister. Kenyatta offered him a piece of land which Kaggia refused. He was then sacked from government and later joined the KPU.

All the people, from the coast to the lake fought for restoration of their lands. At the third Lancaster House Conference in 1963, the two demands of the nationalists were that 20 October be designated as Independence Day and that all grabbed land be restored to their original owners. This was not to be as Kenyatta secretly signed the document acceding to British interests. So now we are back to square one and have to take up the struggle that Pinto and others initiated.

Pinto was a very strong supporter of trade unionism. If he were alive today he would be shocked at the present wage structure, the cost of living and the pathetic condition of the workers. Pinto admired Nkrumah and through Murumbi, he got Tettegah to come to Kenya in 1964-5 and to meet Kenyatta. Pinto would be glad to know that in 1973 the Organisation of African Trade Unions was formed, I was its first secretary-general and served for 13 years and it is not affiliated to the ICFRTU even today. The struggle goes on for the second liberation – that is the best affirmation we can give to Pinto's memory.

*

The reaction to Pinto's assassination was one of utter disbelief, shock and anger. Achieng Oneko was wild. 'No, no, no! Kenyatta must explain! He must explain!' he shouted. Murumbi broke into loud sobs. According to Fitz de Souza, who was then deputy speaker of the Lower House, Pinto had been tipped off two weeks earlier that there was a plot to murder him alongside

Kaggia and Kali because of their secret anti-government activities. After consultations with trusted friends, Pinto had decided to flee to Mozambique. But Murumbi had persuaded him to stay and offered to raise the matter of his safety with Jomo Kenyatta, Mbiyu Koinange and Charles Njonjo.

Legislator Oduya Oprong confronted Mboya and asked, 'What have you people done to Pinto?' Commerce and Industry minister Gikonyo Kiano said he was 'horrified that such a thing could ever happen in this country.' That afternoon, both the Lower House and the Senate adjourned in honour of Pinto. Vice-President Odinga, sobbing, moved the House to tears as he asked for a one-week adjournment. Pio was laid to rest beside his father in the City Park Cemetery on 27 February 1965. The funeral was attended by a huge number of mourners from Kenya as well as Tanzania, Uganda, Zambia, Mozambique and India.

Kisila Mutua, 21, and Chege Thuo, 19, were arrested and charged with the crime. Chege was later acquitted and Mutua was sentenced to hang; the sentence subsequently being commuted to life imprisonment. He was released 37 years later and insisted that he had not killed Pinto. So, then who had pulled the trigger that February morning, and with whose instructions? Chief Justice Ainley delivering his judgement could not help expressing the feelings of many to this day. He said, '. . . it must be conceded that the case wears an unfinished aspect and that we may not have all who were involved in the crime before us . . .' After the verdict on July 15, 1965, Pio's brother Rosario wrote a personal letter to Kenyatta stating that he was not at all happy with the outcome of the trial.

It is to Pio's credit that his friends and colleagues in the socialist movement stayed loyal to him even in death. They defied diplomatic protocol, and in the face of the Kenya Government's indifference, even made secret donations to the Pinto Trust Fund which was set up a week after the murder. The joint trustees were Murumbi, Oneko, Kali and Fitz de Souza. Apart from the many Kenyans, Julius Nyerere of Tanzania, the Chinese and Soviet governments and others donated generously. Emma Pinto and her three daughters, Linda, Malusha and Tereshka emigrated to Canada where they are now settled.

Kamoji Wachira (2005): Gama-Pinto, the Linkman

Kamoji Wachira: Gama-Pinto, the Linkman - Underground Networks in the Fifties[46]

Underground Networks in the Fifties

Impressions from a reunion of descendants

My contribution consists of thoughts and impressions that resulted from an almost accidental reunion that took place in Ottawa, Canada last year – thoughts and impressions on the events and political work of Pio and his friends.

I have emphasised the networks of sympathizers that served both as a backdrop as well as camouflage, in other words, a "stage-curtain" shielding the secret mass-work rolling out on

The idea of a retrospective on Pio Gama-Pinto[1] was too exciting to pass up. I applaud the editors of *Awaaz* for dedicating this special issue to the memory of Pio Gama-Pinto, a true beacon for Kenya if ever there was one[2]. This issue comes not a moment too soon. After a wretched forty years under KANU and a further two years of inexcusable mass deception under NARC – the question as to how we got here and how we might get out may be illuminated a little.

BELOW With ex-detainee colleagues. Left to right, J D Kali, Kungu Karumba, Paul Ngei and Msinga Chokwe

BY KAMOJI WACHIRA

the stage of history and interspersed it with family photographs of Pio with family and colleagues in the 50s and 60s released specially for this article by Emma and Linda Gama-Pinto. Their gesture is gratefully acknowledged here. (it is regretted that not all the individuals appearing on the photographs could be identified)

In May 2004, I learned that Dr Ongong'a Achieng, the current chief of the Kenya Tourist Bureau, was passing through Ottawa on a business mission. Ongong'a is the son of Ramogi Achieng Oneko. Achieng along with Bildad Kaggia, Pio and others formed the militant core of 'young turks' in the movement of the fifties. It quickly occurred to me that his visit had good potential since Pio's family now live here in Ottawa. I contacted Emma to arrange for a reunion. Due to family illness overseas she was out of the country but as luck would have it her elder daughter, Linda, kindly accepted to meet with us. Prior to the meeting I provided Linda with a sprinkling of Ongong'a's background information ". . . son of Achieng Oneko Kenyatta's first Minister of Information . . . your Mum was that minister's personal secretary." In fact, Linda would have already known of the Achieng family

9. Kamoji Wachira's article in Awaaz magazine (2005)

…

In May 2004, I learned that Dr. Ongong'a Achieng, the current chief of the

46   Reproduced from *Awaaz* No. 1 (2005). The Editor thanks *Awaaz* and the author for permission to reproduce the article. This is a shorter version of the original article - Ed.

Kenya Tourist Bureau, was passing through Ottawa on a business mission. Ongong'a is the son of Ramogi Achieng Oneko. Achieng along with Bildad Kaggia, Pio and others formed the militant core of 'young turks' in the movement of the fifties. It quickly occurred to me that his visit had good potential since Pio's family now live here in Ottawa. I contacted Emma to arrange for a reunion. Due to family illness overseas, she was out of the country but as luck would have it her elder daughter, Linda, kindly accepted to meet with us. Prior to the meeting I provided Linda with a sprinkling of Ongong'a's background information ". . . son of Achieng Oneko Kenyatta's first Minister of Information . . . your Mum was that minister's personal secretary." In fact, Linda would have already known of the Achieng family from Emma who still recalls with awe and excitement her days working for Minister Achieng as private secretary.

It was early summer on a very pleasant warm afternoon when the three of us met in a downtown Ottawa hotel lobby. Ongong'a was visibly moved, in fact very deeply moved. He would have been the older of the two children. Meeting now as adults seemed to bring back waves of mixed emotions from the distant past. They hugged each other and exchanged warm greetings. Ongong'a expressed joyfully "how wonderful to see you again finally. . . I knew you as a little girl long ago . . ."

As for me, needless to say, I felt immensely honoured to be present at this unique reunion anticipating at least a few gems of history from the ensuing conversation. In spite of the brevity of the encounter, I was not disappointed. I will share some of them here but first let me set up the context with some background for the benefit of those readers who may not be aware of the role played by the two families in Kenya's mid-century sweep of events. I could not help but reflect, even wonder, as I watched the discussion unfold: Were it not for the vicissitudes of history, these two individuals would not have had reason to be meeting that day.

Few people could have more divergent social backgrounds than them. Linda was born in Nairobi, the first child in a family of educated Indo-Kenyan professionals of Goan affinity. Thanks to the resourcefulness and perseverance of her newly widowed mother (herself born and raised in

India), Linda emigrated to Canada as a young girl with the rest of the family soon after Pio's assassination. Emma was determined to begin a new life in a new land and to ensure that the three young daughters had maximum opportunity to grow, to excel and transcend the tragic loss of their father. As a result, Linda and her sisters, Tereshka and Malusha, have done remarkably well professionally and personally in their adopted country.

Ongong'a was born into a strong, traditional Luo setting and grew up deep in rural Nyanza within a large extended peasant family. His parents, being sticklers for diligence and high achievement, insisted on a good education and high academic achievement in spite of the obvious colonial obstacles against rural Africans at the time. Since his father was a peripatetic political organizer, the young schoolboy, unlike his rural peers, would have enjoyed frequent sojourns in Nairobi, Kisumu and possibly other towns. As an adolescent, thanks to his father, he eventually met and got to know Pio who gradually became something of an uncle to him; sweets, advice, car rides and all. Thus, he would have met the Gama-Pinto girls in the early 1960's when they were not much more than toddlers.

The relationship between Ongong'a and Pio would, however, eventually prove very handy in his political work during the Emergency. Unlike Ongong'a who recalls those times with fondness and considerable emotion, none of the Gama-Pinto girls could possibly be expected to recall either the events or their father in any great detail.

It is important also to recall here the historical circumstances that had brought their fathers, Pio and Achieng, together across the huge racial divide of the times. Like their offspring, the two men had been born into even more diverse and rigid social settings which were common during that eerie period between WW I and the Depression. But, as fate would have it, the two were destined to collaborate intimately on the stage of history - one briefly, brilliantly and tragically, the other courageously and persistently when not painfully locked away for decades by either the settler or Kenyatta regimes.

Through separate meandering paths their lives had converged after WW II as militant members of the Kenya African Union (KAU) and later KANU before it degenerated irreversibly. Achieng had been a precocious and fiercely dedicated anti-colonial fighter practically since his teens. As part of their work within KAU and other early movements the two friends would have also been part of, or in close touch with, a web of semi-clandestine networks of sympathisers that quietly linked African fighters with urban non-Africans. Network members came from diverse backgrounds but included progressive folk of South Asian descent with occupations in business, civil service, the professions and the trade unions.

The term 'networks' is used freely here to mean informal or semi-formal centers of like-minded people with a semi-united general purpose. In this case the purpose was to oppose British colonialism if not overthrow it altogether. They may not all have agreed on specific means of action, but they were united by a fundamental dislike for imperial occupation and the rampant racialist discrimination. They were also aware of topical international events especially regarding the then much hated "yoke of colonialism" as the cliché went across the colonized world. More likely than not, they were well versed in the increasingly militant liberation struggles already afoot after WW II - not least the nationalist fervour generated by Mahatma Gandhi et al in India and by the many congress parties he helped found elsewhere, including in Kenya.

Not far in the background, and still quite secret, the Mau Mau war drums were beginning to roll led by Dedan Kimathi and the famous "Aanake a Forty", again actively linked to Pio and Achieng and their networks. Further Pio, during his travels in Asia, had cultivated an impressive list of overseas supporters and anti-colonial contacts. Soon after independence, these linkages were to prove useful for financial support to Kenya's economic development and mass awareness. Paradoxically, that financial support may also have proved tragically fatal as the independence movement rapidly entered the proverbial stage of consuming its own architects.

This summary hopefully gives the reader a flavour or a hint of the dynamic and fluid political setting into which Pio plunged with such zest on returning from India in 1947. Most people in Kenya in the early 50's were rapidly accepting the fact that the colonial settlers would not sit back and accept the growing rebellion against their hard-won order. There was an air of foreboding amongst all the privileged communities but not so for most Africans and their sympathisers. They sensed a chance to overturn colonial occupation. I myself recall clearly a short-lived, pre-Emergency period of happy anticipation. Pio and Achieng, like the young vanguards then leading Mau Mau in Central Province, must have welcomed the rapidly escalating situation with revolutionary relish. Finally, the colonial contradictions were coming to a head - and why not, better sooner than later - they must have thought. The war for freedom was now inevitable. The Mau Mau war finally broke out into the open in 1951-52. Little did they know what painful fate awaited them only 15 years later, as the many strands of militant interests and counter-interests matured.

In a conversation with Achieng in 1979, he narrated to me how in fact the 'young turks' had prepared themselves mentally for any eventuality. Soon they would all be arrested and locked up in various isolated places without trial or family access by habeus corpus. Achieng and Pio were to meet briefly inside Takwa detention camp on Manda island (Lamu area). Achieng was later tried with the Kapenguria Six at Kapenguria and imprisoned for a total of eight years. Pio was transferred to so-called 'restriction' status at Kabarnet in 1958 and released in1959 after more than four years in prison.

Returning now to our reunion in Ottawa last summer, Linda asked Ongon'ga, "I really did not know my father well. Please tell me, what kind of person was my father?" She was six years of age when her father was assassinated. I was very touched by that question which reminded me of a book I once read in detention entitled "Daddy, we hardly Knew You". Ongong'a, still quite stirred emotionally, was now at a loss for words and took some time to find the right pitch. After all it had been 40 years back, and his was a boy's mind then - the better for vivid recall today. ". . . Pio . . . oh my, he was a simply an unbelievable human being, a happy man with an an easy laugh . . . a most compassionate man, generous to his last cent. He went out of his way to help the poor, fostered many families of detained fighters . . . . Pio worked all day and all night. He was especially good to me . . . gave me small gifts and sweets, rides in his car too. He was a wonderful man indeed . . ."

Obviously, the boy Ongon'g'a loved this man and he was running out of superlatives as he strained to recall the Pio he knew in 1962 or 1963. Linda, now 45 years old, was keen to hear another person's impressions of a father she had only learned about from her Mum. She was eager to dispel images she held of her father as a dour type, an earnest man with a grave demeanour. She was gratified by what she was hearing. This new image pleased her – to learn that he had an easy laugh, that he was a likeable man with such a gentle touch. This alone made the reunion truly worthwhile for her.

Linda also wanted to know what drove her father with such single mindedness that her own family hardly got the full attention of his mind and presence. She was of course raising the perennial dilemma of political activists who are always split between two loves: revolution on the one hand and family on the other. One always gets short shrift and it is almost always the latter.

I managed to slip in a few questions especially about the support networks and could not resist the opportunity to chime in: "Ongong'a tell us of incidents that stand out in your memory of Pio as a political worker".

"There are so many . . . I wouldn't know where to start . . . let's see . . . in 1961 my father was under 'restriction' detention at Kapsabet by the British. As his child I was allowed to visit him occasionally. Somehow Pio and his men [networks] must have known the dates of those visits and obviously involved my mother or uncles in the planning of my visits. On one such visit Pio showed up out of nowhere with his car and drove me all the way to Kapsabet. He dropped me off a distance from the District Commissioner's office and instructed me to go and pick up the official permit required to enter the detention centre where my father was locked up. Permission eventually granted, I walked back, just as I had been instructed, towards his car parked a distance away. He drove some way, stopped, and pulled out an envelope from his coat pocket and carefully stashed it into the well concealed inside left pocket of my shirt. "Do not touch it . . . give the permit to the guards and walk straight into Baba's place". The guards allowed me in, after all what great harm could a small boy do? Looking back, it is amazing to me that on entering the house my father, before even greeting me, rushed straight to me and reached uncannily into the precise pocket under my shirt where Pio had placed the note - as if he had prior knowledge where it would be placed. It must all have been perfectly pre-arranged. He read it with obvious interest and haste, then and only then did he greet me warmly, now asking about home and family. Those were the unchangeable priorities of those young men then, politics then family.

This incident, looking back now, was remarkable - Pio was obviously part of an underground mail or message system that linked detainees with free activists, underground fighters and other networks. Being South Asian he had greater freedom of movement after his own release from detention than any African. Pio had clearly chosen to put this colonial advantage into good use at the service of the movement. I am impressed how he sacrificed himself, at such great risk and expense for the cause of freedom. He never wavered, his commitment was total.

Unfortunately, Ongong'a had to rush to the airport but before he left we took some photographs. Eager to continue the conversation later, he invited the Gama-Pintos to visit Kenya and retrace their roots. I am sure there will be more impressions to gather as the story continues and more information becomes available. For the country and for the family, there are still many unanswered questions on Pio's last few days and on the identity of the real perpetrators of his murder.

Dinesh Singh (1975): Pio - Son of India

By Dinesh Singh MP[47]

No account of the history of modern Kenya will be complete without taking in account Pio Gama Pinto's contribution to the liberation struggle of its people. A staunch nationalist and a socialist, Pio was second to none in upholding human values. He was active, able and unassuming.

One of the first Asians to take part in Kenya's struggle for freedom, Pio completely identified himself with Africa and created an awareness among the people of Asian origin living there that their fortune and future lay in the plains and hills of that great continent and that it was their duty to work for the development of countries where they lived.

Liberation of Kenya from foreign rule being his passion he threw himself into the vanguard of the movement. Barely 5 months after his marriage, in 1954, he was arrested in the infamous Operation Anvil and was put under detention for 4 years on Manda Island along with the "hard-cord" Mau Mau men. Later, he was confined to remote Karbanet from early 53 to October 1959.

In the early days of KANU, Pio was in the forefront of the movement. Also, in the formative stages of trade unionism, he was adviser and helper to the trade unions, enabling them to establish themselves on sound trade union principles and practices. Since he was not attached to any one union, he helped them all without creating any rivalries – a success, which no other trade unionist could achieve.

Again, it was he who initiated a nationalist Press in Kenya and helped its growth. He built up the Lumumba Institute and worked very closely with F.R.E.L.I.M.O . and the Committee of Nine approved by OAU. He was one

---

47   Former deputy minister in Ministry of External Affairs; Minister of State- External Affairs; Minister of Commerce; Minister of External Affairs; Minister of Industrial Development & Internal Trade; Chairman of the Indian Council for Africa; Member of India's Delegation to FAO; 15th Session of the UNO; 16th Session of ESAFA; Tourist Development Council & Innumerable other Organisation.

of those few people who did so much without holding any office.

Deeply concerned about the lot of ordinary people, he made untiring efforts to build a society where differences in wealth should not penalize the poor. He wanted to see development in all parts of the country, especially in areas which had achieved very little development under colonial rule. He advocated rent control in urban areas to protect tenants from being exploited landlords. He also advocated establishment of free health services and free education as a method of assisting the less privileged people in the community. He opposed the practices whereby a few individuals in privileged positions could amass excessive wealth at the expense of the masses. He believed that people in such positions should do more for the masses. And he was a true socialist in precept and practice.

For us in India, Pio is remembered as one of the founders of the Goa National Congress and as one who has contributed greatly in forging close Indo -African relations.

It is a tragedy that Pinto did not live long to see the fruition of his efforts in various fields. He was assassinated 10 years ago. Though he is no longer in our midst, the ideals for which he worked and sacrificed his life are still alive. The light kindled by him is still dispelling the darkness in our society.

Malcolm MacDonald (1975): Pio Pinto

Pio Pinto

I knew Pio well during the vitally important period in Kenya from the opening days of 1963 onwards until the time of his tragic death. The important old British colony was then progressing through the last stage of its transition from dependence to Independence, and the new Kenyan nation was being born. Pio was an extremely able organiser and advocate of the Nationalist cause, and he played a very important part, though mostly quietly "in the wings" beside the public stage, in making that very significant piece of modern history. He continued to influence events and prospects considerably after Independence was attained in December 1963. I sometimes partially disagreed with his ideas and aims after that event, but this made no difference whatever to my high admiration for him. Nor did it alter his and my cordial personal friendship. He was a delightful friend, with a pleasing character and sharp, bright intellect which were enjoyably stimulating. In public affairs he was as capable an organiser of a political movement as I have ever known at any time in any country round the world. Moreover, in his ceaseless, tireless strivings for the causes which he championed he was absolutely sincere, dedicated and honourable. His very premature death was a tragedy for them, as well as for all his colleagues and friends.

~~William MacDonald~~

January, 1975.

10. *Sir Malcolm MacDonald: Pio Pinto*

My father [Rosario Da Gama Pinto] did his best to keep Pio's memory alive. He asked Malcolm MacDonald, former Governor General of Kenya, to write a piece on Pio – Audrey Da Gama Pinto, personal communications, 15-07-1018 – Editor.

I knew Pio well during the vitally important period in Kenya from the opening days or 1963 onwards until the time of his tragic death. The important old British Colony was then progressing through the last stage of its transition from dependence to independence, and the new Kenyan Nation was being born. Pio was an extremely able organiser and advocate of the Nationalist cause, and he played a very important part, though mostly quietly "in the wings" beside the public stage, in making that very significant piece of modern history. He continued to influence events and prospects considerably after independence was attained in December 1963. I sometimes partially disagreed with his ideas and aims after that event, but this made no difference whatever to my high admiration for him, nor did it alter his and my cordial personal friendship. He was a delightful friend, with a pleasing character and sharp, bright intellect which were enjoyably stimulating. In public affairs he was as capable an organiser of a political movement as I have ever known at any time in any country round the world. Moreover, in his ceaseless, tireless striving for the causes which he championed he was absolutely sincere, dedicated and honourable. His very premature death was a tragedy for them, as well as for all his colleagues and friends.

Malcolm MacDonald.
January 1975.
MacDonald Papers
SDMP-LIBPG-5

Lord Fenner Brockway (1974): Pio[48]

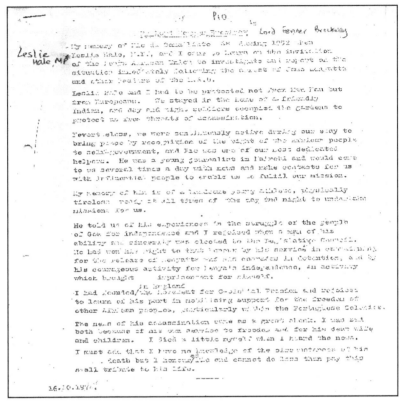

11. *Lord Fenner Brockway: Pio*

My memory of Pio Gama Pinto is during 1952 when Leslie Hale, MP and I came to Kenya on the invitation of the Kenya African Union to investigate and report on the situation immediately following the arrest of Jomo Kenyatta and other leaders of the K.A.U. Leslie Hale and I had to be protected not from Mau Mau but from Europeans. We stayed in the home of a friendly Indian, and day and night soldiers occupied the gardens to protect us from threats of assassination.

---

48   Source: Panaf files.

Nevertheless, we were continuously active during our stay to bring peace by recognition of the right of the African people to self-government, and Pio was one of our most dedicated helpers. He was a young journalist in Nairobi and would come to us several times a day with news and make contacts for us with influential people to enable us to fulfil our mission.

My memory of him is of a handsome young athlete, physically tireless, ready at all times of the day and night to undertake missions for us.

He told us of his experiences in the struggle of the people of Goa for independence and I rejoiced when a man of his ability and sincerity was elected to the Legislative Council. He had won his rights to that honour by his service in campaigning for the release of Kenyatta and his comrades in detention, and by his courageous activity for Kenya's independence, an activity which brought imprisonment for himself.

I had founded in England the Movement for Colonial Freedom and rejoiced to learn of his part in mobilizing support for the freedom of other African peoples, particularly within the Portuguese colonies.

The news of his assassination came as a great shock. I was sad both because of his own service to freedom and for his dear wife and children. I died a little myself when I heard the news.

I must add that I have no knowledge of the circumstances of his death but I honoured Pio and cannot do less than pay this small tribute to his life.

16.10.1974

Makhan Singh (1965): The Assassination of Pio Gama Pinto[49]

THE ASSASSINATION OF PIO GAMA PINTO

※

Pio Gama Pinto was gunned down in his car on Wednesday 24th February, 1965, at the gate of his house, his 18-month old daughter was with him. Two mornings later Makhan Singh made a broadcast, a half-hour report in Hindustani on the Voice of Kenya, recorded by Haroon Ahmed and C L Chaman.

The first time Mr P G Pinto met me was in 1949, after completing his education. He had recently come back from India and was at that time working in Magadi as a clerk. He had come to Nairobi on an outing. During those days our national freedom and trade union movements were going on vigorously. Mr. Pinto told me that he was interested in the movement and was already doing whatever was possible for him under the circumstances. The impression he gave me was that of a good freedom-loving young man. At that time he was in a hurry; so he left after a few minutes.

The second time he met me was a few days before my arrest in 1950. He said he was now ready to take an active part in the freedom struggle and, if necessary, he was prepared to leave his service. I advised him that before doing so he should obtain his certificate of permanent residence so that when he became active the colonial government should not be able to deport him from the

12. Makhan Singh's article on Pinto reproduced from Patel, Z (2006)

49 Reproduced from: Patel, Zarina (2006): Unquiet. Nairobi: Zand

Pio Gama Pinto was gunned down in his car on Wednesday 24ᵗʰ February, 1965, at the gate of his house. His 18-month old daughter was with him. Two mornings later, Makhan Singh made a broadcast, a half-hour report in Hindustani on the voice of Kenya, recorded by Haroon Ahmed and CL Chaman - Patel, Z. (2006).

The first time Mr. P G Pinto met me was in 1949, after completing his education. He had recently come back from India and was at that time working in Magadi as a clerk. He had come to Nairobi on an outing. During those days our national freedom and trade union movements were going on vigorously. Pinto told me that he was interested in the movement and was already doing whatever possible for me under the circumstances. The impression he gave me was that of a good freedom loving young man. At that time, he was in a hurry; so, he left a few minutes.

The second time he met me was a few days before my arrest in 1950. He said he was now ready to take an active part in the freedom struggle and, if necessary, he was prepared to leave his service. I advised him that before doing so he should obtain his certificate of permanent residence so that when he became active the colonial government should not be able to deport him from the country. He agreed and went away after leaving a few political magazines with me.

After a few days (along with Fred Kubai) I was arrested on the 15ᵗʰ May 1950, on account of my political and trade union activities. The arrest was followed by a general strike and along political case, and I was sent into restriction at a small village, Lokitaung, near the boundary of Kenya and Ethiopia.

By this action the colonial government on the one hand wanted to punish me and keep me in complete isolation from the outside world, and on the other it wanted to frighten the other freedom loving Africans and Asians in order to prevent them from taking part in the freedom struggle. But Pinto was not a man who could be frightened. Even after seeing what had happened to me he entered the arena of struggle. Soon after my restriction Mr. Pinto left his service at Magadi, came to Nairobi, obtained his certificate of permanent residence and took plunge in the freedom struggle – so much so that since that day he never thought of retreating from the struggle and always moved forward and forward.

During my restriction while I was still at Lokitaung Mr. Pinto sent me a book by H. G. Wells – *An Outline [history] of the World*. He did so fully knowing that in the eyes of the colonial government even mention of my name was a big crime. On the book he mentioned that it was a present from my Nairobi friends, and also wrote two lines in English to the effect that only that is the man who not only shows the way to others but also to himself walks over the same. The lines not only gave me encouragement but also depicted the way in the way in which Mr. Pinto was himself thinking and acting. Until his last breath he walked over the same path which he had shown to others in course of our national struggle for freedom, human dignity and prosperity for all.

After my release in October 1961, I had the opportunity of working with Mr. Pinto in Kenya Freedom Party and Kenya African National Union (KANU) and I found him politically very sound and very correct. And day and night he worked so hard and so conscientiously that in the course of my own political life I have seen very few persons of that caliber.

Today P. G. Pinto is not with us. He has been taken away from us by the bullets of ghastly assassins, but his wish is alive, and we keep alive his memory for ever by actively and whole-heartedly devoting ourselves to the cause Mr. Pinto fought for all his life – the cause of freedom, peace, human dignity and prosperity for all in Kenya, East Africa, All Africa and the world.

Joseph Murumbi (2015): Pio Gama Pinto: Nationalist and Freedom Fighter[50]

Pio Pinto was an Asian. He was born in Kenya and therefore claimed to be a Kenyan. On the 31ˢᵗ of March 1927, at the age of eight he was sent to India. He went to school in India and he spent nine years there. At the age of seventeen Pio started working, first for the post and Telegraphs Company in Bombay where he got his first taste of a general strike. He was a founding member of the Goan National congress whose objective was Liberation from Portuguese rule.

Bombay was the heart of the Indian struggle for national struggle for national independence. Everything emanated from Bombay- the money for the finance of the Indian Congress as well as its greatest personalities. It was here, I think, that Pio got his first taste of Politics. And owing to his activities against Portuguese rule in Goa, he found his position rather hot. As the Portuguese and British Governments were always in league, no doubt there were recommendations by the Portuguese to the British Government, or the Indian Government under Britain, to get Pio out of India or arrest him. Sensing that danger lay ahead, he returned to Kenya.

Pio was rather an unusual character: honest, dedicated, sincere, and a great nationalist. As Odinga said in a note in a Pamphlet published by the Pan African Press in honour of Pio, "Anyone who met Pio soon forgot his pigmentation because his works and deeds left no doubt that he was a Kenyan Nationalist."

The guiding principle of Pio's life was to maintain liberty and democracy and a fair chance for all, particularly those he loved and respected: the elders who bore the brunt of the struggle for independence, the old men of the KCA, who also joined him in detention. He met them, he lived with them, he was detained with them, and therefore he felt he knew them sincerely, and he never let them down. Although Pio was a poor man (he was really a pauper) he maintained his respect for people. I remember Oneko and I had

---

50   Selection from Thurston, Anne (2015, Ed.): A Path Not Taken: The Story of Joseph Murumbi, Africa's Greatest Cultural Collector and Kenya's Second Vice-President. Nairobi: The Murumbi Trust. The Editor would like to thank the Murumbi Trust, the Murumbi Archives and Alan Donovan for permission to reproduce material on Pio Gama Pinto in this book.

a fund, a thousand to two thousand pounds a term, and this was intended to help those in need. Pio used to produce a list practically every week, and on the list were the names of poor people who had been with him in detention and who were practically starving; they had no jobs and they had families to maintain. Pio used to produce this list and the people listed were to be given twenty shillings, thirty shillings, fifty shillings, a hundred shillings. When we received the list we never questioned it because Pio, we knew, would never let us down. He was not deceitful in any way. He got his money and this money was given to those in need. Besides that, as Secretary of the Pan African Press, he was getting fifty pounds a month, and so was I as secretary to the President and General Manager of the Press. Pio used to tell his wife that his salary was twenty-five pounds, and not fifty, the twenty-five pounds used to be given to the poor people in need.

What motivated Pio to help and honour people?

It was really his principles. As I said in my appreciation of Pio, "Politically his views were beyond many of us in his depth of political understanding and social consciousness. To him socialist meant its true application." Pio lived his Socialism. He lived by his principles, and he died by his principles. He was quick to react to any injustice, and he spent long hours helping other people, but he never helped himself. As a matter of fact, Pio didn't own a house. We suggested that he ought to buy one, but he was very reluctant. Still, he had a family and children, and he needed a roof over his head, so we decided that we would get him a house. Houses in those days didn't cost as much as today. A reasonable three-bed roomed house would cost about 2500. So, we went to Emma and told her that we had decided to buy a house for Pio and that should sour around the town and find one. We would not give the money to Pio because we knew that if the money as in Pio's hands it would soon be distributed to all his friends and those in need. She found a house, we gave her the money to buy it, and then we told Pio we'd bought a house for him.

I cannot but speak with emotion about Pio. He was my sincere friend. If it weren't for Pio, I don't think I would have entered politics. I had returned from Somali and was at a meeting where an Indian politician was speaking.

Pio Gama Pinto, Kenya's Unsung Martyr

I asked a few questions of the speaker and after the meeting Pio came to me and asked me who I was. He naturally didn't know me because I had been in Somali for eleven years. I told him who I was and he took an interest in me. He introduced me to the Kenya study group, and we went regularly to discuss Kenyan's problems. We maintained a close friendship and he urged me on into politics. I became the acting secretary of the party when President Kenyatta and the Central Committee of the Kenya African Union were arrested. When I left for India during the trial, Pio kept me posted of all the events in Kenya by sending me regular press cuttings and reports. I found these invaluable as they kept brief on current affairs and were used for my lectures in different parts of India.

Pio kept constant touch with British politicians, such as Fenner Brockway. Fenner was the Chairman of the movement for Colonial Freedom. He was an old stalwart who took a great interest in the liberation of India and after India's independence he switched his interest to Africa. He was a member of parliament for Slough, and he was commonly known as the "Member of Parliament for Africa "because of his interest. He also stimulated this interest among fellow Members of Parliament in the Labour Movement, and he was responsible for forming the Movement for Colonial Freedom which took a great part in the liberation of Africa from the British.

Pio sent Brockway regular Letters, reports, and these of course were sent to a cover address, Mrs. Ella Reed, wife of the correspondent of the Hindustan Times. So this information was channeled to Fenner and to Mr. Reed, who kept the Indian papers informed of activities in Kenya and who actually visited Nairobi during the Emergency.

When I arrived in London, Fenner Brockway handed me a lot of Pio's reports in England. How Pio found the time to do all this is remarkable. We know because he was dedicated. He believed in the cause, he was more African than many other Africans, and he used his intelligences and training very effectively in providing the right information that we needed in London and that we used as the basis for questions in the House of Commons.

For instance, he sent us information that the Government in Kenya was using Maasai Warriors in the security forces to fight the Mau Mau forces.

Pio managed to speak to Mr. John Tameno and convince him that it was wrong for the Maasai to participate in a war that was not theirs. Tameno managed to convince the warriors that they were fighting for a cause which was not their own. They had no quarrel with the Kikuyu and thus should not follow the British Government, or the Colonial Kenya Government, in their efforts to suppress a true nationalist movement. The warriors then withdrew.

In his reports Pio also mentioned the conditions on detention camps. The people who were brought to the camps were kept out in the open with one blanket, subject to the cold and hazards of the weather, and this necessitated prompt action. It was possible to stop this immediately, and the detainees were properly housed. There were numerous other incidents where Pio's reports caused a lot of stir among government officials, and they knew of his activities to a certain extent.

Pio's background included many other activities. He, with Peter Wright who was later deported from Kenya, assisted in forming the KAU African Study Circle, of which Odede was the Chairman and I was the secretary. This study circle filled a gap caused by the arrest of the president and other national leaders, it prevented the national movement from disintegrating, and it was a great help to us during the trial of Jomo Kenyatta.

Pinto was very active in helping, particularly young newspapermen who used to publish broadsheets in those days. And of course, they couldn't afford a duplicating machine. I think he also helped them financially in a limited way in buying them paper, but he was working in the Asian Congress office where he had a duplicating machine, and he used to type these broadsheets for them, sometimes, invariably he rollered these himself. In those days we didn't have electric duplicating machines. You had to turn them with your hand and Pinto was instrumental in getting thee broadsheets out. And these broadsheets were sometimes banned. Well, in those days if a broadsheet was banned you had a month to cease publication. So, after that month the same broadsheet came out in another name. They continued right through out. And, Pinto was the man behind these people, encouraging them, helping them to write these broadsheets, helping them to duplicate it, and sometimes financially he used to help them as well, and he was trying

Pio Gama Pinto, Kenya's Unsung Martyr

to also get a change amongst the Indians. And it was he who organized the young Indians who came forward to help us, there were several of them, I don't remember their names now, but he is the one who kept prodding them, and telling them your future is not with the Indian people. Your fathers are conservatives in their attitude toward the Africans. Your future lies in the country, and therefore you should reach an accommodation with the Africans and do all you can to help them and identify yourselves with the struggle. In that way lies your security, the security of the country.

In 1952, in the latter part of the year, Pio resigned from the post as Secretary of the Indian National Congress to become the editor of the Daily Chronicle and Correspondent of the Press Trust of India and All India Radio. Of course, these duties did not prevent Pio from keeping a close liaison with political and trade union leaders who were not yet arrested. He was also responsible for the formation of the Kenya League which was made up of Young Indians who were disturbed at the reactionary trends of the Indian National Congress; the League was formed to try to counter this reactionary trend. Pio was also General Secretary of the East African Students Federation. And during the Lancaster House Conference, he assisted in the formation of the Kenya Freedom Party and worked as its Assistant Secretary. The Kenya Freedom party was dissolved as soon as KANU opened its doors to non-Africans.

After his release from detention and restriction, Pio worked very closely with KANU. Together with Odinga, Mboya and Gichuru, he founded *Sauti ya KANU* which saw us through the first general elections. In 1962 he worked as commercial manager of the Pan Africa press Limited which published Sauti ya Mwafrika and *Pan Africa*. During the election campaigns he also served as an honorary secretary of the KANU Nairobi Election Committee which was a sponsor for the campaign involving certain seats in the House of Representatives.

Pio developed an interest in Mozambique whilst he was in India and on his return to Kenya he tried to mobilize the Mozambican workers who were engaged in sisal estates on the coast. He assisted in the formation of the Mozambique National Union which was linked with the newly formed FRELIMO.

PIO PINTO AND KAU

As I said before, Pio found time to engage himself in a variety of interests, and it needed a lot of tact, a lot of intelligence, and a lot of hard work to maintain his contacts and work for other people. Pio always worked for other people, he never worked for himself. He was always writing petitions, memoranda for Members of Parliament, helping people out of their problems, trying to find money to assist them, going to see the families of people who were away from Kenya on some job or the other. I remember when as Foreign Minister I was out of the country, he used to visit my wife Sheila and ask whether she needed money or take her out for a meal and make her feel comfortable whilst I was away. He did this for many people and when people were sick in hospital, he would visit them.

The time came for pio to take a more active interest in politics, and as there was a specially elected seat vacant, and candidates were elected by the House of Parliament as a whole, Pio applied for this position-offered himself as a candidate. In his modes way in a circular letter to all members of Parliament, he had this to say, "It is essential that you should be aware as far as practicable the past activities of the potential candidate as a guide of what to expect him in the future. "Now, Pio had done quite a lot, there is no doubt that he devoted his entire time, his life, as a matter of fact till his death, to working for Kenya. I have never met a more dedicated man than Pio. He was elected, a specially elected member of parliament. It was a joyous occasion, and in view of his popularity with the members, as soon as the announcement was made, Pio was hoisted shoulders high by the Members. It was a sign of appreciation for what he had for Kenya, for individual members and for the people as a whole.

PINTO'S DEATH

February the 24th 1965 will always stand out in my memory as a sad day when I lost a very sincere friend. Both Sheila and I were very much affected by Pio's death, and every year on that day we visit Pio's grave with a bouquet of flowers to make him know that we still remember him. There are others too- I don't know who they are-who on the many occasions when I've been to his grave on the 24th of February have put flowers there. It was a sad day when Pio died. I was at home having a shave when Achieng Oneko rang to say he had information that Pio had been beaten up at his home and for me to go up and see what happened. As I was not ready yet, I sent my driver and a man called Cheche who worked for me to go and see what had happened. I would follow. I immediately dressed and rushed up to the house and parked my car besides Pio's gate. Pio's car was parked just a little outside the gate, and I saw Pio in there and I thought he was hurt. I rushed to him and I said, "Pio what has happened, what has happened?" And the police officer told me, "Don't say anything to him, he is dead. "It was tremendous shock. His wife was in the office (she used to work for Achieng Oneko), but his mother-in-law to do but make the best of it, So we sent for his wife, and the news soon got around that Pio was dead.

The whole day we had people coming to the house. They were poor people, friends of Pio, people he had helped, people who had been with him in detention, and the place was jammed the whole day. The next day we buried Pio. People from far and wide in Kikuyu came to the funeral. There were people in the church where we had the requiem mass, there were people who went to the wrong cemetery, the forest Road Cemetery; but Pio was buried in the City Park, the main cemetery, and that was jammed with people. There were many foreign ministers from the neighboring territories like Oscar Kambona, Sam Udaka, and others who were in Nairobi at the time. They all came to the funeral. It was really pathetic to see elderly Kikuyu weeping for a man who helped them in need, a man who was their colleague in detention, and a man who had never forgotten them. The public response was tremendous and even today people speak of respect whenever the name of Pio Pinto is mentioned. All that is now past, but Pio will always be remembered as one of the first patriots who gave their lives for freedom and democracy. In view of the subsequent assassinations of Tom Mboya, and J.M. Kariuki, it is interesting to note that Rosario Da Gama Pinto, Pio's brother. In a letter to President Kenyatta, appealing for a public enquiry to be held in addition to the trial, to get to the bottom of Pio's death, wrote, "I sincerely hope that you would kindly consider this appeal with a view to remedying this unhappy situation which might encourage similar assassinations and outrages against persons and families of public spirited individual who are really dedicated to the implementation of African Socialism." Rosaria was very much affected by this, and in the end he left for India. Pio's wife Emma and the children have also gone to Canada. Emma felt she couldn't stay in Kenya and with the help of Paul Martin, the Canadian Foreign Minister, I managed to get her permission to immigrate to Canada where she has now become a citizen and is quite happy and living with her mother; the children are now grown up.

An interesting sidelight to Pio's popularity, Africapix, and East African picture agency, made a film of Pio's funeral and Ivor Davis who owns Africapix gave the family a free copy of the film. As he put it in his letter, the 9th of April 1965, "This is a small tribute to a man for whom we at Africapix had a great regard."

That was the life of Pio Pinto, a great Patriot, a great nationalist, great friend and one whose name will live in the annals of Kenyan history.

Pinto in his Own Words

A Rising Politician's
Autobiography.

☆

Mr. P. G. PINTO

A DETAINEE'S LIFE STORY
(By HIMSELF)

Mr. P. G. Pinto was born in Nairobi in 1927. He was educated in India and returned to Kenya in 1949. While in India he took an active part in the Goa National Congress and was one of its founder members and a member of its National Executive. In 1950 he returned to Kenya and in 1951 joined the E.A. Indian National Congress as its paid Secretary. He helped in reorganising the E.A. Labour Trade Union after the arrests of Makhan Singh and Fred Kubai. Later he developed close relations with leaders of the Kenya African Union, the Kikuyu Independent Schools Association, the Karing'a Independent Schools Association and the African Orthodox Church. In 1952 he helped in founding the Kenya League and was its Hon. Asst. Secretary at the time of its proscription. In 1953 Mr. Pinto took over the editorship of the "Daily Chronicle" and was the East African correspondent of All-India Radio.

Mr. Pinto was arrested and detained on 19th June, 1954, and taken to Takwa Detention Camp on Manda

13. Pinto: A Detainee's Life Story

Pinto in his Own Words

Pio Gama Pinto (1963)[51]: A Detainee's Life Story

MR. P. G. PINTO: A DETAINEE'S LIFE STORY

(By HIMSELF)

Mr. P.G. Pinto was born in Nairobi in 1927. He was educated in India and returned to Kenya in 1949. While in India he took an active part in the Goa National Congress and was one of its founder members and a member of its National Executive. In 1949 he returned to Kenya and in 1951 joined the E.A. Indian National Congress as its paid Secretary. He helped in reorganizing the E.A. Labour Trade Union after the arrests of Makhan Sign and Fred Kubai. Later he developed close relations with leaders of the Kenya African Union, the Kikuyu Independence Schools Association, the Karing'a Independent Schools Association and the African Orthodox Church. In 1952 he helped in founding the Kenya League and was its Hon. Ass. Secretary at the time of its proscription in 1953 Mr. Pinto took over the editorship of the *Daily Chronicle* and was the East African correspondent of All-India Radio.

Mr. Pinto was arrested and detained on 19th June 1954 and taken to Takwa Detention Camp on Manda Island. His detention was suspended on 29th December 1957, and he was transferred to Kabarnet township in Baringo District on 24th January 1958. He remained at Kabarnet until 31st July 1959, when his restriction order and detention order were revoked, and he was allowed to return to Nairobi.

After returning from exile Mr. Pinto immediately set about arranging financial assistance for his comrades still in detention at Lodwar, Hola and Marsabit. In 1960 with Messrs. Oginga Odinga, Tom Mboya and James Gichuru, he founded the KANU organ *Sauti ya Kanu* a Swahili weekly. He was also a founder of the Kenya Freedom Party and its first Assistant Secretary. In 1961, with Hon. M. C. Chokwe, he assisted in the formation

---

51   Source: Patel, Ambu H. (comp) 1963: Struggle for Release Jomo and his Colleagues. Nairobi: New Kenya Publishers. pp. 155-157.

of the Mozambique African National Union in Mombasa.

After the release of Mzee Jomo Kenyatta, Mr. Pinto assisted in the establishing of Pan African Press Limited whose first Directors were Hon. Joseph Murumbi as its General Manager. Mr. Pinto is now a member of the Central Legislative Assembly of East Africa and the Director and Secretary of the Pan African Press Limited.

*

NO SOLUTION TO KENYA PROBLEMS WITHOUT JOMO

Jomo Kenyatta is the leader of all those in Africa who have waged a struggle against colonialism and imperialism. He was one of the founders of the Pan African Movement, and the democratic and progressive forces in Africa have suffered a severe set-back as a result of his unjust imprisonment and restriction. There can be no solution to many of the problems which confront Kenya unless Jomo Kenyatta is released. Economic and political stability, and Kenya's relationship within the proposed E. A. Federation must await Kenyatta's release. By depriving African political leaders of their freedom, Britain is violating the principles underlying the U.N. Charter of Human Rights and numerous agreements to which she is a signatory.

P. G. PINTO,
Nairobi,
1st August 1960

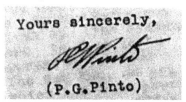

14. *Pinto's signature*

Pio Gama Pinto (1963): To All KANU Members of the House

TO ALL KANU MEMBERS OF THE HOUSE OF REPRESENTATIVES

From P.G. Pinto- Candidate for a KANU ticket for a Specially Elected Seat.

I hope you will not consider it presumptuous of me to give you a brief biographical sketch of myself. I feel compelled to resort to this expedient for two reasons: firstly, there are a large number of Kanu Elected Members whom I have not had the privilge of meeting and, secondly, it is essential that you should be aware, as far as is practicable, the past activities of a potential candidate as a guide of what you can expect of him in future. If you consider my past justifies your expectations of a good citizen of Kenya who has the true interests of the masses of this country at heart, then I request you to vote for me as one of your twelve Specially Elected Members to the House of Representatives.

I was born in Nairobi in 1927 and studied in India from 1938 to 1949. I returned to Kenya in 1949 and began devoting all my time to Kenya politics from 1951. In my capacity as paid Secretary to the Kenya Indian Congress I worked in close association with the leaders of the Kenya African Union (KAU). Together with Peter Wright (who was deported from Kenya) I assisted in the formation of the K.A.U. Study Circle with Messrs. Odede and Murumbi as the Chairman and Secretary of the Circle. It was the leaders of this Study Circle who filled in the gap caused by the arrest of Hon. Jomo Kenyatta and other national leaders and prevented the national movement from disintegrating following upon the trial and imprisonment of our national leaders. Late in 1952 I resigned my post with the Congress and worked as Editor of the <u>Daily Chronicle</u> and correspondent of the Press Trust of India and All India Radio. These duties did not prevent me from working with the political and trade union leaders who had not yet been arrested. In addition to assisting in the defence of Hon. Jomo Kenyatta, his colleagues and many other patriots I maintained close liaison with British Members of Parliament, keeping them fully posted on the situation in Kenya with particular reference to some of the attrocities taking place.

On 19th June 1954 I was arrested and detained under the Emergency Regulations. From June 1954 to February 1958 I was detained at Takwa Special Detention Camp, Manda Island. In February 1958 I was transferred from Manda Island to Kabarnet in Baringo District under a Restriction Order. I was finally set free towards the end of 1959.

......./

15. Pinto's memo to all KANU Members. 1963

Pio Gama Pinto, Kenya's Unsung Martyr

Dear Friend,

I hope you will not consider it presumptuous of me to give you a brief biographical sketch of myself. I feel compelled to resort to this expedient for two reasons: firstly, there are a large number of Kanu Elected Members whom I have not had the privilege of meeting and, secondly, it is essential that you should be aware, as far as is practicable, the past activities of a potential candidate as a guide of what you can expect of him in future. If you consider my past justifies your expectations of a good citizen of Kenya who has the true interests of the masses of this country at heart, then I request you to vote for me as one of your twelve Specially Elected Members to the House of Representatives.

I was born in Nairobi in 1927 and studied in India from 1938 to 1949. I returned to Kenya in 1949 and began devoting all my time to Kenya politics from 1951. In my capacity as paid Secretary to the Kenya Indian Congress I worked in close association with the leaders of the Kenya African Union (KAU). Together with Peter Wright (who was deported from Kenya) I assisted in the formation of the K.A.U, Study Circle with Messrs. Odede and Murumbi as the Chairman and Secretary of the Circle. It was the leaders of this Study Circle who filled in the gap caused by the arrest of Hon. Jomo Kenyatta and other national leaders and prevented the national movement from disintegrating following upon the trial and imprisonment of our national leaders.

Late in 1952 I resigned my post with the Congress and worked as Editor of the Daily Chronicle and correspondent of the Press Trust of India and All India Radio. These duties did not prevent me from working with the political and trade union leaders who had not yet been arrested. In addition to assisting in the defence of Hon. Jomo Kenyatta, his colleagues and many other patriots, I maintained close liaison with British Members of Parliament, keeping them fully posted on the situation in Kenya with particular reference to some of the atrocities taking place.

On 19th June 1954 I was arrested and detained under the Emergency Regulations. From June 1954 to February 1958 I was detained at Takwa Special Detention Camp, Manda Island. In February 1958 I was transferred from Manda Island to Kabarnet in Baringo District under a Restriction Order. I was finally set free towards the end of 1959.

While working with the African National Movement, I did all I could to build up the progressive front among Asians in Kenya. I was a founder member of the Kenya League which was formed to combat the reactionary trends in the Kenya Indian Congress shortly after the Declaration of the State of Emergency. I was also General Secretary of the East African Students Federation. Both these progressive and largely Asian organisations were banned during the Emergency. During the first Lancaster House Conference, I assisted in the formation of the Kenya Freedom Party and worked as its Asst. Secretary. The Kenya Freedom Party was dissolved as soon as KANU opened its doors to Non-Africans.

Since my release from detention and restrictions, I have been closely associated with the publicity work of KANU. Together with Messrs. Odinga, Mboya and Gichuru I founded "SAUTI YA KANU" which saw us through the last General Elections. From January 1962 I have worked as Commercial Manager of the PAN-AFRICAN PRESS LTD., which publishes "SAUTI YA MWAFRIKA" and "PAN-AFRICA".

For the last 10 weeks of the recent Election Campaign I worked on a full-time basis (in an honorary capacity) as Secretary of the KANU NAIROBI ELECTION COMMITTEE which was responsible for the campaign involving 7 seats to the House of Representatives and 1 seat to the Senate.

In addition to my interest in local politics, I have been closely associated in the struggle against Portuguese fascism both in India and Africa. In March 1961, together with Mr. M. Chokwe, I assisted in the formation of the Mozambique African National Union which has since linked up with the newly founded FRELIMO (Mozambique National Liberation Front). I shall always do what I can to contribute my mite in the struggle against

Portuguese and South African fascism.

As a loyal KANU Member who has been closely associated with the Party since its inception at Kiambu I am pledged to uphold the Party's policy. I shall be privileged, if given the opportunity, to work with you, under the leadership of Mzee Kenyatta, in the task of nation reconstruction.

Yours sincerely,

(P.G. Pinto)

Yours sincerely,

P.G. Pinto
P.O. Box 8064,
Nairobi.
29th May 1963.

Pio Gama Pinto (1963): Glimpses of Kenya's Nationalist Struggle

Glimpses of Kenya's Nationalist Struggle

— By P.G. Pinto —

Mr. P. G. Pinto was detained from June 1954 to August 1959. Prior to his detention he edited a local bilingual daily, and was closely connected with KAU leaders and the Independent Schools Association.

After his release, he was active in the formation of KANU and, with KAU leaders, founded the KANU organ, Sauti ya Kanu.

Later, he was associated in the founding of Pan-African Press Ltd, of which he is now one of the Directors. He was elected to the Central Legislative Assembly in August this year.

DECEMBER 12th 1963, marks the end of 68 years British colonial rule and the emergence of Kenya as an independent nation. In these 68 years, the struggle for national independence has been conducted on many fronts.

It is impossible in an article to do justice to the heroic efforts of individuals and organisations who participated in the struggle for the liquidation of colonialism.

All that can be done is to afford the reader a brief insight of the intensive struggle waged by various organisations against imperialist domination abetted by white settlerism.

"Fit for Whites"

In 1902 Commissioner Elliot declared Kenya a fit place for European settlement. The construction of the railway linking the seaport of Mombasa to Kampala had been completed, and arguments were not lacking to suggest that the only way to make the railway pay itself was to encourage the settlement of Europeans by every conceivable means.

What followed has been aptly referred to as the "Great Land Grab". Adventurers and speculators displayed considerable enterprise in acquiring huge areas of land for little or nothing, and then parcelling it out to their fellow countrymen at considerable profit to themselves.

The whole process was accompanied by astute jingoism with demands for "responsible Government" under European hegemony alternating with demands for the introduction of laws existing in South Africa which were found eminently suitable to ensure an abundant supply of cheap labour.

The Kikuyu, and to an extent the Wakamba and Masai, were the first to suffer the full consequences of these depredations. It was natural that the Kikuyu, effectively sandwiched between the farms alienated to Europeans, or reserved for their "exclusive use and ownership",

should be the first to revolt against these obnoxious measures.

Towards the end of 1919 an organisation called the East African Association was formed under the Presidency of Harry Thuku and the Treasurership of Ismael Ithongo.

After touring the Central Province Harry Thuku was able in 1921 to convene a meeting at Dagoretti, near Nairobi, of Chiefs and Headmen.

THE MEETING AUTHORISED HARRY THUKU TO DRAW UP WHAT IS PROBABLY THE FIRST AFRICAN PETITION TO THE BRITISH GOVERNMENT PROTESTING AGAINST FORCED LABOUR, THE INIQUITOUS' HUT AND POLL TAXES, THE ALIENATION OF THEIR LANDS TO EUROPEANS, AND THE ENACTMENT OF THE REGISTRATION ORDINANCE.

The Petition ended by enquiring of the British Government whether the oppressive measures enacted against Africans was the Government's way of acknowledging the faithful service rendered by the Carrier Corps, consisting largely of Africans, in the war effort against the Germans in Tanganyika.

The Kenya Government's response was to launch an attack on Harry Thuku and his associates which culminated in the arrest of Harry Thuku on March

14, 1922. Thuku was held in custody at a Police Station close to the Norfolk Hotel in Nairobi.

On learning of the arrest of their leader, thousands of Africans began assembling near the Police Station where he was detained, and demanded his release.

Exasperated by the refusal of Chief Secretary Sir Charles Bowring to release their leader, the unarmed crowd of several thousands, led by a woman called Mary Muthoni, attempted to pull down the wall which consisted of aluminium sheets.

Opened Fire

THE POLICE OPENED FIRE AND KILLED OVER 30 PERSONS.

The Government banned the E. African Association and deported Thuku to Kismayu, a remote area in the Northern Province, from where he was released in 1931.

Two other persons, Waiganjo Ndotono and George Mugekenyi were deported and restricted to Lamu and Kwale Districts.

The methods employed by the Colonial Government in Kenya in dealing with the genuine grievances of Africans on this occasion was to form the pattern for dealing with similar occasions in future.

IN 1923 THE GOVERNMENT ALLOWED THE FORMATION OF A POLITICAL BODY PROVIDED IT CONFINED ITS MEMBERSHIP TO A SINGLE TRIBE.

This policy was again to be adopted by the British Government during the State of Emergency when political organisations were allowed to function provided they were confined to districts. In this way the British Government hoped to foster tribal divisions within the country.

The Motive

In allowing Africans to form political organisations at this time the Colonial Government was not motivated by the desire to promote the interests of the people.

At this time the Settler leaders imagined that they could use the Africans in their fight against the Indians who began to demand equality of treatment.

ACCORDINGLY, IN 1925 THE KIKUYU CENTRAL ASSOCIATION WAS FORMED WITH JOSEPH KANGETHE AS PRESIDENT, JESSE KARIUKI AS VICE-PRESIDENT, JOB MUCHUCHU AS TREASURER AND H. GICHUIRE SECRETARY.

The Kikuyu Central Association conducted a vigorous campaign against the many oppressive laws enacted to transform Kenya into a feudal state. Leading members of the KCA joined the Local Native Councils in an effort to use them as platforms to carry out their attacks against the exploitation of their people.

In 1926 Mzee Jomo Kenyatta was elected Secretary of the K.C.A, and shortly after founded the first African weekly, MUIGWITHANIA.

In 1928 Mzee Jomo Kenyatta was chosen to represent African grievances to the British authorities in England.

HE WAS RECALLED IN 1931, BUT IN VIEW OF PUB-

(PLEASE TURN OVER)

16. Pinto: Glimpses of Kenya's Nationalist Struggle (1963)

December 12, 1963 *Pan* African - Uhuru Souvenir PAN AFRICAN - pp.27-39. By P.G. Pinto

Mr. P. G, Pinto was detained from June 1954 to August 1959. Prior to his detention he edited a local bilingual daily, and was closely connected with KAU leaders and the Independent Schools Association.

After his release, he was active in the formation of KANU and, with KAU leaders, founded the KANU organ, Sauti ya Kanu.

Later, he was associated in the founding of Pan-African Press Ltd. of which he is now one of the Directors. He was elected to the Central Legislative Assembly in August this year.

December 12th, 1963, marks the end of 68 years British colonial rule and the emergence of Kenya as an independent nation. In these 68 years, the struggle for national independence has been conducted on many fronts.

It is impossible in an article to do justice to the heroic efforts of individuals and organisations who participated in the struggle for the liquidation of colonialism.

All that can be done is to afford the reader a brief insight of the intensive struggle waged by various organisations against imperialist domination abetted by white settlerism.

Fit for Whites

In 1902, Commissioner Elliot declared Kenya a fit place for European settlement. The construction of the railway linking the seaport of Mombasa to Kampala had been completed, and arguments were not lacking to suggest that the only way to make the railway pay itself was to encourage the settlement of Europeans by every conceivable means.

What followed has been aptly referred to as the "Great Land Grab". Adventurers and speculators displayed considerable enterprise in acquiring huge areas of land for little or nothing, and then parcelling it out to their fellow countrymen at considerable profit to themselves.

The whole process was accompanied by astute jingoism with demands for "responsible Government" under European hegemony alternating with demands for the introduction of laws existing in South Africa which were found eminently suitable to ensure an abundant supply of cheap labour.

The Kikuyu, and to an extent the Wakamba and Masai, were the first to suffer the full consequences of these depredations. It was natural that the Kikuyu, effectively sandwiched between the farms alienated to Europeans, or reserved for their "exclusive use and ownership", should be the first to revolt against these obnoxious measures.

Towards the end of 1919 an organisation called the East Africa Association was formed under the Presidency of Harry Thuku and the Treasurer-ship of Ismael Ithongo.

After touring the Central Province, Harry Thuku was able in 1921 to convene a meeting at Dagoretti, near Nairobi, of Chiefs and Headmen.

The meeting authorised Harry Thuku to draw up what is probably the first African petition to the British government protesting against forced labour, the iniquitous hut and poll taxes, the alienation of their lands to Europeans, and the enactment of the registration ordinance.

The Petition ended by enquiring of the British Government whether the oppressive measures enacted against Africans was the Government's way of acknowledging the faithful service rendered by the Carrier Corps, consisting largely of Africans, in the war effort against the Germans in Tanganyika.

The Kenya Government's response was to launch an attack on Harry Thuku and his associates which culminated in the arrest of Harry Thuku on March 14, 1922. Thuku was held in custody at a Police Station close to the Norfolk Hotel in Nairobi.

On learning of the arrest of their leader, thousands of Africans began assembling near the Police Station where he was detained and demanded his release.

Exasperated by the refusal of Chief Secretary Sir Charles Bowring to release their leader, the unarmed crowd of several thousands, led by a woman called Mary Muthoni, attempted to pull down the wall which consisted of aluminium sheets.

Opened Fire

The police opened fire and killed over 30 persons.

The Government banned the East African Association and deported Thuku to Kismayu, a remote area in the Northern Province, from where he was released in 1931.

Two other persons, Waiganjo Ndotono and George Mugekenyi were deported and restricted to Lamu and Kwale Districts.

The methods employed by the Colonial Government in Kenya, in dealing with the genuine grievances of Africans on this occasion, were to form the pattern for dealing with similar occasions in future.

In 1923 the government allowed the formation of a political body provided it confined its membership to a single tribe.

This policy was again to be adopted by the British Government during the State of Emergency when political organisations were allowed to function - provided they were confined to districts. In this way the British Government hoped to foster tribal divisions within the country.

The Motive

In allowing Africans to form political organisations at this time the Colonial Government was not motivated by the desire to promote the interests of the people.

At this time the Settler leaders imagined that they could use the Africans in their fight against the Indians who began to demand equality of treatment.

Accordingly, in 1923 the Kikuyu Central Association was formed with Joseph Kang'ethe as president, Jesse Kariuki as vice president, Job Muchuchu as treasurer and Henry Gichuire as Secretary.

The Kikuyu Central Association conducted a vigorous campaign against the many oppressive laws enacted to transform Kenya into a feudal state. Leading members of the KCA joined the Local Native Councils in an effort to use them as platforms to carry out their attacks against the exploitation of their people.

In 1926 Mzee Jomo Kenyatta was elected Secretary, of the KCA and shortly after founded the first African weekly, *Muigwithania.*

In 1928 Mzee Jomo Kenyatta was chosen to represent African grievances to the British authorities in England.

He was recalled in 1931, but in view of publicity he had secured for Kenya during his stay in London, Mzee Kenyatta was asked to return to London in 1932, accompanied by Parmenas Githendu, to continue the fight for African rights.

During Mzee Kenyatta's absence from Kenya his place was filled by George Kiringothi Ndegwa who acted as Secretary and Editor.

Independent Schools

In the meantime, Protestant Missionaries decided to launch their campaign against female circumcision.

On October 15, 1929, resolutions were passed in Church Council requiring parents of African children seeking admission to schools to give a written undertaking that they were against the custom of female circumcision.

Anyone refusing to give this undertaking was required to remove his child from school and was excommunicated.

Government officials supported the stand taken by the Missionaries, and it appeared to the Africans that yet again the Missionaries had allied themselves to the Colonialists to suppress them.

The time and manner in which the Missionaries decided to enforce their views on female circumcision led to the formation of the Kikuyu Independent Schools Association, the Karinga Independence Schools Association, Githunguri Teachers College and the African Independent Orthodox Church.

For not only were the children of such parents denied schooling in Mission schools, but they were not allowed to be baptised — a proper illustration of the sins of the fathers descending on their children, only that in this instance the parents were not prepared to allow their children to become victims of Missionary folly.

At the time of the declaration of the State of Emergency in October 1952, over 175,000 children were receiving their education at these Independent Schools, and many of the best fighters and nationalists graduated from them.

KCA leaders took an active part in supporting the Independence Schools and the Orthodox Church, and in raising funds for their maintenance.

Every possible obstruction was placed in way of KCA leaders. But the influence of the KCA began to grow, particularly when the Kenya Land Commission under the Chairmanship of Justice Carter felt that their terms of reference precluded them from redressing the land grievances of Africans, and went on to recommend the legalisation of an iniquitous system whereby 16,000 square miles of land was reserved for the exclusive use of 3,000 Europeans and their descendants,

KCA leaders, despite the restrictions placed on their activities, made common cause with the Wakamba Association and the Taita Association.

In 1938, the Wakamba, under the leadership of Samuel Muinde, organised a mammoth protest march to Government House against the confiscation of over 2,000 cattle. Muinde was arrested and deported to Baringo District.

The Second World War provided the Government at the instigation of Settlers with the opportunity it needed. In May1940, the KCA was proscribed on the grounds that its leaders were in touch with Italians.

Twelve Kikuyu, eight Wakamba and two Taita were arrested and detained in remote parts of the country until the end of the war.

James Beauttah's Arrest

Among those arrested was James Beauttah who, on the day of his arrest, was actually organising the collection of funds for the purchase of an aeroplane as a contribution of Fort Hall District to the war effort!!

The persons arrested were tried in camera by a former judge, Sir Charles Belcher who also owned a farm in Kenya. Among those who played a prominent role in securing the conviction of the accused was the son of a highly respected clergyman, the well-known archaeologist, Leakey. Apparently, Leakey used his position as interpreter in a way which was later, during the Kapenguria trial, found to be highly questionable, and resulted in his removal from the job of interpreter.

The banning of Kikuyu Central Association and the arrest of Kikuyu,

Wakamba and Taita leaders in 1940 represents one phase of the nationalist struggle in Kenya.

The intervening period between the proscription of the KCA and the formation of the Kenya African Union in 1946 was fully exploited by the settlers representatives to entrench their position in the policy-making bodies, and use their political power to make the position of Africans, whether on the farms or in towns, unbearable.

One of the great pioneers of the political struggle for independence was Harry Thuku. In 1919 the East African Association was formed under his presidency in 1921 he drew up the first African petition to the British Government. In March the following year he was arrested and banished to a remote part of the Northern Province where he was kept in detention for 10 years, being eventually released only on condition that he abstained from political activities.

Africans had by now come to an understanding that non-violent, constitutional agitation had serious limitations and that new methods must be evolved to avoid the collapse in political organisation which characterised the banning of the political association and the arrest of Its leaders.

The disabilities from which Africans suffered might be listed as the wholesale alienation of their lands, highly discriminatory scales of pay in the Civil Service, the ban on the growth of cash crops, the transformation of Reserves or "Native Land Units" into reservoirs of cheap labour, the imposition of a tax structure which compelled Africans to seek work on terms and conditions dictated by their employers, an educational and economic system which discriminated in favour of the rich and powerful and against the poor, a change from a subsistence economy and shifting cultivation to a money economy and static farming without the provision or acquisition of new techniques, resulting in a considerably lower standard of living, and the disintegration of tribal society without the benefit of new values, and the absence of any voice in the Legislature or any of the policy-making institutions.

The overcrowded, poverty-stricken reserves were expected to provide social security for the disabled or retired urban worker.

Humiliation

Finally, the laws of the country were designed to subject the African to humiliation through the Registration and Liquor Laws, while the strong colour bar practiced in hotels was an affront to his dignity as a man.

The aftermath of World War II brought even greater suffering to the mass of Africans. Prior to the War, the World economy experienced a series of depressions and recessions.

The prices of agricultural commodities on the world market were low. There was little incentive for the farmer to grow more or to invest in machinery.

As a result, the European settler adapted the situation to his needs by practicing what is known as 'kaffir farming'. Under this system a labourer is to grow as much as he can cultivate or to graze a large number of cattle, in return for nominal wages.

The scarcities caused by the war and the resultant demand for agricultural produce changed the situation. 'Kaffir farming' was described as dangerous. Laws were enacted to limit the area of cultivation and the number of sheep or cattle a 'squatter' could retain on the farm.

The provision of large sums of money in the shape of loans enabled the settler to introduce mechanisation.

He, therefore, set about devising ways and means to 'evict' as many labourers and 'squatters' from his farm — labourers and 'squatters' who had been enticed, and sometimes often compelled, to leave their traditional homes in the reserves.

Desperate

By leaving his traditional home over many years, the African had lost his traditional land. The end of the War found him in a desperate situation with nowhere to go to.

The position in the towns was similar. Wages had increased, but the increase was hardly commensurate with the increased cost of food, or the scarce bed- space housing. Unemployment was rife and the 'spiv law' forced him to be on the run. Victory over fascism and the victory for democracy had no meaning for him.

On the termination of hostilities a group of Africans living in Nairobi formed an association for the purpose of discussing the problems confronting the country.

Their activities were given further impetus when the British Government, claiming that African interests were adequately represented through the sole European missionary appointed to the Legislative Council, grudgingly conceded the necessity of replacing the European Missionary by an African.

In 1906 when the Kenya Legislative Council was constituted European settlers had been given four seats. By 1919 they had increased their representation to 11 and secured the right of election on racial rolls. Asians were given two seats and African interests were represented by a European Missionary.

In 1944 African district councils were invited to submit a list of names for the consideration of the governor, and he appointed Mr. Eluid W. Mathu to the Kenya Legislative Council,

Prominent in the group of Africans who decided to call the Association the Kenya African Study Union (KASU), were Peter Mbiyu Koinange, James Gichuru, Albert Awino, Joseph Katithi, Tom Mbotela, James Beauttah, Harry Nangurai, Fred Kubai, Jesse Kariuki, Francis Khamisi and Ambrose Ofafa.

Harry Thuku of KCA fame also associated with the group in its early stages, but the Harry Thuku who was exiled in 1922 and the Harry Thuku who was released in 1931 were two different persons.

Before being released, Thuku was compelled to give all kinds of assurances that he would not indulge in politics or in anti-Government activities. He lost his old fire and contented himself with becoming a prosperous farmer.

KASU soon discovered that sweet reasonableness weighted with all the logic in the world did not have the slightest effect in removing the racial disabilities from which Africans suffered. "Paramountcy" of African interests, as contained in the Devonshire Paper of 1923, was a myth.

The Guardian discovered that the interests of her own children conflicted with that of her African ward, and in the process the ward suffered badly.

KAU Formed

In the elections held towards the end of 1945, the Union felt that it had studied enough, and decided to form a political union. It was called the Kenya African Union (KAU) and its first office bearers were James Gichuru, W.W.W. Awori, Francis Khamisi, Fred Nganga and Joseph Kathithi.

Branches were established throughout the country. The Union started a weekly newspaper which was appropriately called *Sauti ya Mwafrika* with Mr. Khamisi as its first Editor.

In 1946 the Union decided to send a two-man delegation, consisting of Mr. Gichuru and Mr. Awori to London, with a memorandum covering the grievances of the people. In the event, only Mr. Awori could make the trip, and as soon as he arrived he established close contact with Mzee Jomo Kenyatta who, in between the work of keeping the British informed on the Kenya problem, was taking a leading part in organising the Pan- African Movement in association with leading figures such as Mr. Nnamdi Azikiwe, Kwame Nkrumah, Professor Dubois and George Padmore.

Mzee Jomo Kenyatta returned to Kenya in September 1946 and early in 1947 he was elected president of KAU.

Jomo Takes Over

Mzee Kenyatta's assumption of the Presidentship of the Union gave it vigour and direction. All the old KCA leaders and members who were doubtful about the effectiveness of the new organisation joined KAU, and meetings were held throughout the country in an effort to impress the Government with the necessity of finding a solution to African grievances.

The Government, encouraged by the settlers, turned a deaf ear to African demands. They were completely oblivious of the existence of tens of thousands of Africans who gained a lot of experience during the war. It was significant that leaders of KAU, at national and party level, had seen service in the Middle East, Burma, and other theatres of the War.

Instead of understanding the nature of the transformation taking place, settler leaders were even more vociferous than ever in their demands for "self-government" under European hegemony.

In 1949 the Electors' Union, which represented European political interests, produced the "Kenya Plan" which was treated as a blueprint for substituting Colonial Government, rule with European Settler rule.

Trade Union Struggle

The machinery of oppression was further strengthened, and the answer to all African demands was "no compromise".

The memorable Dockworkers Strike of 1948 led by Chege Kibachia, and the 1950 Nairobi General Strike, following upon the arrest of Fred Kubai and Makhan Singh, were used as opportunities to press for the enactment of legislation prevalent in South Africa and Southern Rhodesia.

TRADE UNION PIONEERS Makhan Singh (left) and Fred Kubai (right). Both spent a decade in prison and detention: Makhan Singh for 10 years following the banning of the East African T.U.C. Fred Kubai was charged with attempted murder and acquitted. But he was arrested again with Jomo Kenyatta and found guilty at the infamous Kapenguria trial.

Even the minor concessions granted to African demands were more than offset by the grant of increased representation to European settlers in the Executive Council, the Legislative Council, and complete control of local government authorities through the County Council Ordinance.

The circumstances which led to the Nairobi General Strike in 1950 illustrate the attitude of the Government.

Trade Union Congress (TUC) Banned

At the instigation of European settlers, the Government banned the newly formed East African Trade Union Congress and arrested Fred Kubai and Makhan Singh, the President and Secretary of the organisation.

The workers retaliated by observing a general strike which was only broken after ten days of government- sponsored terror, involving the use of fire-arms and extensive beating.

Makhan Singh was charged with sedition and deported to Lokitaung,

Lodwar and Maralal where he was to remain for over 10 years.

Fred Kubai was charged with 'attempted murder', but his case was dismissed, and he returned to become the Vice-President of KAU. Earlier, Chege Kibachiu who led the Mombasa Dock Workers strike in 1948 was tried in secret and deported to Baringo where he was to remain for nine years.

It had become increasingly obvious that "constitutional", "non-violent" methods of fighting for one's rights were absolutely futile in dealing with the Settler-Colonial combination which was charged with the administration of the country. Organised violence was the only answer to such a situation.

Despite this belief which was held by a large number of African nationalists, it was nevertheless decided to do everything possible to bring the British Government to its senses by demonstrating the strength of the national movement by peaceful means.   .

Meetings were held by Mzee Jomo Kenyatta throughout the country and KAU branches were established everywhere.

The earliest convert to the new nationalist crusade in Nyanza was Jaramogi Oginga Odinga who was then battling against odds trying to organise a vast co-operative venture of which he was the Managing-Director, with Achieng Oneko as its Secretary.

After a meeting between Mr. Oginga Odinga and Mzee Jomo Kenyatta it was decided that Achieng Oneko should relinquish his appointment as Secretary of the Luo Thrift Corporation and as Editor of *Ramogi* to take up the job of Secretary-General of KAU and to join Peter Mbiyu Koinange in a KAU delegation with the responsibility of presenting a mammoth petition signed by two million people to the British Parliament.

Oginga Odinga

Jaramogi Odinga also agreed to serve on the Central Committee and

Governing Council of KAU, and at the last meeting of the Governing Council of KAU held in September 1952, he was deputed by Mzee Jomo Kenyatta to act as its chairman.

Instead of appreciating the strength of the nationalist forces and the need for radical reforms, the Government launched a counter-offensive in the shape of trumped up charges against prominent nationalists.

The first victims were the veteran politician James Beauttah and the Rev. Peter Kigondu who were charged with inciting crowds to destroy cattle crushes.

Rev. Kigondu was one of the first African priests to be ordained and was over 70 years of age when the Government decided to prosecute him. Mr. James Beauttah was one of the founders of K. C. A. and was then Vice-President of KAU.

Both of them were given stiff prison sentences and on the expiry of their sentences were detained for eight years in special Detention Camps, located in the most in hospitable parts of the country, under the Emergency Regulations.

The next victim was Jesse Kariuki, one of the founders of KCA, who had acquired the title "macho ya KAU," meaning "the eyes of KAU". Kariuki was found guilty under the Deportation Act and was restricted at Marsabit for 11 years.

Finally, towards the end of September 1952, the Government decided to arrest and charge a man who was second only to Mzee Jomo Kenyatta in terms of mass popularity: Ex-Senior Chief Koinange Mbiyu, for the murder of Chief Waruhiu.

Senior Chief Koinange was ever 80 years of age at the time of his arrest and although he was found innocent together with his son John Mbiyu Koinange, he was detained and restricted to a remote part of the country, only to be allowed to return to his beloved home in Kiambaa when he was on his death-bed.

Pio Gama Pinto, Kenya's Unsung Martyr

In spite of repression launched against KAU, it continued to grow from strength to strength. Public meetings were being attended by twenty and thirty thousand people, and the money collected at these meetings was sometimes in excess of £1,000 at each rally. At all these meetings Mzee Jomo Kenyatta called upon the people not to be provoked into violence and appealed to the colonialists to change their negative and destructive approach.

European leaders successfully forced the British Colonial Secretary, Mr. James Griffiths who was then visiting the country, to accede to their demand for parity of representation in the Legislative Council with all the other races. In the Constitutional changes which were introduced, African representation was increased to 6, Asians to 6, Arabs to 2 and Europeans 14. Africans, however, continued to be indirectly nominated by the Governor, while Europeans were given the right of electing their representatives.

Kenyatta Arrested

Mzee Jomo Kenyatta's appeal to the British government was spurned. Instead, on the night of October 20, 1952, the government arrested him and charged him with the management of Mau Mau.

A state of Emergency was declared, Lancashire Fusiliers were flown into Kenya from Egypt, and the 4th Uganda Battalion of the Kings' African Rifles drafted into the country. Over 2,000 Europeans joined the Kenya Police Reserve, and all European reservists were under orders to rejoin the notorious Kenya Regiment.

Other KAU leaders to be arrested and charged jointly with Mzee Kenyatta were Achieng Oneko, the General Secretary, Paul Ngei, the Asst. General Secretary, Fred Kubai, the Vice-President, Bildad Kaggia, President of the Labour Trade Union of East Africa and Secretary of the Nairobi Branch of KAU, and Kungu Karumba, the Chairman of the Divisional KAU Sub-Branch in Kiambu.

"Jock Scott"

Simultaneously, the Government launched what they called "Operation Jock Scott" aimed at taking into custody all KAU leaders, and leaders of the African Independent Orthodox Church, the Kikuyu and Karinga Independent Schools Association, Glthunguri Teachers' Training College, and the proscribed KCA

Mr. Kiringothi Ndegwa after suffering restriction during the war was earlier sentenced to 1½ years rigorous imprisonment for continuing to work for K.C.A despite its proscription.

All these persons were served with governor's detention orders and most of them were detained or restricted without trial till the end of the emergency.

On October 21,1952, the Government introduced into Nairobi a large number of 'askaris' from the Northern Frontier Province, who were charged with the task of terrorising the population.

Africans in Nairobi were indiscriminately beaten without any rhyme or reason.

Papers Banned

This Special Force from N.F.P. was then taken to Kiambu, Fort Hall, Embu and Nyeri to repeat their performance. In the Reserves they excelled not only by beating people but also raping women, destroying property, and pillaging the homes of the detained or arrested leaders.

On October 24, 1952, the Government banned 9 newspapers and 43 "broadsheets." A curfew was imposed from 7 p.m., and the organ of imperialist interests in Kenya, the *East African Standard* announced that "the situation was under control." By the October 31, arrests in Nairobi totalled 2,309, Rift Valley 700, Central Province 561, and Nyanza 36.

The *East African Standard* eulogised the efforts and the "wonderful response" of European women in working at the Police Stations. Praise was showered on those who rallied to defence of 'law and order' and not a word was mentioned either of the ban on newspapers, nor the draconic measures imposed to control the nationalist press.

The Exodus

On October 27, however, a *Standard* report drew the attention of the public to a "most disturbing element." Apparently, information was being received of an "exodus into the Aberdares", and it was stated that "large quantities of food were being bought and goats and cattle" were being driven there.

Within four days of the Declaration of the State of Emergency, Government officers were seen relaxing over their gin and tonics fully confident that the "show of force" had done the trick. They were soon to suffer the shock of their lives.

Study Circle

Some time in August 1952, a Study Circle consisting of members of KAU Central Executive Committee and others had been established for the purpose of preparing papers which could be considered by the K.A.U Executive. Among other things, this Study Circle organised a meeting of leaders from Kenya, Uganda and Tanganyika which was held under the Chairmanship of Mzee Jomo Kenyatta. Representatives from Uganda included Ignatius Musazi and Abubakar Mayanja, the President and Secretary of the Uganda National Congress.

JOMO KENYATTA UNDER ARREST He remained proud, vigorous, defiant. Through all the years of imprisonment, detention and restriction he was confident of final victory.

The Chairman of the Study Circle was a Representative Member of the Legislative Council, Walter Odede, and the Secretary, Joseph Murumbi. Other regular members were Bildad Kaggia, Peter Wright, Fred Kubai, Paul Ngei, John Miller, J, D. Kali and this writer.

It was, therefore, natural that immediately following the arrest of the complete KAU Executive and the majority of the Governing Council, the vacuum created by the removal of the main office bearer a should be filled by Messrs. Walter Odede, Joseph Murumbi and W. W. W. Awori, who was also a Representative Member.

At a Press Conference held on October 28, 1952, the three new office

Pio Gama Pinto, Kenya's Unsung Martyr

bearers denied that KAU was a purely Kikuyu organisation, expressed their full confidence in the leadership of Mzee Jomo Kenyatta and other arrested persons, and demanded the repeal of Emergency Regulations and the appointment of a Royal Commission to go into the question of African grievances.

The Defence

The new office bearers of KAU immediately set about organising the defence of Mzee Kenyatta and his colleagues. In spite of the fact that no meetings could be held, KAU branches throughout the country began collecting money for the defence of their leaders.

A team of lawyers was engaged headed by the redoubtable D. N. Pritt Q.C. and including H. O. Davies from Nigeria, Diwan Chamanlal from India, and A. R. Kapila from Kenya, later to be joined by F. R. S. de Souza and Jaswant Singh.

The Government, alarmed by the amount of attention which the trial was drawing throughout the world, banned the entry of other lawyers from Ghana, Nigeria, Sudan and India who had offered their services in the defence of justice and truth.

Crooked Evidence

Everyone is aware or the chicanery and subterfuge to which the government resorted in their efforts to secure a conviction. The judge appointed to hear the historic case was a man of strong prejudices and deep vengeance and disdained to hide his feelings.

Years later, the main witness in the case against Mzee Kenyatta, an unprincipled scoundrel by the name of Rawson Macharia, admitted that he had committed perjury in his evidence. Yet, it was on Macharia's evidence, and the evidence of other professionally-coached witnesses, that Mzee Kenyatta and his colleagues were convicted.

In a statement made in November 1958, Rawson Macharia admitted that the evidence he gave at the trial "was false", and that he had been "promised certain' conditions" if he gave this false evidence.

He revealed that the inducements consisted of "(a) an air passage to the United Kingdom at £278, (b) a two year course in local| government at a university at £1,000, and (c) subsistence for two years at £250".

Macharia alleged that similar offers were made to other government - sponsored witnesses in the case. Macharia was tried for perjury, found guilty and sentenced to imprisonment.

What Thacker Said

The attention of readers is now drawn to the following extracts from the Judgment delivered by Justice R.H. Thacker at Kapenguria on 8th April 1953:

> The second and equally important matter in this trial is the (question of the credibility to be attached to the many witnesses. If the prosecution witnesses are not believed, that must be an end to the prosecution; alternatively, if there is a reasonable doubt whether they are telling the truth, then again there must be an end to the prosecution. If the accused and their witnesses are believed, the prosecution, of course, must fail. The question, therefore, of credibility is of the utmost importance in this case, and I have endeavoured to observe the demeanour of such of all the witnesses, including that of the accused, who have appeared before me.

> "Although my finding of fact means that I disbelieve ten witnesses for the defence and believe one witness for the prosecution, I have no hesitation whatever in doing so. The prosecution witness, Rawson Macharia, gave his evidence well and in my opinion truthfully; and except on one minor point, already mentioned, which I do not

regard as important, was not shaken under cross-examination. All the defence witnesses were evasive, and I am satisfied were not telling the truth. I therefore find as a fact that Kenyatta was present at a ceremony of oath-taking, that he administered the oath to which I have referred to two people and endeavoured to administer it to Rawson Macharia.

In his Affidavit made in November 1958, Rawson Macharia alleged that several days before the Kapenguria trial, he, together with other Government witnesses, were thoroughly coached into the evidence they were required to give.

Mr. Dingle Foot, M.P. Q.C., after interviewing Macharia at this time declared that he "was satisfied that his extremely circumstantial narrative called for the closest investigation". Needless to say, there was neither an investigation nor a judicial inquiry.

The criminal complicity of many senior civil servants in every department of the Colonial Government in thwarting the course of justice, and acting as the official rubber-stamp of reactionary, racial-minded politicians and administrators has been a characteristic feature of the Government of Kenya.

Admittedly, in the course of nine years of the Emergency, individual Europeans like Colonel Young, Peter Bossock, D.G. MacPherson and others who had the misfortune to work in so-called "rehabilitation camps" exposed injustices that were being committed.

They invariably suffered for their candour at the hands of those at the helm of affairs in this country.

A New Enquiry?

There is nothing to prevent the independent Government of Kenya from instituting a fresh Commission of Inquiry into the allegations made by Rawson Macharia. This is not proposed merely with the intention of raking up the past.

This is proposed in the knowledge that there are in Kenya today people occupying important positions in the government and in other walks of life who have not eschewed their diabolical methods of revenging themselves on Mzee Kenyatta and many of his colleagues.

They cannot reconcile themselves to the fact that things have changed beyond repair. Hence their attempts to build up inter-tribal fear and hatred, their attempts to support, finance and direct pseudo-gangsters to indulge in so-called L.F.A. activities.

These elements have proved over a period of many years that they will stop at nothing in order to sabotage the Government of this country. They constitute the biggest threat to the security of the state and must be brought under the closest control and surveillance from December 12, 1963.

In June 1959 Mrs. Barbara Castle M.P, quoted ex-Superintendent D.G. Macpherson, who was head of the C.I.D. from 1954 to 1956 as saying: "I had to investigate the deaths by violence of several unfortunate inmates of {Detention Camps). I was told by the Commissioner to stop investigations into such things. I refused. It was the main reason I left Kenya a disgusted man".

Mr., Richard Catling, the present Inspector-General, who was then Commissioner of Police since 1954, denied the allegation.

The consequences of the Kapenguria trial which resulted in the imprisonment of Mzee Jomo Kenyatta and his colleagues had the widest repercussions.

The proscription of the only African political organisation, KAU, followed soon after, and the Government embarked on a determined course which sought to erase the names of their beloved leaders from the minds of the people.

The heroic struggle of Dedan Kimathi and his warriors for the freedom of Kenya and the release of their leaders cannot be compressed in a few paragraphs.

Suffice it to say that Dedan Kimathi's courageous leadership against the might of a dwindling empire fired the imagination of freedom fighters throughout the length and breadth of Africa,

Kimathi and his lieutenants proved to the Colonialists in Africa that colonialism was unprofitable   and that once a people had determined to be free there is no obstacle they will shirk in the pursuit of their goal of freedom. The mistakes they made are the mistakes which belong to their age.

Griffiths Case

The brutality of the forces which sought to destroy them has been well described during the trial of Captain Griffiths of "five bob a man" fame, or in the press reports of "people shot while trying to escape". There is no need to recapitulate here the sadistic tortures and inhuman treatment meted out indiscriminately to the local population. .

Perhaps, the worst action taken by the government was the mass eviction of tens of thousands of innocent men, women and children from the Rift Valley province. The vast majority of these people had been in the Rift Valley for two or three decades. They had lost their customary right in the reserves, where land consolidation and the provision of title deeds replaced the old system of communal tenure. The desperate position of these uprooted people can well be imagined.

Side by side with the terrorisation of the African people in the Reserves and the towns went the policy of arresting and detaining anyone who exhibited the slightest degree of political consciousness.

Following the fiasco which attended the Government's efforts to convey a facade of judicial sanction to the arrest and imprisonment of Mzee Jomo Kenyatta and his five colleagues, the Government resolved to use the simpler expedient of detaining citizen without the necessity of bringing them before a Court of Law.

As a sop to world opinion, the Government appointed an Advisory Committee with a quasi-judicial status, for the alleged purpose of investigating the allegations on which a person was detained. From personal experience, the writer can vouch for the fact that this tribunal was a ludicrous farce.

How It Worked

In June 1954 this writer was served with a Detention Order, and shortly after appearing before the Advisory Committee was detained at Takwa Special Detention Camp on Manda Island. Among the allegations contained in the charge sheet were; (a) That I had knowledge of illegal arms traffic; (b) That I assisted Mau Mau in drafting documents and arranged for the printing of membership cards of the 'African Liberation Army'; and (c) had given assistance to the non-militant wing of the Mau Mau in planning 'its subversive campaign'.

The onus of proving the contrary rested with this writer, and he was informed that the only way he could do it was to prove (a) his loyalty to the British Government and its policies; (b) the steps he took to abet the criminal activities of the authorities; and (c) his sympathy for European settlers and South Africa!

The only reason for recounting this sordid episode which casts a poor reflection on British methods of securing justice is to draw attention to the fact that 80,000 Africans who were detained were accorded similar 'justice'.

From October 1952 to early in 1956, African political opinion was silenced. Messrs. Blundell, Havelock and Harris representing the so-called 'moderate' wing of European settlers, and Messrs. Culwick and Briggs, representing the 'hardcore' section, thought the occasion presented a wonderful opportunity to press to a successful conclusion the fight for "freedom from Colonial Office rule", with transfer of power to those "who know the African".

Meetings were organised by European settlers to pass votes of "no confidence" against Sir George Erskine, the British local Commander-In-Chief, who with soldier-like candour told a Press Conference that he did not see the war against Africans reaching a successful conclusion unless the Africans were given greater political concessions.

When surrender terms were offered to African freedom-fighters a section of the settlers put up notices on their farms reading "No Surrender Here", while others called upon Europeans to resign from the Kenya Police Reserve. The first surrender talks were sabotaged by units of the Kenya Regiment, consisting exclusively or European settlers.

The writer was himself engaged in arranging a scheme which would have avoided further massacres of untrained, badly equipped, and starving freedom-fighters when he was arrested and detained. The British Government which apparently gave its consent to the scheme pleaded its ignorance of my activities at that stage.

The trade union movement did not escape the attention of the authorities. In a series of successive sweeps, trade union leaders who protested against various Emergency Regulations which curbed the freedom of workers, were arrested and detained. But shortly Mr. Tom Mboya, who made his entry into the trade union movement, secured the support of British and American Trade Union leaders to prevent further arrests.

The Fight Back

Mr. Mboya used the trade union movement effectively as a platform to draw attention to the despotic measures enacted by the Government, and it was only the support he enjoyed abroad which' prevented his arrest.

Another person who played a leading part at this time in frustrating the settler-inspired policies of the Government was Jaramogi Oginga Odinga. As President of the Luo Union he toured the country tirelessly warning Africans not to allow themselves to be drawn into the imperialist strategy which sought to exploit tribalism.

TOM MBOYA; He built up the Kenya Trade Union Movement, used it as a weapon to fight for African rights

Like the struggle of the freedom fighters in the forests and towns, the struggle in Detention Camps against the attempts of the Authorities to demoralise and destroy the political faith of detainees requires a book to itself.

Camp Conditions

Yet a brief mention is called for the circumstances which led to the brutal murder of detainees at Hola, in compliance with a diabolical plan evolved by a sadist called Cowan, who was shortly to be rewarded with an M.B.E. for his distinguished services.   .

The conditions at Manyani and Mackinon Road Camps, especially when the Detainees' spokesmen consisted of James Njoroge Koinange and George Githunguri, are indescribable.

Josiah Mwangi Kariuki in his book 'Mau Mau Detained' has given details of conditions in these and other Camps.

Despite the considered views of Sir George Erskine and other prominent people, the British Government's colonial policy with respect to Kenya remained static. In 1954 Colonial Secretary Oliver Lyttleton introduced the Lyttleton Plan which did little more than increase European representation in the Executive Council and add a Government stooge by the name of Ohangu to adorn the Council, as a concession to African Interests.

In 1956, eight Africans were elected on the basis of a restrictive franchise. The eight African Representative Members played a leading part in securing the abrogation of the Lyttleton Plan.

They elected Jaramogi Ogjnga Odinga as their chairman and their first action was to declare the Lyttleton plan "null and void."

These eight Africans, who included Tom Mboya, Ronald Ngala and Daniel Moi, had been elected on the basis of recommendations contained in the Coutts Report, which although falling short of universal franchise, was a great advance on previous methods evolved for selecting Africans.

African Voice

These eight African Members spoke with knowledge and confidence, born out of the realisation that they had the backing of their people, and for the first time the Imperialist controlled Legislative Council resounded with a voice expressing the aspirations and hopes of the eight million African people.

The eight African Elected Members, under the Chairmanship of Jaramogi Oginga Odinga, worked as a- united team, and demanded the restoration of civil liberties and the right to form a political organisation, as a condition of support for any Government policy.

As a result, Mr, Lennox Boyd, the Colonial Secretary, was compelled to introduce a new Constitution which, among other things, provided for an increase in African Representative Members to 14, and the election of four Specially Elected Members from each of the three racial groups, on the basis of an electoral college composed of the Elected and Official Member of the Legislative Council.

The Constitution also provided for the establishment of a Council of State which was supposed to ensure that the laws passed in the Legislative Council did not contain provisions which discriminated between races.

The African elected members staged a positive boycott of the elections of the twelve specially elected members as their choice rested with the European official and unofficial members of the legislative council.

Not unexpectedly, when the 14 African Representative Members refused to co-operate with the Government or in its formation, the four African Specially Elected Members offered to adorn the Government benches and become the apologists of official policy.

From 1957 onwards, the hardcore section among Europeans realised that they must abandon their claims to European leadership and abandon the prospect of responsible Government under European hegemony.

Ably abetted by the so-called 'moderates', they contented themselves by fighting a rear-guard action aimed at delaying in dependence opposing the release of Mzee Jomo Kenyatta and sowing the seeds of division among the African leaders.

Parity of representation with all the other races represented their anchor-sheet, and once that had been lost, they realised that it was only a question of time before their influence would shrink into insignificance.

In 1958 the African Representative Members in association with their Asian and Arab colleagues sent a delegation to London under the Chairmanship of Ronald Ngala to press for the drastic, revision of the Constitution.

Tanganyika, under the brilliant leadership of President Julius Nyerere, was already firmly on the road to Responsible Government, and African leaders in Kenya were in no mood to lag behind.

Tribal System

In 1956, the demand of the African Members to be allowed to form a political organisation was met by the British Government by allowing the formation of political bodies on a district basis.

As most of the districts coincide with tribal areas, the British government set out to implant tribalism in its most virulent form into the body politic of Kenya.

This move was to have the most dangerous consequences for Kenya, and the country is still suffering from the effects of this policy.

Political organisations such as the Nairobi African District Congress, the Nairobi Peoples' Convention Party, Baringo Independence Party, Central Nyanza District Congress, Mombasa African Democratic Union, mush-roomed overnight.

Except for Central Nyanza, all the other political organisations elected their Legco Member as their respective President, and observers of the political scene foresaw difficulties which would arise at a meeting of so many 'Presidents' when the time came to form a single political organisation.

Divisions

The African Representative Members in association with their Asian and Arab colleagues formed an organisation Central Elected Members Organisation (CEMO). It had one rather eccentric European Representative, Mr. S. V. Cooke, as a member. CEMO was hardly born when an unfortunate split occurred in the ranks of the African Representative Members, which was based more on personality differences than any differences in policy.

When permission was granted for the formation of nation-wide parties, African Representative Members were divided into the Kenya National Party and the Kenya Independence Movement.

Differences which cropped, up between supporters of KNP and KIM at public meetings were given a tribal twist.

The imperialist press in Kenya and European politicians were quick to seize the opportunity to excite tribal animosities to the maximum and every report which helped to inflame tribal feelings found a suitable place in the European - controlled press.

The differences which arose between the KNP and KIM created unnecessary bitterness within the ranks of the African Representative Members, and placed national leaders who were either in detention or being released in a very difficult position in view of the over-riding necessity to bring about unity.

Neither the KNP nor KIM were mass political organisations. Both represented a union of district political organisations which had still to merge their Identity with the parent bodies.

OGINGA ODINGA: He organised KAU in Nyanza, kepi the Luo people loyal to the national cause. Then he led the demand for Jomo Kenyatta's release.

However, the approach of the Lancaster House Conference held in January and February, 1960 in London forced the African Members to come together. Mr. Ronald Ngala was elected Chairman and agreement reached on the demand for the immediate introduction of Responsible Government, the release of Mzee Jomo Kenyatta and other restricted leaders, and ending the State of Emergency.

Major Victory

The conclusions of the first Lancaster House Conference represented a major victory for the nationalist forces and Kenya was now placed firmly on the road to independence.

Changes in the Constitution included the introduction of adult franchise on a common roil, the appointment of a cabinet headed by a Chief Minister with responsibility for all the Ministries except Legal Affairs, Finance, Internal Security and Foreign Affairs which continued to be under the control of the British Government.

Unfortunately, the spirit of unity which existed in London was not reflected in the events, which took place on the return of the African Elected Members to Kenya. In London they had agreed to sink their differences, dissolve KIM and KNP and form a single political organisation.

On March 27, 1960 a meeting was called at Kiambu Township of all political organisations in Kenya in accordance with a decision of the African representative members in London.

Notable absentees were Daniel Moi, Masinde Muliro and Ronald Ngala. Taita Towett arrived with a delegation of Kalenjin tribesmen, but half-way through the proceedings, he staged a walk- out.

Birth of KANU

At this historic meeting which continued for two days, Mzee Jomo Kenyatta was unanimously elected President of KANU, despite the fact that he was still under restriction at Lodwar, more than 500 miles from the place they were holding the meeting.

Mr. James Gichuru was elected Acting President, Jaramogi Oginga Odinga as Vice-President, Tom Mboya as General Secretary, Ronald Ngala as Treasurer, Daniel Moi and Arthur Ochwada as Assistant Treasurer and Assistant Secretary, respectively.

It had been decided that all district organisations be dissolved, and their assets transferred to KANU.

Within a few days, Messrs, Ngala, Masinde Muliro, Tipis, Towett, and Moi announced the formation of KADU, which was to consist of the union of the Kalenjin Political Alliance, the Masai United Front, the Baluhya Political Union and the Coast African Peoples Union. The separate tribal organisations were to retain their identity and so, from the very start, KADU based its political approach on tribalism.

In March 1961, elections were held under the new Constitution. Although KANU polled 604,578 votes it only secured 22 seats as against KADU which polled 143,079 votes and secured 11 seats.

The reason for this disparity lay in the fact that the Constituency Delimitation Commission consisting of two senior officials Walter Coutts and Erick Griffiths Jones gave great advantage to the sparsely populated areas where KADU support was likely to be greater.

The Administration and Senior Officials had already decided to work for KADU, and everything was done to assist KADU officials and penalise KANU officials.

Although KANU had a substantial majority over KADU it was precluded from forming the Government unless the authorities released Mzee Jomo Kenyatta who had now been moved to Maralal.

KADU's Betrayal

It is at this stage that KADU, actively abetted by the so-called "moderate" European leaders who had won their seats on the basis of support from KANU, committed a treacherous act which was to force them to become the servile tools of imperialism.

While discussions were proceeding between KANU and the Government Sir Patrick Renison on the formation of a KANU Government, provided Mzee Jomo Kenyatta was released unconditionally, the third All African Peoples' Conference had been convened at Cairo in the United Arab Republic.

At this Conference Ronald Ngala, who was even elected leader of the Kenya Delegation, gave a categorical assurance on behalf of his Party that he would abide by the resolution passed by the Conference calling for the release of Mzee Jomo Kenyatta as a prerequisite to any co-operation with the British Government, including the formation of a Government.

Ngala and his colleagues had repeatedly given this assurance to the Kenya public.

Within a matter of days, however, Ngala and his colleagues, with the active assistance of Messrs. Blundell, Havelock, R. Macleod and Porter, succumbed to the 'tempting offer' of chief ministership and betrayed his pledges.

A host of nominated Members were created in order to give the minority Government a suitable majority.

JAMES GICHURU. - A KAU pioneer, he later became first President of KANU when the organisation was refused registration under detained Kenyatta's presidency. On Mzee's release, Gichuru vacated the office.

Although the State of Emergency was ended on January 12, 1960, the Government enacted two Bills, the Preservation of Public Security Bill and the Detained and Restricted Persons (Special Provisions) Bill, in November 1959.

These Bills were aimed in the words of the Governor, to "reinforce the substantive law, to ensure that it provides a fully effective first line of defence against incipient lawlessness", and "to continue to hold those remaining detained and restricted persons whom it has not yet proved possible to release...."

Release Campaign

The formation of an unrepresentative minority Government buttressed by official support only served to make matters worse. The campaign for Mzee Kenyatta's release was stepped up throughout the country. Hitherto, the main excuse advanced by the Government to deprive Mzee Kenyatta and his colleagues of their freedom was that their return was opposed by people in their areas, and, more particularly, by the so-called "loyalists".

In a series of KANU- sponsored meetings held throughout the central province and the Rift Valley, which were attended by former government supporters, resolutions were passed demanding the release of Mzee Kenyatta and his colleagues

The minority Government fearing the reaction of the masses, arranged the transfer of Mzee Kenyatta from Lodwar to Maralal on April 4, 1961. The KADU Government, however, followed the Colonial Government's policy of alternating concessions with repressive measures.

Operation "Milltown" was mounted in which over a hundred persons were arrested and detained without trial at Hola and Lamu on the grounds that they threatened the personal security of Ngala.

Free at Last!

Mzee Jomo Kenyatta was moved to his home in Kiambu on August 15, 1961, and became a free man at 9 a.m. on Tuesday, August 21, 1961, when he was served with the Instrument revoking his Restriction Order.

The days that followed must have been among the happiest ones in Mzee Kenyatta's life. Tens of thousands of people, using every mode of transport, flocked to his home at Gatundu to pay tribute to the man who for nearly forty years symbolised the aspirations of the nationalist movement in the country.

Mzee Kenyatta rose to the occasion. Both at Maralal and at his home in Gatundu he gave the lie to the vicious propaganda deliberately fostered by imperialists that he was too old and incapable of leadership.

At Press Conferences and in personal interviews he disclosed his firm grasp of local and international affairs.

Unfortunately, despite the fact that it was clear that Mzee Kenyatta enjoyed the support of the overwhelming majority in the country, the KADU leaders, power - drunk and completely under the influence of their European advisers, rejected Mzee Kenyatta's appeal for unity.

KADU leaders prated about democracy and indulged in blatant tribalism. Conveniently forgetting the undemocratic and opportunistic means they had adopted in forming the Government, they joined the imperialist chorus in denigrating the very man who, a short while ago, they claimed was their leader.

On October 28, 1961, Mzee Jomo Kenyatta was unanimously elected President of KANU. It should be noted that when KANU originally applied for registration under the Societies Ordinance on June 5, 1960, it was refused registration, which was tantamount to proscribing it, on, the grounds that Mzee Kenyatta was named as its President. KANU was registered on June 11, 1960, when Mr, James Gichuru's name was cited as President.

While KADU leaders must share the blame for the unnecessary delays in the country's march towards independence, they may be excused for their understandable ignorance of imperialist tactics of divide-and- rule.

All of them fell prey to the subtle flattery and newly-found concern for the 'rights of minority tribes' which was the stock-in- trade of senior govern- ment officials, headed by Sir Patrick Renison.

KADU leaders apparently consigned to oblivion the fact that the so-called backwardness of the tribes they claimed to represent, the relative lack of educational and economic facilities existing among the Masai, Digo, Giriama etc. was the responsibility of the Government and its officials, whom they now regarded as their mentors.

Settler Intrigue

As even more important factor which contributed to KADU's errors was the fact that their leaders could not possibly appreciate the extent to which certain Government officials and European settlers would go in order to ensure the political destruction of Mzee Kenyatta and other leaders of the banned KAU.

An awareness of this factor is essential in understanding the attitude of some officials and European settlers towards KANU even today, and the history of these events may be briefly recapitulated in a separate article.

The history of events which followed the release of Mzee Jomo Kenyatta is too well known to require a detailed repetition.

In December 1961 KANU held its first delegates conference where members of parliament who had undertaken to vacate their seats on the return of Mzee Kenyatta were to redeem their pledge.

Elected Unopposed

Although it was decided that Kariuki Njiiri should resign his seat, the initiative was taken by Muinga Chitasi Chokwe, a former detainee who was the last Vice-President of the Kenya African Union, to be followed by Jaramogi Oginga Odinga, Jackson Angaine and Ngala Mwendwa.

Mzee Kenyatta was elected unopposed and led the KANU Delegation to the Second Lancaster House Conference held in London from February 14 to April 6, 1962.

Once again, the Settler clique, led by Messrs. Blundell and Havelock, and a number of senior officials, did everything possible to prevent the formation of a national government.

All kinds of concessions were wrung out of KANU by effectively employing the worst tactics of political blackmail. The choice before KANU was either the acceptance of provisions within the Constitution which could, in certain circumstances, pave the way towards the disintegration of the country, or to accept them for the time being in the hope that the masses of Kenya would return them to power with a big majority.

Not satisfied with imposing conditions under duress, the Colonial Government went so far to insist that Jaramogi Oginga Odinga should be excluded from the list of Ministers who were to serve in the National Government.

The Colonialists have never been able to forgive Jaramogi Oginga for having initiated the struggle for the release of Mzee Kenyatta, and for his consistent anti-colonial, anti-imperialist policies.

KANU Victory

Mzee Kenyatta's faith in the masses of Kenya was not misplaced. In the General Elections held in May 1963, KANU won a sweeping victory with 72 seats out of a total of 112 seats. The election of National Members, coupled with defections from KADU and the reunion of the APP, brought KANU's strength in the House of Representatives to 93, as opposed to KADU's 31.

On June 1, amidst indescribable scenes of joy, Mzee Kenyatta's ministers were sworn in, and in October the Prime Minister led a delegation to London to finalise the arrangements for the country's independence on December 12, 1963.

Historic Document

Within four days of assuming the Premiership Mzec Kenyatta, together with President Julius Nyerere and Prime Minister Milton Obote, signed a historic document calling for the formation of a federation embracing the territories Of Uganda, Tanganyika and Kenya, and appointing a Working Committee to draft the necessary details aimed at giving concrete expression to the resolutions passed at the recent Addis Ababa Conference for Pan-African unity.

As the Union Jack is lowered at 23.59 hours on December 11, and the Black, Red and Green flag of independent Kenya rises to take its place at midnight, the thoughts of many thousands in the vast stadium will go back to their comrades in the forests, in detention camps, in the streets of Nairobi and all over Kenya, who gave their most precious possession — their lives — in the bloody struggle against the forces of reaction and imperialism, so that those of us witnessing this ceremony may live in a better Kenya —freed from the hated colonial system, with its concomitant of the exploitation of man by man.

Kenya's Uhuru must not be transformed into freedom to exploit, or freedom to be hungry, and live in ignorance. Uhuru must be Uhuru for the masses — Uhuru from exploitation, from ignorance, disease and poverty.

The sacrifices of the hundreds of thousands of Kenya's freedom fighters must be honoured by the effective implementation of KANU's policy —a democratic, African, socialist state in which the people have the rights, in the words of the KANU election manifesto, "to be free from economic exploitation and social inequality"

Pinto – A Selection of Quotes

All quotes are taken from Pinto's article: Glimpses of Kenya's Nationalist Struggle, *Pan Africa.* 12-12-1963 and other writings of Pinto.

Dedan Kimathi

Dedan Kimathi's courageous leadership against the might of a dwindling empire fired the imagination of freedom fighters throughout the length and breadth of Africa. Kimathi and his lieutenants proved to the colonialists in Africa that colonialism was unprofitable and that once a people had determined to be free there is no obstacle they will shirk in the pursuit of their goal of freedom.

*

Land

In 1902 Commissioner Elliot declared Kenya a fit place for European settlement... What followed has been aptly referred to as the "Great Land Grab". Adventurers and speculators displayed considerable enterprise in acquiring huge areas of land for little or nothing, and then parcelling it out to their fellow countrymen at considerable profit to themselves.

-

Perhaps, the worst action taken by the government was the mass eviction of tens of thousands of innocent men, women and children from the rift valley province. The vast majority of these people had been in the rift valley for two or three decades. They had lost their customary right in the reserves, where land consolidation and the provision of title deeds replaced the old system of communal tenure. The desperate position of these uprooted people can well be imagined.

*

Terrorising and detaining

Side by side with the terrorisation of the African people in the Reserves and the towns went the policy of arresting and detaining anyone who exhibited the slightest degree of political consciousness.

*

Detention

Following the fiasco which attended the Government's efforts to convey a facade of judicial sanction to the arrest and imprisonment of Mzee Jomo Kenyatta and his five colleagues, the Government resolved to use the simpler expedient of detaining citizen without the necessity of bringing them before a Court off Law.

...

In June 1954 the writer was served with a Detention Order, and shortly after appearing before the Advisory Committee was detained at Takwa Special Detention Camp on Manda Island. Among the allegations contained in the charge sheet were; (a) That I had knowledge of illegal arms traffic; (b) That I assisted Mau Mau in drafting documents and arranged for the printing of membership cards of the 'African Liberation Army'; and (c) had given assistance to the non-militant wing of the Mau Mau in planning 'its subversive campaign'.

The onus of proving the contrary rested with the writer, and he was informed that the only way he could do it was to prove (a) his loyalty to the British Government and its policies; (b) the steps he took to abet the criminal activities of the authorities; and (c) his sympathy for European settlers and South Africa!... 80,000 Africans who were detained were accorded similar 'justice'.

*

Pio Gama Pinto, Kenya's Unsung Martyr

Avoiding massacres

The writer was himself engaged in arranging a scheme which would have avoided further massacres of untrained, badly equipped, and starving freedom-fighters when he was arrested and detained. The British Government which apparently gave its consent to the scheme pleaded its ignorance of my activities at that stage.

*

Struggle in the forests, towns and detention camps

Like the struggle of the freedom fighters in the forests and towns, the struggle in Detention Camps against the attempts of the Authorities to demoralise and destroy the political faith of detainees requires a book to itself.

*

National political parties

In 1956, the demand of the African Members to be allowed to form a political organisation was met by the British Government by allowing the formation of political bodies on a district basis. As most of the districts coincide with tribal areas, the British government set out to implant tribalism in its most virulent form into the body politic of Kenya. This move was to have the most dangerous consequences for Kenya, and the country is still suffering from the effects of this policy.

*

Imperialist Press

The imperialist press in Kenya and European politicians were quick to seize the opportunity to excite tribal animosities to the maximum and every report which helped to inflame tribal feelings found a suitable place in the European - controlled press.

*

Freedom from economic exploitation and social inequality

As the Union Jack is lowered at 23.59 hours on December 11, and the Black, Red and Green flag of independent Kenya rises to take its place at midnight, the thoughts of many thousands in the vast stadium will go back to their comrades in the forests, in detention camps, in the streets of Nairobi and all over Kenya, who gave their most precious possession — their lives — in the bloody struggle against the forces of reaction and imperialism, so that those of us witnessing this ceremony may live in a better Kenya —freed from the hated colonial system, with its concomitant of the exploitation of man by man.

Kenya's Uhuru must not be transformed into freedom to exploit, or freedom to be hungry, and live in ignorance. Uhuru must be Uhuru for the masses — Uhuru from exploitation, from ignorance, disease and poverty. The sacrifices of the hundreds of thousands of Kenya's freedom fighters must be honoured by the effective implementation of KANU's policy —a democratic, African, socialist state in which the people have the rights, in the words of the KANU election manifesto, "to be free from economic exploitation and social inequality"

*

Violence/ Non-violence

[in 1940 Kikuyu Central Association was proscribed... in 1946 Kenya African Union was formed]... Africans had by now come to an understanding that non-violent, constitutional agitation had serious limitations and that new methods must be evolved to avoid, the collapse in political organisation which characterised the banning of the political association and the arrest of Its leaders.

-

[After 1950 General Strike, charges against Makhan Singh and Fred Kubai] It had become increasingly obvious that "constitutional", "non-violent" methods of fighting for one's rights were absolutely futile in dealing with the Settler-Colonial combination which was charged with the administration of the country. Organised violence was the only answer to such a situation.

*

Grievances

The disabilities from which Africans suffered might be listed as the wholesale alienation of their lands, highly discriminatory scales of pay in the Civil Service, the ban on the growth of cash crops, the transformation of Reserves or "Native Land Units" into reservoirs of cheap labour, the imposition of a tax structure which compelled Africans to seek work on terms and conditions dictated by their employers, an educational and economic system which discriminated in favour of the rich and powerful and against the poor, a change from a subsistence economy and shifting cultivation to a money economy and static farming without the provision or acquisition of new techniques, resulting in a considerably lower standard of living, and the disintegration of tribal society without the benefit of new values, and the absence of any voice in the Legislature or any of the policy-making institutions.

The overcrowded, poverty-stricken reserves were expected to provide social security for the disabled or retired urban worker.

*

Colonial State terrorism

On October 21, 1952, the Government introduced into Nairobi a large number of 'askaris' from the Northern Frontier Province, who were charged with the task of terrorising the population. Africans in Nairobi were indiscriminately beaten without any rhyme or reason.

Pinto seen through his correspondence

Pinto to Brockway: 12-01-1953

17. Pio Gama Pinto to Fenner Brockway (12-01-1953)

THE KENYA INDIAN CONGRESS

SUCCESSOR TO
THE EAST AFRICAN INDIAN NATIONAL CONGRESS

P.O. Box No. 186
TELEPHONE 3467

TELEGRAMS;
"INDIAN CONGRESS"

DESAI MEMORIAL.
VICTORIA STREET,
NAIROBI.

KENYA COLONY.

(20)

12th January, 1953.

Dear Fenner,

It was good to hear from you after a prolonged silence. I presume that you felt that it might not be safe to write to me directly, and I think you are right. I am a bit surprised to learn that you are not kept as well informed as I had imagined. Awori told me that was keeping you posted with cuttings etc. through the Head Office. It was for that reason that I discontinued sending you cuttings. Murumbi was away at Kapenguria for most of the time, and on his return he had to take up his job with his employees because things were a bit too uncertain to permit him taking up a full time job with the K.A.U. at the Head Office. It will be a pleasure to be of service to you and to Mr. Hale, and I shall do my best to keep you informed of events in Kenya. It might be possible for you in your next letter to tell me what exactly you want. Will you be satisfied, for instance, with cuttings from local papers, reports of atrocities etc. etc. It is difficult to make a detailed study of say the labour conditions, because although I am at the moment only employed on a part-time basis in the Congress, I have any amount of other work to do. Please, however, make it a point to write to me at the following address:-

note =

Mr. R. Gama Pinto,
Hutchings Biemer
P.O.Box 408,
Nairobi.

I have already sent you cuttings through Mrs. Ela Reid, and shall continue to send you material c/o. her address until you can provide me with another cover address. I do not know whether the address you gave me i.e. Mrs. J. Wood, is a cover address.

When you read the cuttings a number of questions will suggest themselves to you and your colleagues. The attitude of the Government would, however, appear to be most irresponsible in allowing the Settlers and their supporters unlimited opportunities to make the most fantastic statements at a criticial juncture in the present crisis. The Congress has issued a weak rejoinder. It is apparent that the present campaign by the settlers is directed towards the forthcoming Session of the Legislative Council, when it is proposed to follow the policy of repression to the hilt. Practically every vernacular paper has been banned. My own "Afrika Mpya" was the last casuality. No reason is given. I have not even received an official intimation to the effect that the

12th January 1953.

Dear Fenner,

It was good to hear from you after a prolonged silence. I presume that you felt that it might not be safe to write to me directly, and I think you are right. I am a bit surprised to learn that you are not kept as well informed as I had imagined. Awori told me that was keeping you posted with cuttings etc. through the Head Office. It was for that reason that I discontinued sending you cuttings. Murumbi was away at Kapenguria for most of the time, and on his return, he had to take up his job with his employees because things were a bit

too uncertain to permit him taking up a full-time job with the K.A.U. at the Head Office. It will be a pleasure to be of service to you and to Mr. Hale, and I shall do my best to keep you informed of events in Kenya. It might be possible for you to tell me exactly what you want. Will you be satisfied, for instance, with cuttings from local papers, reports of atrocities etc. etc. It is difficult to make a detailed study of any the labour conditions, because although I am at the moment only employed on a part-time basin in the Congress, I have any amount of other work to do. Please, however, make it a point to write Ito me at the following address:

> Mr. R. Gama Pinto,
> Hutchings Biemer
> P.0.Box 408,
> Nairobi.

I have already sent you cuttings through Mrs. Ela Reid and shall continue to send you material c/o. her address until you can provide me with another cover address. I do not know whether the address you gave me i.e. Mrs. J. Wood is a cover address.

When you read the cuttings a number of questions will suggest themselves to you and your colleagues. The attitude of the Government would, however, appear to be most irresponsible in allowing the Settlers and their supporters unlimited opportunities to make the most fantastic statements at a critical juncture in the present crisis. The Congress has issued a weak rejoinder. It is apparent that the present campaign by the settlers is directed towards the forthcoming Session of the Legislative Council, when it in proposed to follow the policy of repression to the hilt.

Practically every vernacular paper has been banned. My own "Afrlka Mpya" was the last casualty. No reason is given. I have not even received an official intimation to the effect that the District Commissioner has considered it in the interests of peace and good order to ban my paper. The authorities are trying to stifle all opposition by 1) refusing to give licences to owners of cyclostyling machines on the grounds that the "Registrar" "after consulting the Member" considers that "the applicant is likely to keep or use a printing press for unlawful purposes, or for the printing of any document prejudicial to, or incompatible with, peace or good order in the Colony;..."; and 2) by proscribing the newspapers as soon as they appear without giving any reasons whatsoever. Meanwhile, the Europeans are given a free hand to carry out their campaign for a Settler-dominated Government of Kenya. I am sending you the official gazette banning the publications.

I am collating data on the schools closed by the administration, and will shortly let you have the relevant details in regard to the number of children affected, number of schools closed, number of teachers arrested 1 etc.

Reports reaching me from the Police Camps and other concentration camps indicate that the position of the detainees is getting worse. During the first sweeps, the detainees were given no shelter whatsoever. Some had to be content with blankets and to remain in the open air during the nights in barbed wire encampments. In the detention camp at Kajiado where most of the political prisoners are detained, the detainees have submitted a petition to the Governor. H.E. the Governor visited the camp,on the 5rd of January, and the detainees put forward certain demands concerning the deplorable conditions prevailing in the camp, and the urgent necessity of putting them on a trial. We are receiving reports of the bad conditions in other camps located in the Reserves. In some cases, the relatives of the Prisoners are forced to bring food for those detained by the Police. There are camps in the Kiambu Reserve in which the inmates and the goats and cattle confiscated by the Police are herded in the same encampment.

There is one point in particular which requires the urgent consideration of the public in England. Hundreds of Kikuyu are being tried for Mau Mau offences in Magistrate Courts. These Courts have recently been empowered to use powers which were normally reserved only for the Supreme Court. They sentence people to 7,10 and even 12 years hard labour. However, in most cases, there is no defence for the poor Kikuyu who are charged with the offences. How are ignorant tribesmen to put up a defence against an educated prosecutor who may have got his facts from a Headman or Home Guard who in turn may have
some ulterior motive in getting rid of the person charged? This is a most urgent problem.

I shall write to you again in the course of the next two days. Meanwhile, here's wishing you all the very best.

Greetings from all of us.

Yours sincerely
P. G. Pinto
Pinto to Brockway: 14-01-1953

THE KENYA INDIAN CONGRESS

SUCCESSOR TO
THE EAST AFRICAN INDIAN NATIONAL CONGRESS

P.O. Box No. 186
Telephone 3467

TELEGRAMS:
"INDIAN CONGRESS"

DESAI MEMORIAL
VICTORIA STREET,
NAIROBI,
KENYA COLONY.

14th January, 1953.

My dear Fenner,

I have already sent you 3 airmail letters c/o. Mrs. Ela Reid. I have not received any acknowledgement to my letters so far - hope you have been receiving them.

A new development took place this morning. The Government cancelled the Registration of the Tribune Press. This means that Tribune will not be produced on the Press. No reasons have been given. We are, however, endeavouring to get the paper our on the cyclostlying machine. Sharda is sick since the last 6 weeks. He is down with a bad attack of Pneumonia which at one time was thought to be Pleurisy. He is better now but it will be some time before he can leave his bed. Please inform Mr Kingsley Martin & Mr Colin Legum of this event.

I am enclosing a copy of the memorandum which a deputation composed of Asians and Africans have prepared and sent to H.E. the Governor with a request that it form the basis of an discussion between the deputation and the Governor. The persons responsible for the preparation of the memorandum, and who have given it their consent and signature are, among others, Mr. Nazareth, Mr. D.D. Puri, Hon. Odede, Murumbi, Awori, Councillor Ofafa, A.B. Patel, Hon. Chanan Singh and several other notable Indian lawyers and businessmen. It is not known whether the Governor will receive the deputation.

I hope you will bear in mind the question of the absence of legal assistance for Africans who may be sentenced to 7,10 or even life sentences without any provision of defence.

Convey my regards to Mr. Hale & others.

Yours v. sinc.

enclosed Qff.

I am having the Petition signed by people in all walks of life. Please inform Leon Szur.

18. *Pio Gama Pinto to Fenner Brockway (14-01-1953*

14th. January 1953

My dear Fenner,

I have already sent you 3 airmail letters c/o. Mrs. Ela Reid. I have not received any acknowledgement to my letters so far - hope you have been receiving them.

A new development took place this morning. The Government cancelled the Registration of the Tribune press. This mean that Tribune will not he produced on the Press. No reasons have been given. We are, however, endeavoring to get the paper our on the cyclostyling machine. Sharda is sick since the last 6 weeks. He is down with a bad attack of pneumonia which at one time was thought to be pleurisy. He is better now but it will be some time before he can leave his bed. Please inform Mr. Kingsley Martin and Mr Colin Legum of this event.

I am enclosing a copy of the memorandum which a deputation composed of Asians and Africans have prepared and sent to H.E. the Governor with a request that it form the basis of a discussion between the deputation and the Governor. The persons responsible for the preparation of the memorandum, and who have given it their consent and signature are, among others, Mr. Nazareth, Mr. D.D. Puri, Hon. Odede, Murumbi, Awori, Councillor Ofafa, A.B. Patel, Hon. Chanan Singh and several other notable Indian lawyers and businessmen. It is not known whether the Governor will receive the deputation.

I hope you will bear in mind the question of the absence of legal assistance for Africans who may be sentenced to 7, 10 or even life sentences without any provision of defence.

Convey my regards to Mr. Hale & others.

Yours v. sinc.

Handwritten note: I am having the enclosed petition signed by people in all walks of life. Please inform Leon Szur[52]

---

52   Leon Szur, Communist activist in South Africa and author of *What is Neo-colonialism*. Central Council, Movement for Colonial Freedom, 1962: London.

Rsxx Nairobi
18th January, 1953.

Dear Fenner,

I wrote you 3 letters care of the following address:
Mrs Ela Reid, Flat 1, 45 Eaton Place, London S.W.1
I hope you have received them all. I had asked you in my first
letter to let me have another cover address. Mrs Reid is the wife
of Mr Alec Reid of the Hindustan Times, Delhi.

From the cuttings and from my personal talks with Mr John
Tameno, M.L.C. the most disturbing feature is the attempt on the
part of Government to create antagonisms between the Masai
and the Kikuyu by encouraging the Moran to take part in raids
on the Kikuyu in the Aberdares and other places. Tameno has actually
toured several areas and protested to the District Commissioner, Sweetman,
at Ngong against the attempts to stir up trouble. He tells me that
he was responsible in getting the administration to send back Masai
Moran from Laiktokitok. The Masai Elders told him that they had
been told by the Government Officials to fight the Kikuyu, and when they
refused they were warned that their sections would suffer. The Elders
therefore thought it wise to advise the Moran to do what the Administration
desired of them. Tameno, as you will observe from a perusal of the
Standard reports of the proceedings of the Legislative Council, raised
the matter in the Council.

The Legislative Council passed by a majority the
Bill imposing the death sentence on those who administered the Oath
involving the murder of anotherperson. Incidentally, Mr Mathu is
absent from the present Session of the Council, and gives the excuse
that he has "fallen ill". Although the African members were the only
ones who opposed the Bill, there is evidence to suggest that they agreed
to the provisions of the Bill when it was discussed at a meeting
of the Unofficial Members Organisation. In fact, it was only on the
insistance of an Indian Member, that the "death penalty" was to be
confined only to those cases where it was proved that the Administrator
administered an oath involing the murder of another man. The European
Unofficials were pressing for death penalty for all Oath Administrators.
The African Members for obvious reasons opposed the Bill in the open
Legislative Council. I have had occasion to see personally the
"confidential" minutes of the Unofficial Members organisation. When
we discussed the matter with certain African Members they tried to explain
it of as a part of a bargain for the abolition of the colour bar in the
services. I am giving you these details so that you and Mbiu should
know just how far you can go with some of our friends. At the moment,
we want them more than they want us and as such should not precipitate
any crisis by levelling accusations etc. Murumbi and others
agree to this course.

19. Pio Gama Pinto to Fenner Brockway (18-01-1953)

Nairobi
18th January 1955.

Dear Fenner,

I wrote you 3 letters care of the following address:

Mrs Ela Reid, Flat 1, 45 Eaton Place, London S.W.1

I hope you have received them all. I had asked you in my first letter to let me have another cover address. Mrs. Reid is the wife of Mr. Alec Reid of the Hindustan Times, Delhi.

From the cuttings and from my personal talks with Mr. John Tameno, M.L.C. the most disturbing feature is the attempt on the part of Government to create antagonisms between the Masai and the Kikuyu by encouraging the Moran to take part in raids on the Kikuyu in the Aberdares and other places. Tameno has actually toured several areas and protested to the District Commissioner, Sweetman, at Ngong against the attempts to stir up trouble. He tells me that he was responsible in getting the administration to send back Masai Moran from Laitokitok. The Masai Elders told him that they had been told by Government Officials to fight the Kikuyu, and when they refused they were warned that their sections would suffer. The Elders therefore thought it wise to advise the Moran to do the Administration desired of them. Tameno, as you will observe from a perusal of the Standard reports of the proceedings of the Legislative Council, raised the matter in the Council.

The Legislative Council passed by a majority the bill imposing the death sentence on those who administered the oath involving the murder of another person. Incidentally, Mr. Mathu is absent from the present session of the council and gives the excuse that he has "fallen ill". Although the African Members were the only ones who opposed the Bill, there is evidence to suggest that they agreed to the provisions of the Bill when it was discussed at a meeting of the Unofficial members of the organization. In fact, it was only on the insistence of an Indian Member, that the "death penalty" was to be confined only to those cases where it was proved that the Administrator administered an oath involving the murder of another man. The Europeans Unofficials were pressing for death penalty for all Oath Administrators. The African members for obvious reasons opposed the Bill in the open Legislative Council. I have had occasion to see personally the "confidential" minutes of the Unofficial Members organisation. When we discussed the matter with certain African Members they tried to explain it of as a part of a bargain for the abolition of the colour bar in the services. I am giving you these details so that you and Mbiu should know just how far you can go with some of our friends. At the moment, we want them more than they want us and as such should not precipitate any crisis by levelling accusations etc. Murumbi and others agree to this course.

Reports of atrocities are coming in, and we are having them translated and kept in order for use in the near future.

As a result of the recent ban on papers, nearly all the African papers have been closed down, and the Tribune Press has had its registration withdrawn. This is a hard blow to all of us. The funny thing is that neither the Registar nor the District Commissioners think it necessary to give any reasons, or even quote the damaging passages, when they ban the papers or withdraw registration. There are papers like "WIHUGE" which reproduce nothing but reports from the E. A. Standard and some foreign paper. They are purely "newspapers" and do not air any views. They, moreover, get all their news from the Standard. Sharda always has the English translations of the Kikuyu papers made before printing the material. All this just shows that the Government is determined to stifle and stamp out even- ordinary newspapers, so that the people should only read the stuff dished out by the semi-official organ of the Government, Baraza.

"Wihuge" was banned along with "Afrika Mpya". Meanwhile, the European newspapers are permitted full freedom to print whatever they like, and the Settlers are having meetings all over the country demanding "self-Government under European leadership".

Governor has not yet seen the deputation of Indo-African leaders. He is

Pio Gama Pinto, Kenya's Unsung Martyr

I understand very busy touring and was to pay a visit to Uganda as well.

I have just had a Masai Moran Officer in my room, and he has given me details of the incident involving the Masai. He tells me that two officers by the names of Sweatman (c/o Masai Province) and a certain Walford Walker who has just returned from U.K. went to Loitokitok - a place near the Tanganyika Border near Moshi, and after a short conference in a tea room (probably over a glass of rum) with a few headmen, packed some Moran in trucks and took them over two hundred miles from their homes to the Aberdares. The whole process is unconstitutional from the practice followed hitherto by the Masai whenever any important decision is to be adopted. It is the usual practice for such matters to be decided by the Masai Council which is composed of representatives from over 17 Sections. These Sections have their own Councils which are subject to the over-all jurisdiction of the Masai Council which may be held at Ngong, Norok or Kajiado.

In this particular instance the Moran were packed off to the Aberdares without even consulting the local Section Council of Elders, and the parents of the Moran were ignorant of the decision. If the Masai had actually decided to perform these policing duties, why should it be necessary for Government to import Masai Moran hundreds of miles from the Aberdares when thousands of Moran were handy at Narok? Anyway, you have now got the facts, and can place whatever interpretation you wish.

All the best.

Yours v. sincerely

Pinto

Dear Fenner,

Thanks a lot for your letter. I am glad you have tabled a
question on the closing of the Tribune. You can get all your facts
from Mr Kingsley Martin who has been kept well informed by Mr Shard

You will be surprised to learn that the C.I.D. in plain
clothes raided Sharda's press this morning on the plea that they we
looking for "subversive literature". Quite naturally, they did not
find anything of an incriminating nature. I would not be surprised
if this act on their part is a direct consequence of your
enquiries in London. ~~Itxisxquitextheoongeivshisxxthatxthexyxwill~~
~~is~~ Sharda is petitioning the Governor in a few days time ar will
be sending you a copy of the Petition.

I am enclosing cuttings of the protest demonstrations ma
by Europeans. It was broadcast last night on the Nairobi Radio, alt'
not published this morning, that an Officer of the Kenya Police R'
had actually issued orders that all Europeans who were accosted
the roads should be informed of the demonstration and asked to
it. ~~It~~ If you read the reports of the mass meetings held you
observe a reference to some European who was shoved out of the
The gentleman happens to be a Welsh Barrister by the name of Peter
Evans - apparently the Europeans could not stick his presence at the
meeting.

Yesterday, Tameno, Awori and about 5 representatives of
the African Charitable Trust had an interview with the Member for
Education. The Authorities did not seem anxious to commit themselv
in any way. The ~~at~~ only alternative is that the Independent School
will have to apply for registration individually. That is the
to find out which schools will be allowed to function and wh
Government intends to close. Thereafter, legal proceedings co
instituted if there is an attempt to appropriate the property
people who own the schools. Hon. Chanan Singh is helping the
concerned with the case. Nazareth suggested that he would be a bette
person because of his deep knowledge of the subject.

The people here are very anxious to get somebody to reorgan
the schools from the United Kingdom. Do you think it would be possi
for you to suggest the name of someone who has had educational expe
and who could undertake this work. It would be wonderful if we coul
get somebody with the spirit of Mr Stonehouse. Please discuss the
matter with Mbiu and let us know soon because the ~~it~~ people are ver
anxious to have this piece of information. You could let us know
the terms and conditions ~~sx~~ which the person will accept. Murumbi a
myself have also been discussing the question of co-operatives. Th
is a lot of scope for ~~weekly~~ work on this field, but we lack the
personnel. Let us know at your earliest the possibilities of getti
people for work on the educational and co-operative spheres. I a
enclosing a note for Mbiu from a friend.

I have received a letter from Mr Reid asking me to continu
sending him the cuttings to be passed on to you. In a way it is a
excellent idea because Reid makes very effective use of the stuff
I send on the Hindustan Times which is attracting an increasing amou
of interest among the Settlers, and because it has the effect of
getting us sympathy and support ~~is~~ from India. If you have not
objection, I shall continue sending the cuttings through Mr Reid,
and use the other address for private correspondence.

Thats all for the present -

Yours sincerely.

20. *Pinto to Brockway (28-02-1953)*

28th January 1953

Dear Fenner,

Thanks a lot for your letter. I am glad you have tabled a question on the closing of the Tribune. You can get all your facts from Mr. Kingsley Martin who has been kept well informed by Mr Sharda

You will be surprised to learn that the C.I.D. in plain clothes raided Sharda's press this morning on the plea that they were looking for "subversive literature". Quite naturally, they did not find anything of an Incriminating nature. I would not be surprised if this act on their part is a direct consequence of your enquiries in London, Sharda is petitioning the Governor in a few days' time and I will be sending you a copy of the Petition.

I am enclosing cuttings of the protest demonstrations by Europeans. It was broadcast last night on the Nairobi Radio, although not published this morning, that an Officer of the Kenya Police had actually issued orders that all Europeans who were accosted [on] the roads should be informed of the demonstration and asked to [join] it. If you read the reports of the mass meetings held you will observe a reference to some European who was shoved out of the meeting. The gentleman happens to be a Welsh Barrister by the name of Peter Evans — apparently the Europeans could not stick his presence at the meeting.

Yesterday, Tameno, Awori and about 5 representatives of the African Charitable Trust had an interview with the Member for Education. The Authorities did not seem anxious to commit themselves in any way. The only alternative is that the Independent School will have to apply for registration individually. That is the [way] to find out which schools will be allowed to function, and which Government intends to close. Thereafter, legal proceedings can be instituted if there is an attempt to appropriate the property of the people who own the schools. Hon. Chanan Singh is helping the people concerned with the case. Nazareth suggested that he would be a better person because of his deep knowledge of the subject.

The people here are very anxious to get somebody to reorganize the schools from the United Kingdom. Do you think it would be possible for you to suggest the name of someone who has had educational   experience and who could undertake this work. It would be wonderful if we could get somebody with the spirit of Mr. Stonehouse. Please discuss this matter with Mbiu and let us know soon because the people are very anxious to have this piece of information. You could let us know the terms and conditions which the person will accept, Murumbi and myself have also been discussing the question of co-operatives. There is a lot of scope for work on this field, but we lack the personnel. Let us know at your earliest the possibilities of getting people for work on the educational and co-operative spheres, I am enclosing a note for Mbiu from a friend.

I have received a letter from Mr Reid asking me to continue sending him the cuttings to be passed on to you. In a way it is an excellent idea because Reid makes very effective use of the stuff I send on the Hindustan Times which is attracting an increasing amount of interest among the Settlers, and because it has the effect of getting us sympathy and support from India. If you have no objection, I shall continue sending the cuttings through Mr Reid, and use the other address for private correspondence,

That's all for the present.

Yours sincerely.

SAUTI YA KANU

PEOPLES PRESS LIMITED (IN FORMATION)
Directors & Editorial Board:— J. S. Gichuru, Oginga Odinga M.L.C., Tom Mboya M.L.C.

FIELD HOUSE
VICTORIA STREET
NAIROBI

P.O. Box 6814
TELEPHONE: 22614

Pinto

Date....7/1/61........196...

Ref: Mr. Joseph Murumbi,
Moroccan Embassy
London.

My dear Joe,
I am delighted at this opportunity of being able to write to you. Quite honestly I have been expecting a note from you – but apparently you are under the impression that you might be endangering my position by doing so. Let me assure you that I am in fairly close contact with all those of my brothers whom I left behind at Takawa Camp and are now dispersed all over at Hola, Manjalat and Mahitaung.

My good comrade Chokwe will explain everything to you. He was in detention with me for several years and since his release we are in very close touch.

Where is your family? Please give them my love and do write to me regularly. If you wish I would be delighted to make you our official correspondent for London. Drop me a note to my above address.

21. Pio Gama Pinto to Joseph Murumbi (07-01-1961)

FIELD HOUSE   P.O.BOX 6814
VICTORIA STREET
                                                       TELEPHONE 2261

NAIROBI
Date: 7-1-1961

Ref
Mr Joseph Murumbi,
Moroccan Embassy
London.

My dear Joe,
I am delighted at this opportunity of being able to write to you. Quite honestly, I have been expecting a note from you - but apparently you are under the impressions that you might be endangering my position by doing so. Let me assure you that I am in fairly close contact with all those of my brothers whom I left behind at Takwa camp and are now dispersed all over at Hola, Marsabit and Lokitaung.

My good comrade Chokwe will explain everything to you. He was in detention with me for several years and since his release we are in very close touch.

Where is your family? Please give them my love and do write to me regularly. If you wish I would be delighted to make you our official correspondent for London. [Make a] note of my above address.

If you meet Mbiyu please give him my best wishes and tell him that he should get in touch immediately with the Ethiopian Embassy and arrange for the protection of his two sons who are apparently stranded in Addis. I gave them a bit of help before their deportation to Addis and enclose their photographs.

J.D Kali and Mugo [Muratha] send you their best wishes. We are all working together. Many of our boys are now back from detention and imprisonment and we are working very hard.

Lastly, give Chokwe and Gichuru all the help and assistance you can and see that you engage a proper channel of communication for the future. I am sure you will be allowed to return together with Mungai, at any time in the next couple of months.

Pass my regards to Stonehouse, Temera, Fenner and any of our mutual friends.

Yours in the struggle for freedom

Pio

(P.G Pinto) My wife and brothers send you all their best wishes. You must have heard that my father died when I was in detention.

Pinto's letter to Joseph Murumbi (27-03-1961)[53]

My dear Joe,

Forgive me for not having written to you earlier. We were all very busy during the elections. I do not know exactly how well you are informed on Kenya politics. I realise that when one is in Kenya one is liable to become so immersed in its problems as to be oblivious of the bigger problems facing the anti-colonialist forces throughout the world: and by colonialism I imply not merely the political subjugation of a territory but, what may be more important and far-reaching in its consequences, the economic subjugation of a territory, sometimes referred to as neo-colonialism. I realise that when one is in London the problems of Kenya are one of the many problems which one has to face. We here are forced to concentrate on Kenya and its immediate problems because there is little that we can do to affect other issues. You, on the other hand, with all the powerful connections you have built up through your dedication to the cause of striving for the freedom of African states, are in a position to assist the progressive forces in the federation and other territories.

Please let me know whether you get the E.A. Standard or whether you would like me to send you cuttings every week by air. I am very anxious that you should be kept reasonably well-informed on the situation in Kenya because it will not be very long before you are called upon to play a much more important part in the affairs this country. These[54] were printed by me and you will note that I did not forget to include the photos of our real heroes in the long and arduous struggle we have had to wage.

I think Chokwe told you that I and my group are in close touch with our brothers still in restriction- whether at Lodwar, Lokitaung, Marsabit or Hola (now called Galole) and J.D. Kali, the last editor of the KAU organ. It will not surprise you to learn that I am working [with] the old group i.e. Mugo,

---

53   Reproduced from Thurston, Anne (2015, Ed.): A Path Not Taken: the Story of Joseph Murumbi, Africa's Greatest Cultural Collector and Kenya's Second Vice-President. Nairobi: The Murumbi Trust. The Editor would like to thank the Murumbi Trust, the Murumbi Archives and Alan Donovan for permission to reproduce material on Pio Gama Pinto in this book.

54   It is not clear what Pinto is referring to here but seems to be important documentation undertaken by Pinto.

Chokwe, J.D and many others who were known to you. I am sure you were delighted to learn of Chokwe's great victory at Mombasa. Although Odede lost badly in the general elections, he secured the highest number of votes for the national seat. F.R.S. de Souza was also elected to one of the two national seats for Asian non-Muslims.

In February we started a Kikuyu newspaper called "WIYATHI" which means freedom. The editor is Wilfred Kabue, the old editor of Muramati, which was banned during the Emergency. Wilfred has recently come out of Galole and was with us in Manda Island.

KANU could have done much better during the elections but it suffered badly from indiscipline and personality attacks. Surprisingly, the worst offenders were those who should have known better- the chaps we refer to as the degreewallas. Vicious personality attacks or character assassinations, invoking tribalism of the worst type, circulating unsigned scurrilous cyclostyled sheets, etc. were all a part of a campaign. Our whole group rallied around Tom, not because we were not aware of some of his shortcomings, but it would have been foolish to ignore his sterling services to the country or to allow opportunists of the first order to take his place. There is much I would like to tell you, Joe, but it must wait until such time as we meet again. The most heartening thing about the whole campaign was that the old Kikuyu political elders - those who were with us in detention at Manda and were the persons who founded KCA and other organisations - saw through the tactics of these educated tribalists and refused to have anything to do with them. You are no doubt aware of the results.

Although I have been closely involved in Kenya politics, I did not think it was fair to forget our Portuguese friends!!! Sometime before the Santa Maria episode we have been planning the formation of the Mozambique African National Union. There are about 8000 Mocambiquans in Kenya and about 500,000 Mocambiquans in Tanganyika - most of them employed in sisal estates. As it is impossible for us to organise in Mocambique itself where Portuguese fascism rules supreme, we decided to organise in East Africa firstly. We accordingly held an inaugural meeting at Mombasa and although the Government refused us a public meeting, we launched the union after a series of meetings with delegates of people of Mocambique origin from a number of places in Kenya, and also from Dar, Tanga and Pemba. Chokwe acted as the convener.

Unfortunately, most of the people who have been forced to migrate from Mocambique are labourers. You are, no doubt, fully aware of Portuguese policy to deny them any education and to force them to migrate so that they can support the home economy by sending in money and paying their taxes. As such it will be necessary to do most of the organizational work for them in the beginning. We plan to train them in any numbers. Their lack of education, on the other hand, should not detract from their sense of patriotism and unity of purpose, which is so often found wanting among our so-called miseducated Goans who are never at a loss in producing arguments designed to delay action on every conceivable projects.

Among our other activities is to give the maximum publicity to Portuguese atrocities in Mocambique. Angola is now on the map, but something must also be done to stir up public opinion on the conditions in Mocambique and to assist the Mocambiquan in their struggle against the fascist dictatorship. Through the E.A. Goan League we have been in touch with Mr. Nyerere and have been assured full support. I understand that a conference is to take place at Casablanca. If there is a possibility, Chokwe and I would very much like to attend the conference. I received a return ticket from the Egyptian Govt, to attend the All African Peoples Conference currently being held at Cairo but gave my ticket to a KANU Legco. Member by the name Lawrence Sagini, representing Kisii, as the poor chap was very anxious to go and also because I did not think it is advisable to leave Kenya at a time when nearly all the leading KANU politicians are away. A chap by the name CABRAL wrote to my brother that they had only one ticket available which they felt should be used by a Mocambiquan. My brother explained the difficulties and I feel that if they object is to get something concrete done for the people of Mocambiquan origin they might be induced to change their minds. Please let me know the possibilities. Cabral, incidentally, works for the Goal League in London.

Before I conclude, a little bit of news of our mutual friends. Kaggia and

Pio Gama Pinto, Kenya's Unsung Martyr

Ngei are fit at Lodwar. I received letters from both. Achieng is still restricted at Kapsabet. He has asked us to visit him and we applied for permission. Lawrence Karugo, John Mbiyu Koinange, and Babu Kamau are still at Marsabit. They recently sent a petition to the Government complaining at conditions there. Jessie Kariuki and Dedan Mugo, also at Marsabit, were fined shs.80/- each for violating some stupid restriction imposed on them.

Mugo, Kali, Lillian Njeri (Your supporter in KAU days), and many other friends send you their very best wishes.

Should you write of a confidential nature, please address it to,

Mrs. Emma Gama Pinto
c/o. Jos Hansen& Schoene Ltd.
P.O.BOX 30196
Pioneer Building, Govt.Road, Nairobi

Wish you all success in the work you are doing.

Yours in the struggle,
Pio
P.S. Fitz, Oscar & Rosario send you their best wishes.

Pmb

This Conference deplores and condemns the efforts of Western European Nations who are attempting the economic subjugation of Afro-Asian countries through the E.C.M. The Conference member states & political organisations of the danger of association with the E.C.M. and calls for concrete measures to combat the efforts of former colonial powers to further neo-colonialism. This Conference is of the opinion that the International Conference on trade & development being convened by the UNO next year should provide the opportunity for Afro-Asian countries to work out positive measures to foster trade among themselves and safeguard their economies from the machinations of the Western cap. countries.

✻

This Conference of the Afro-Asian Solidarity Committee meeting at Moshi
a) Having regard to the need for promoting economic development in the underdeveloped countries of Asia and Africa and also the vital necessity for closer cooperation in the economic field. that appeals to the Great Powers to disarm in the interests of peace and the necessity to divert the vast expenditure on armaments towards alleviating the misery and poverty in the underdeveloped countries

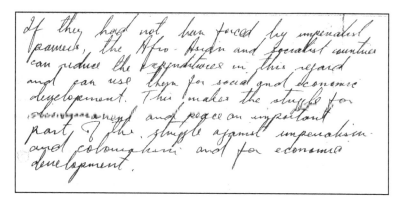

22. Pinto's handwritten notes, Conference of Afro-Asian Solidarity. Moshi, 1963

CONFERENCE OF AFRO ASIAN SOLIDARITY
Moshi, 1963

This Conference of the Afro- Asian solidarity committee meeting at Moshi:

Having regard to the need for promoting economic development in the underdevelopment countries of Asia and Africa and also the vital necessity for closer cooperation in the economic field, appeals to the great powers to disarm in the interests of peace and the necessity to divert the vast expenditure on armaments towards alleviating the misery and poverty in the underdeveloped countries:

> This conference deplores and condemns the efforts of Western European Nations who are attempting the economic subjugation of Afro-Asian countries through the E.C.M [European Common Market]. The conference warns member states and political organizations of the dangers of association with the E.C.M and calls for concrete measures to combat the efforts of former colonial powers to further neo-colonialism.

> This conference is of the opinion that the international conference in trade and development being convened by the UNO next year

should provide the opportunity for Afro-Asian countries to work on positive measures to foster trade among themselves and safeguard their economies from the machinations of the western capitalist countries.

If they had not been forced by imperialist powers, the Afro-Asian and socialist countries can reduce the expenditures in this regard and can use them for social and economic development. This makes the struggle for disarmament and peace an important part of the struggle against imperialism and colonialism and for economic development.

Selected Points from Pinto's Correspondence with Lord Fenner Brockway

A Complete Revolutionary

It is perhaps best to let Pinto himself show the various activities he was involved in and the number of issues he was concerned about. A brief glimpse into the revolutionary warrior is provided in his letters and reports, a few quotes from these are reproduced below to show what an extraordinary person Pio Gama Pinto was. In his letter to Fenner Brockway, (Kenya National Archives) Pinto reveals the political activist devoting himself to ensure that the world was informed and supported the struggle of working people in Kenya, at the same time revealing a number of activities that he was involved in: (Source: Kenya National Archives files (3) Miscellaneous Correspondence, 1952-1972)

Detention

Mr Thompson and Mr Dingle Foot visited the concentration camp at Kajiado yesterday. You are probably away that the majority of active K.A.U. members and office bearers have been detained at Kajiado. (26-01-1953).

∗∗

Divide and Rule Policy

Awori and Odede returned from Nyanza this afternoon. They returned victorious because the attempts on the part of the District Commissioners and some other government authorities to discredit them for their part in the KAU failed miserably. The D.C. seeing which way the wind was blowing would not even allow the meeting to be held, although he had earlier given permission for the meeting in the expectation that his stooges would carry the day. The people of Nyanza, the Luo and the Baluyha, gave them a big oration and refused to hear what DC had to say. I hope this demonstration we'll have a restraining influence on certain D.C.s who are apt to misjudge the character and intelligence of the people. (26-01-1953).

*

Another good piece of news is that the Masai Morans have been withdrawn. Tameno made strong protests, and supervised the withdrawal personally. I understand at the Government now contemplates recruiting the Masai Moran individually. It is not expected that they will achieve great success in their efforts to foster tribal ill-will.
(26-01-1953).

***

Laws and the Legal System

There is one point in particular which requires the urgent consideration of the public in England. Hundreds of Kikuyu are being tried for Mau Mau offences in Magistrate Courts. These Courts have recently been empowered to use powers which were normally reserved only for the Supreme Court. They sentence people to 7,10 and even 12 years hard labour. However, in most cases, there is no defence for the poor Kikuyu who are charged with the offences. How are ignorant tribesmen to put up a defence against an educated prosecutor who may have got his facts from a Headman or Home Guard who in turn may have some ulterior motive in getting rid of the person charged? This is a most urgent problem.

And the letter ends in a typically Pinto style. In spite of the large amount of work he was involved in, he ends: "I shall write to you again in the course of the next two days". No political work can be left undone or postponed, even if it means staying up the whole night to complete it all. Kenya has not seen another person like Pio Gama Pinto to this day.

Education
A deputation of Africans consisting of Awori, Gikonyo, Tameno, Kimani, Mugo and Kabui will be waiting upon the Member for Education tomorrow. I hope they will succeed in convincing the Member of the need to reopen the schools closed down by the government under independent management but strict government supervision. (26-01-1953).

*

The people here are very anxious to get somebody to reorganise the schools from the United Kingdom. Do you think it would be possible for you to suggest the name of someone who has had educational experience and who could undertake this work? … Please discuss the matter with Mr. Mbiu and let us know soon because the people are very anxious to have this piece of information… Murumbi and myself have also been discussing the question of cooperatives. There is a lot of scope for work in this field, but we lack the personnel… I am enclosing a note for Mbiu from a friend. (28-01-1953).

***

Education and situation in schools
I am collating data on the schools closed by the administration and will shortly let you have the relevant details in regard to the number of children affected, number of schools closed, number of teachers arrested.

Pinto (Pinto, P.G. 1953) shows his concern for providing education to Kenyan children and young people agin in 1953 where he seeks support for education in a letter to Fenner Brockway:

> ... Representatives of the African Charitable Trust had an interview with the Member for Education. The authorities did not seem anxious to commit themselves in any way. The only alternative is that the Independent Schools will have to apply for registration individually...The people here are very anxious to get somebody to reorganise the schools from the United Kingdom. Do you think that it would be possible for you to suggest the name of someone who has had educational experience and who could undertake this work. It would be wonderful if we could get somebody with the spirit of Mr. Stonehouse. Please discuss the matter with Mbiu and let us know soon because the people are very anxious to have this piece of information. ... Murumbi and myself have e have also been discussing the question of co-operatives. There is a lot of scope for work in this field, but we lack the personnel. Let us know at your earliest the possibilities of getting people for work on the educational and co-operative spheres.

P.O.Box No. 186,
Nairobi.
8th April, 1952.

Dear Mr. Fenner Brockway,

I note that in your last letter dated 24th March, you have conferred a doctorate upon me. Mr. P. Ratansi will no doubt inform you that it is not so. I am, however, very much encouraged after having read your letter, and look forward to receiving a detailed communication from Mrs. Klopper.

I am enclosing for your information some cuttings from the Standard which illustrate the outlook of certain elements in the Colony towards a reference to "human rights in the Colonies". I am also enclosing a cutting from the East African Standard giving details of the the police refusal a public meeting which was scheduled to be held on the Van Riebeeck Day. This instance alone proves the absolute lack of civil rights in Kenya. So far the Congress has had no reply to its letter to the Superintendent of Police (Nairobi District), enquiring into the reasons for withholding the Permit to hold a joint meeting. It is proposed to have a joint meeting of the Executives Committees of the K.A.U. and the Congress for the purpose on Wednesday, the 9th inst., for the purpose of passing a resolution of protest against the arbitrary action of the Police authorities.

There is a rather important point which I would like to bring to your notice in connection with the above. Since the last two months or so, the Government has banned meetings and public demonstrations in the Nyeri and Forthall districts. Among the reasons given are the disturbances which followed the refusal of cattle-owners to have their cattle inoculated, and reports of widespread arson for which the Mau Mau is held responsible. The Mau Mau, as you are probably aware, is a secret organisation which has been proscribed. The East African Standard has been writing editorials advocating strong measures against the Mau Mau. As the Standard is regarded as the semi-official organ of the Government, we can expect the forces of "law and order" to take their clue from the public indignation expressed through the Standard to launch a movement in which they will not be very discriminating in distinguishing the Mau Mau from the K.A.U. In fact, as is evident from the report of the trials, a move is afoot to involve the K.A.U. so that there can be an excuse to either ban it altogether in a particular area, or to make it impossible to function actively by imposing all sorts of restrictions necessary for holding meetings.

23. Pinto to Brockway (08-04-1952)

Conditions in prisons and concentration camps

Reports reaching me from the Police Camps and other concentration camps indicate that the position of the detainees is getting worse. During the first sweeps, the detainees were given no shelter whatsoever. Some had to be content with blankets and to remain in the open air during the nights in barbed wire encampments. In the detention camp at Kajiado where most of the political prisoners are detained, the detainees have submitted a petition to the Governor. H.E. the Governor visited the camp on the 5rd of January, and the detainees put forward certain demands concerning the deplorable conditions prevailing in the camp, and the urgent necessity of putting them on a trial. We are receiving reports of the bad conditions in other camps located in the Reserves. In some cases, the relatives of the Prisoners are forced to bring food for those detained by the Police. There are camps in the Kiambu Reserve in which the inmates and the goats and cattle confiscated by the Police are herded in the same encampment.

Internationalism

Central African Federation. You will observe from the cuttings I have enclosed that steps are being taken to link East Africa with the Federation to the South. Mr. J. Otiende, the General Secretary of the K.A.U., has already addressed a communication to the Nyasaland African Congress with a copy to the N.Rhodesian African Congress on the subject of establishing closer liaison with their respective organisations. It is intended at some future date to hold a conference (without giving any publicity) of the territories to be included within the Federation.

Central African Federation. You will observe from the cuttings I have enclosed that steps are being taken to link East Africa with the Federation to the South. Mr. .J. Otiende, the General Secretary of the K.A.U., has already addressed a communication to the Nyasaland African Congress with a copy to the N. Rhodesian African Congress on the subject of establishing closer liaison with their respective organizations. It is intended at some future date to hold a conference (without giving any publicity) of the territories to be included within the Federation.

10-03-1952

Through the columns of the Tribune I presume you are familiar with the situation as it exists within the Congress. Mr. Nazareth succeeded in getting his resolution for "blocking" the seats through the Session held on the 26th and 27th Jan. He is now busy trying to evolve a method or plan which will ensure that the resolution is implemented effectively by the Standing Committee which has been empowered to devise ways and means to implement the resolution. The sub-Committee which was appointed at the last meeting of the Standing Committee to report on "ways & means" has agreed with a proposal put forward by Mr. Nazareth which would secure the implementation of the resolution. He suggested that Congress nominate 4 Indians who do not belong to the category of "prospective candidates" or eligible candidates, or past Councillors. The only qualification should be their absolute integrity. It may not be so easy for Mr. Nazareth to get it his proposals through the Standing Committee, nor is it certain that after it has received the sanction of the Congress it will dissuade certain "aspirants" from contesting the elections and fighting against Congress nominees. As you are probably aware, powerful forces within the Indian community are working hard to secure the reversal of the policy adopted during the past three years. It will therefore be clear to you that, so far as the Congress is concerned, it will be consumed to a great extent with its internal quarrels. If the policy hitherto followed is reversed, it will lead to much frustration, and even those who in the past took keen interest in the affairs of the community will be tempted to withdraw from politics. It will also effect the little prestige it possess with the Colonial Office, because it will be evident that an organisation which retreats at the very moment when its threats become applicable cannot count for much. In view of the above, it will be so obvious that as far as effective opposition to Government is concerned, it will have to come from some other quarters. Thex

Through the columns sums of the Tribune I presume you are familiar with the situation as it exists within the Congress. Mr. Nazareth succeeded in getting his resolution for "blocking" the seats through the session held on the 26th and 27th Jan. He is now busy trying to evolve a method or plan which will ensure that the resolution is implemented effectively by the Standing Committee which has been empowered to devise ways and means to implement the resolution. The sub-Committee which was appointed at the last meeting of the Standing Committee to report on "ways & means" has agreed with a proposal put forward by Mr. Nazareth which would secure the Implementation of the resolution. He suggested that Congress nominate 4 Indians who do not belong to the category of "Prospective candidates" or eligible candidates, or past Councillors. The only qualification should be their absolute integrity. It may not be so easy for Mr. Nazareth to get it his proposals through the Standing Committee, nor is it certain that after it has received the sanction of the Congress it will dissuade certain "aspirants" from contesting the elections and fighting against Congress nominees. As you are probably aware, powerful forces within the Indian community are working hard to secure the reversal of the policy adopted during the past three years.

It will therefore be clear to you that, so far as the Congress is concerned, it will be consumed to a great extent with its internal quarrels. If the policy hitherto followed is reversed, it will lead to much frustration, and even those who in the past took keen interest in the affairs of the community will be tempted to withdraw from politics. It will also affect the little prestige it possesses with the Colonial Office, because it will be evident that an organisation which retreats at the very moment when its threats become applicable cannot count for much. In view of the above it will be obvious that as far as effective opposition to Government is concerned, it will have to come from some other quarters.

Kenya Indian Congress

T.U. Bill. You must be acquainted with the provisions of the new TU. Trade Union Bill. In collaboration with D.K., I have been able to prepare a memorandum for the East African Labour Trade Union of East Africa. A copy of this memorandum will be sent to you by air mail in the course of the next 3/4 days. I do not know whether you have a copy of the Bill with you, but in case you have not got one I shall be only too pleased to send you a copy. We have sent a copy to the Fabian Colonial Bureau. I do not know whether you can do anything about the extremely restrictive clauses which are a feature of the Bill. Under the proposed Bill trade unions are maxxxxxxxxxxxx under the complete mercy of the Registrar.

I was wondering whether you could assist the trade unions here to secure their affiliation to the International Confederation of Free Trade Unions. It would be very much appreciated if you could give us some advice on this matter. Following the disturbances which took place in May 1950, trade union activity has slowed down considerably but efforts are now being made to resuscitate these unions.

Van Roobeeck Day - April 6th. Both the Kenya African Union and the Congress have agreed on a programme to be observed on April 6th, in support of the movement being launched in South Africa. The following is the programme:-

1. All those going to Churches, Mosques or Temples will be asked to offer their prayers for the success of the movement launched by the African National Congress, and for the failure of the Union Government's policy of Apartheid.

2. Mass meetings to be held all over the country under the auspices of the K.A.U. and other organisations.

3. Wherever possible, meetings to be preceded by processions.

4. The people will be called upon to observe the day as a day of mourning. For this purpose an appeal will be made to the people asking them to wear something black-preferably a black feather-which will constitute a visible emblem of mourning.

The K.A.U. has already communicated with the the Northern Rhodesian African Congress asking xxxxxxxxxxxxxxxxx in asking them to adopt a similar programme if they have not already thought of some such protest demonstration. Letters have also been xxxxx written to the two newspapers in Nigeria, representing the two main parties, asking them to consider a similar programme. I was wondering whether you could not, through the Congress of Peoples against Imperialism, make an approach to the organisations affiliated to the Congress with a view to enlisting their support for the above programme. Alternatively, although the time is short, could you please arrange to send the Kenya African Union the addresses of representative institutions who, you feel, would be interested in participating in the above movement. The K.A.U. has yet to develop liaison with organisations political organisations in other African territories and it would be of assistance to them if you they knew that exactly whom they are approaching.

T.U. BILL. You must be acquainted with the provisions of the new Trade Union Bill. In collaboration with D.K., I have been able to prepare a memorandum for the Labour Trade Union of East Africa. A copy of this memorandum will be sent to you by air mail in the course of the next ¾ days. I do not know whether you have a copy of the Bill with you, but in case you have not gone I shall be only too pleased to send you a copy. We have sent a copy to the Fabian colonial Bureau. I do not know whether you can do anything about the extremely restrictive clauses which are a feature of the Bill. Under the proposed Bill trade Union are under the complete mercy of the Register.

I was wandering whether you could assist the trade unions here to secure their affiliation to the international Confederation of Free Trade Unions. It would be very much appreciated if you could give us some advice on this matter. Following the disturbance which took place in May 1960, trade union activity has allowed down considerably but efforts are now being made to resuscitate these unions.

Van Riebeeck Day - April 6

Both the Kenya African Union and the Congress have agreed on a programme to be observed on April 6th in support of the movement being launched in South Africa. The following is the programme:

> 1. All those going to Churches, Mosques or Temple will be asked to offer their prayers for the success of the movement launched by the African National Congress, and for the failure of the Union Government's policy of Apartheid.
> 2. Mass meetings to be held all over the country under the auspices of the K.A.U. and other organizations.
> 3. Wherever possible, meetings to be preceded by processions.
> 4. The people will be led upon to observe the day as a day of mourning. For this purpose an appeal will be made to the people asking them to wear something black-preferably a black feather-which will constitute a visible emblem of mourning.

The K.A.U has already communicated with the Northern Rhodesian African Congress asking them to adopt a similar programme if they have not already thought of some such protest demonstrations. Letters have also been written to the two Newspapers in Nigeria, representing the two main parties, asking them to consider a similar programme. I was wondering whether you could go through the Congress of Peoples against imperialism, make an approach to the organizations affiliated to the congress with a view to enlisting their support for the above programme. Alternatively, although time is short, could you please arrange to send the Kenya African Union the addresses of representative institution who, you feel, would be interested in participating in the above movement. The K.A.U has yet to develop liaison with political organization's in other African territories and it would be of assistance to them if they knew exactly whom they are approaching.

10-03-1952

***

Press
Glad you tabled a question [in the British House of Commons] on the closing of the *Tribune*. You [...] your facts from Mr. Kingsley Martin who has been kept well informed by Mr Sharda   ...   CID in plain clothes raided Sharda's press this morning looking for "subversive literature" - probably a direct consequence of your enquiries in London. Sharda is petitioning the Governor in a few days' time and will be sending you a copy of the Petition. (28-01-1953).

*

Have received a letter from Mr. Reid asking me to continue sending him cuttings to be passed on to you. Reid makes effective use of the stuff in the *Hindustan Times* which is attracting an increasing amount of interest among the Settlers and gains us sympathy and support in India. If you don't object I'll continue sending the cuttings through Reid and use the other address for private correspondence. (28-01-1953).

*

When you read the cuttings a number of questions will suggest themselves to you and your colleagues. The attitude of the Government would, however, appear to be most irresponsible in allowing the Settlers and their supporters unlimited opportunities to make the most fantastic statements at a critical juncture in the present crisis. The Congress has issued a weak rejoinder. It is apparent that the present campaign by the settlers is directed towards the forthcoming Session of the Legislative Council, when it in proposed to follow the policy of repression to the hilt.

Practically every vernacular paper has been banned. My own *Afrlka Mpya* was the last casualty. No reason is given. I have not even received an official intimation to the effect that the District Commissioner has considered it in the interests of peace and good order to ban my paper. The authorities are trying to stifle all opposition by 1) refusing to give licences to owners of cyclostyling

machines on the grounds that the "Registrar" "after consulting the Member" considers that "the applicant is likely to keep or use a printing press for unlawful purposes, or for the printing of any document prejudicial to, or incompatible with, peace or good order in the Colony;..."; and 2) by proscribing the newspapers as soon as they appear without giving any reasons whatsoever. Meanwhile, the Europeans are given a free hand to carry out their campaign for a Settler-dominated Government of Kenya. I am sending you the official gazette banning the publications.

***

Trade Unions and Labour Conditions

Labour conditions: Dear Fenner, … It will be a pleasure to be of service to you and to Mr. Hale, and I shall do my best to keep you informed of events in Kenya. It might be possible for you to tell me exactly what you want. Will you be satisfied, for instance, with cuttings from local papers, reports of atrocities etc. etc. It is difficult to make a detailed study of any the labour conditions, because although I am at the moment only employed on a part-time basin in the Congress, I have any amount of other work to do

Emma Gama Pinto's Perspective: Life with and without Pio

Emma Gama Pinto: Remembering Pio[55]

Remembering Pio   — by Mrs Pinto

As far back as I can remember, Pio was always gentle, kind, thoughtful and quiet. He managed with a minimum number of hours sleep and drove himself like a slave - reading, writing and organizing. He was not the marrying-kind, and I often wondered on what impulse he decided to wed. Pio's first love was his 'cause'. As an idealist he had several wherever he happened to be in his adolescent years. He abhorred persecution of those unable to defend themselves and readily championed their cause.

I met Pio about September 1953 and we married in January 1954. If it wasn't breaking the 'colour-bar', or meeting the local chiefs, he was out on the field practising for the 220 yard, 440 yard or hop-step-jump events for the coming championship. He was a good sportsman and had represented Kenya in the Indian Ocean Games a few years before.

Pio was honest in a funny way - he told me he did not make much to support me and I should therefore start thinking about getting a job myself! No frills - just a blunt statement with a wide smile. Since my first few weeks as a bride was akin to being a grass-widow, I felt it might be best if I did not stay home and twiddle my thumbs.

Home, to Pio, was a one room bed-sitter with minimum furnishing. A small portable one-burner stove was all the 4 ft.x 4 ft. kitchen could boast of. My parents who had flown in from India for the wedding were shocked. They presented us with a car, washing machine, a sewing machine and   a substantial cash cheque for the wedding.

Early in June, my husband was arrested under the Emergency Regulations. He was then editor of the Daily Chronicle and Secretary of the Indian Congress in Nairobi. As the situation in Kenya was getting from bad to worse, Pio sent information to friends aboard in England and the UAR (Joseph Murumbi and Mbui Koinange). They pleaded the cause from their vantage positions where there was freedom of   press and speech. He smuggled releases to important people in many countries so that they could be apprised about the true conditions in Kenya.

I saw my husband for about five months for just 10 minutes before he was whisked away to an unknown destination. About a week later I heard that he was in Manda Island. I requested the Minister for Defence to allow me to visit Pio. I was told that since my husband was in sympathy with the Africans he would be treated like one. Besides, Pio wanted no privileges that the other inmates of the prison camp did not enjoy.

Pio told me later that he built a small shelter against the scorching sun and a simple bed. The land was destitute of vegetation and there were no facilities when he got there. A daily ration of food was barely enough to suffice for one meal. He went on a hunger strike, but after 9 days realized that it would get the prisoners nothing more. They could die like dogs for all the authorities cared. The prisoners were sullen and dejected. Pio met some of his old friends there - Achieng Oneko and others and they set about improving the morale of the 9,000 men on the island prison. They organized games and set about trying to catch fish, turtles and the like to supplement their impoverished diet. Hardly anyone received mail. After pleading with the authorities, I was allowed to write to my husband once a month but the letter would be censored. His reply was also censored. The prisoners did not receive any news of the world or their own country - they were isolated. I received permission to send Pio some literature. He asked for the works of Shakespeare and Shaw. Later Pio said that those books kept him from committing suicide. Everything he had, he shared with his friends - even my letters!

---

55   Submitted to June Milne of Panaf Books on 30-06-1972.

As far back as I can remember Pio was always gentle, kind, thoughtful and quiet. He managed with a minimum number of hours sleep and drove himself like a slave – reading, writing and organizing. He was not a marrying-kind, and I often wondered on what impulse he decided to wed. Pio's first love was his 'cause'. As an idealist he had several wherever he happened to be in his adolescent years. He abhorred persecution of those unable to defend themselves and readily championed their cause.

I met Pio about September 1953 and we married in January 1954. If it wasn't breaking the 'colour bar' or meeting the local chiefs, he was out on the field practicing for the 220-yard, 440 yard or hop-step-jump events for the coming champions. He was a good sportsman and had represented Kenya in the Indian Ocean games a few years before.

Pio was honest in a funny way - he told me he did not make much to support me and I should therefore start thinking about getting a job myself! No frills – just a blunt statement with a wide smile. Since my first few weeks as a bride was akin to being a grass-widow, felt it might be best if I did not stay home and twiddle my thumps.

Home, to Pio, was a one room bed-sitter with minimum furnishing. A small portable one-burner stove was all the 4 ft. by 4ft. kitchen could boast of. My parents who had flown in from India for the wedding were shocked. They presented us with a car, washing machine, a swing machine and a substantial cash cheque for the wedding.

Early in June, my husband was arrested under the emergency Regulations. He was then editor of the Daily Chronicle and a secretary of the Indian National Congress in Nairobi. As the situation in Kenya was getting from bad to worse, Pio sent information to a friend aboard in England and the UAR (Joseph Murumbi and Mbiyu Koinange). They pleaded the cause from their vantage position where there was freedom of press and speech. He smuggled releases to important people in many countries so that they could be apprised about the true conditions in Kenya.

I saw my husband of about five months for just 10 minutes before he was whisked away to an unknown destination. About a week later I heard that he was in Manda Island. I requested the minister for Defence to allow me to visit Pio. I was told that since my husband was in sympathy with the Africans he would be treated like one. Besides, Pio wanted no privileges that the other inmates of the prison camp did not enjoy.

Pio told me later that he built a small shelter against the scorching sun and a simple bed. The land was destitute of vegetation and there were no facilities when he got there. A daily ration of food was barely enough to suffice for one meal. He went on a hunger strike, but after 9 days realized that it would the prisoners nothing more. They would die like dogs for all the authorities cared. The prisoners were sullen and dejected. Pio met some of his old friends there – Achieng Aneko and others and they set about improving the morale of the 9,000 men on the Island prison. They organized games and set about trying to catch fish, turtles and the like to supplement their impoverished diet. Hardly anyone received mail. After pleading with the authorities, I was allowed to write to my husband once a month but the letter would be censored. His reply was also censored. I received permission to send Pio Literature. He asked for the works of Shakespeare and Shaw. Later Pio said that those books kept him from committing suicide. Everything he said, he shared with his fiends – even my letters!

Pio was the only Asian detained under the Emergency Regulations. Makhan Singh has also been detained but for other reasons and was not at Manda Island. True to his old self, Pio did not waste time. Here were hundreds of old men who had been working for years to achieve freedom from oppression; who had been instrumental in sending delegations (Kenyatta, Murumbi, Koinange) abroad to plead their cause. Pio secretly took notes – he interviewed many of the 'old guard' and his copious notes were smuggled out and hidden in various villages whenever a prisoner was released. The years dragged by and at last in February 1958 Pio was released from detention but put under restriction in a tiny village 8,000 ft. above sea level. Karbanet became our home for almost 2 years.

At last I was permitted to join my husband. We were given a two-bedroom house with spare furniture and less than sh. 50 on which to live. We were not supposed to speak to anyone except the 'administration staff of the district', which consisted of about a dozen people, most of whom were not really interested in the ex-detainee.

After assuring the district commissioner that he was not subversive, Pio was allowed to do odd jobs in the administration office. We were able to hear about what was going on in Nairobi and although he managed to hide his political interest, Pio was again the moth circling the light.

At the recommendation of my doctor, Pio was allowed to travel to Nairobi for the birth of our first child in case of the need for blood transfusion due to my Rh-negative condition. On the joy of being with people again! Pio visited me briefly at the nursing home and finding that all was well, kept in touch by phone for the rest' of his short leave, and spent his time catching-up on the true nature of the situation in the country. That was Pio! This leopard hasn't changed its spot or even blurred them.

Fortunately, during the years of detention, I had read avidly about the struggle in South Africa, and the aspirations of the Africans had given me an understanding of my husband fervent desire to exert his utmost energies on their behalf. To the utter consternation of my friends, I refused to lift a finger to change him. His ideals were high, and I admired his courage. I was happy to share him with the country that needed him.

We had little finances. Pio sadly confessed that the money given by my father had been used as part – payment on a printing press which he wanted to operate as the voice of the people. The press was lost as soon as Pio was arrested. On his release from restriction in early 1960 Pio asked Mr. Oginga Odinga to help him buy a house. It was more a hotel – we had people coming and going and dropping in for a meal at all hours. Pio would have political refugees from Angola or South Africa spend a night or two, and listen to their accounts about the situation.

Pio rigged a study in one room. He had large desks and bed there. He worked ceaselessly. No African who came to the house was turned away – if they needed school fees for their children, advice, or just a letter written

Pio Gama Pinto, Kenya's Unsung Martyr

to a relative or government official, Pio lent a hand. They were his brothers – and I mean brothers. He knew the weaknesses of some of them but felt that they would see reason soon enough even if temporarily they did not put their country first. From the start of his interest in Kenya politics, Pio understood clearly that the African cause must be carried by Africans. He identified himself with the Africans completely and secretly suffered mental anguish that he was not born African. He preferred to work behind the scenes, but he did not work in isolation. He consulted with lawyers, economists and politicians before planning his work. He chose his non-African friends carefully for what they could contribute to the cause.

Although many Asians were politically uncommitted during the emergency, Pio hit their pocket –books for funds to care for the families of the detainees. Pio drew out the good in most people; many said it was his modesty and sincerity that moved them. Lawyers took on African cases at no charge; gave jobs to tribesmen on the government suspect list; supplied clothing to destitute families, and Dr. Yusuf Eraj spent half his clinical time on patients sent by Pio who could not pay a cent.

Pio was the unofficial speech writer for many of the leaders that emerged at UHURU. When party politics started to drive a wedge between the leaders, Pio was torn with concern for the fundamental needs of the man-in-the-street.

Despite the fact that Pio vehemently worked against those opposed to the African freedom movement, he did not harbor rancor against any individual. I never once heard him raise his voice in anger or swear at anyone, he called them blind or stupid in their policies. If anyone lived by the cliche 'the pen is mightier than the sword', it was Pio. He was once given a pistol for protection… He promptly buried it in the garden; later when he heard that one of his African friends was in danger, he recovered the weapon and gave it to his friend for protection. The safety of his African friends and leaders was a constant worry to him. He would drive miles out into the country to warn his friends of possible arrest. He risked his own life to hide Achieng Aneko (later Minister of Information, Broadcasting and Tourism) for almost a month when things looked dangerous. Knowing how lonely it must be for Achieng, he hid him under a blanket and we drove him to a Drive-In movie to cheer him up!

During the KANU first election campaign, Pio freely gave of his time, money and car. The party was victorious, but the car was a write-off.

By June 1963 we had three daughters, but Pio was still not a doting father. He bought the candy and took the youngest for a ride each morning just to the end of the drive-way, a mere 75 yards, on his way to work. There was no slackening of the work in re-organizing the party and studying parliamentary papers to advise his friends. He was back at his try to get a newspaper to voice the African viewpoint, Sauti ya KANU was soon in print. Pio had learnt to read and write Swahili in Manda and was able to edit the paper. It was rough going as he was more or less chief cook and bottle washer.

I believe the Lumumba Institute was also his brain-child. He sold the idea and his African friends made it possible to get the building erected. However, it was never put to the use intended by Pio – to train party branch officials.

Pio was going to retire early to write a book on Kenya. While he lived he was honest so his book would have been something of value.

The assassin's bullet in February 1965 took away a husband and father, but more so, a patriot of Kenya.

Emma Gama Pinto
30-06-1972.
-

> *Pinto's ideals were high, and I admired his courage. I was happy to share him with the country that needed him - Emma Gama Pinto.*[56]

---

56   Quoted in: Nowrojee, Pheroze (2007): Pio Gama Pinto: Patriot for Social Justice. Nairobi: Longhorn Publishers.

Emma Gama Pinto interviewed by Frederick Noronha (2000)

'Pio's total focus was to work to fight colonialism'

The comments in italics in the text below are by the interviewer. Vita Books would like to thank Frederick Noronha[57] for permission to reproduce the interview.

Introductory Note by Frederick Noronha - notes in brackets are also by him:

> Emma Gama-Pinto was reluctant to talk about her years gone by. As she put it, "I have received many requests for interviews and it is because the recall of the past is painful that I have tended to stay away from such requests."
>
> Not without reason. She is the widow of a prominent African patriot of Goan origin, Pio Gama Pinto. An MP in post-colonial Kenya, her husband Pio was assassinated some three-and-half decades ago. This Leftist politician from Kenya was killed when not yet 40 and left behind three small children.
>
> Pio Gama Pinto's role has been widely acknowledged in Africa. Back home he is a largely unknown figure. Then Kenyan Vice-President Oginga Odinga had commented: "No description of the history of Kenya would be complete without an assessment of Pio Gama Pinto's contribution to our struggle. Pio was a solid Kenyan patriot. His assassination leaves a gap in our struggle for complete freedom that few men -- none that I know -- can fill."
>
> She said she completed a short autobiography two years ago at the insistence of her three daughters. Emma, who currently lives in Canada, agreed however to answer questions from Frederick Noronha.

---

57   The Editor would like to thank Frederick Noronha for permission to reproduce this interview.

Below are extracts of the interview:

How do you and the daughters remember Pio today?

My daughters Linda, Malusha Marie and Tereshka were all under the age of 7 when Pio was assassinated and therefore have no coherent memory of their dad. From the time of Pio's release from 'Restriction' in Karbanet, he threw himself into the political scene, albeit surreptitiously at first because he had to report to Police HQ every week for four months.

Pio was continually meeting with his Kenya elected officials, and his ex-detainee friends for grass-roots input. He rarely spent time with the children. When I commented about him earning the title of "absentee father", he replied that when they grew older he would read to them the works of Shakespeare.

Incidentally, I had sent him Shakespeare when he was in Detention in Manda Island. Pio had told me that Shakespeare had helped him to retain his sanity in those long years away from any type of reading material.

I remember Pio as a person relentless in his pursuit of fair play for the unfortunate. He knew first-hand how thousands of Kikuyu, Meru and Embu men suffered in the Detention Camp in Manda Island and reminded me that we must do whatever we could to help.
Mentally, Pio wore blinkers like a racehorse -- his total focus was on working for the liberation of countries under foreign rule. He received newspapers from these countries and seemed glued to his typewriter sending off letters or articles to the leaders of the freedom movement.

His aim was a unified approach across Africa. He enlisted the help of other African countries which had attained Independence.

In order to bridge the family separation caused by Pio's long work hours for KANU, Oginga Odinga (*Kenyan Vice President, whose close lieutenant Pinto was*) informed Pio sometime in 1962 that he would purchase a house for us.

As soon as we moved into 6 Lower Kabete Road, Pio set up office in a spare room. He typed until the early hours of the morning when there were no interruptions. I did, of course, miss out on normal family outings, and so on, but Pio's earnestness of purpose gave me the understanding to let him have the freedom to follow his ideals. I had a few Goan friends whom I visited with my daughters. Besides, I had my twin sister Joyce with whom I had a very close and happy relationship.

Do you feel that the role played by your late husband is recognised or known by the people of Goa, and the Goan expatriate community as a whole?

Pio and I had attended a few Goan social functions after his release, and even though several men came forward to hear about his "detention" there was little evidence of their sympathy for the detainees.

When the Portuguese anthem was played at the end of an occasion, Pio could guess where the allegiance lay. He had painted a sketch of Kenya's road in the struggle for freedom and left it to them to pursue a course. Mr. J. M. Nazareth Q.C. and a few others were already on the road.

Later we did not attend Goan functions, so I was not aware of the view they had of Pio. Even after Pio's assassination I did not feel that I belonged to the Goan community. I do not fault the community - it is just that we had other interests and concerns. I was happy with any Asian who understood and helped Pio's work.

Pio and a small group of Kenya politicians including Tom Mboya and Joe Murumbi flew to India around 1961 and met with Pandit Nerhu. The agenda included the Liberation of Goa as well as funds for a printing press in Kenya (*to provide the African political view point*). Funds were granted, and Pio set up the Pan African Press. Subsequently, Pio and Fitz De Souza attended Goa's Liberation celebrations. Pio spent so much of his time travelling that I was not always aware of his trips or details of his working papers. There are some Goans who applaud Pio's small contribution for Goa.

Could you tell us some interesting reminiscences with a political link?
When Mozambique was in the throes of its freedom movement, Pio was in touch with members of (*the main group fighting colonial rule*) FRELIMO. One evening, Pio announced to me that he was expecting two men from Mozambique. They would be spending a night with us as they were en route to Europe for discussions.

The second incident was actually precipitated by me when I was personal secretary to Achieng Oneko, Minister for Information, Broadcasting and Information. One day Field Marshall Okello suddenly walked into my office unannounced and informed me that he wished to speak to the Minister. How this man was able to enter a security enforced building is a mystery.

Earlier that year (1964) the world was awakened to the news that in a bloodless coup d'etat in Zanzibar by Field Marshall Okello, the Sultan's Government had been overthrown. Achieng Oneko who was not at all pleased called Vice President Oginga Odinga for advice. I did not know at that time that Okello was a hot potato.

In the meantime, I returned to my office and casually invited the Field Marshall to have dinner with my family that night and he accepted. I thought that as a journalist Pio would welcome an exclusive interview. When I called Pio with the news, he was aghast, but I had no way of contacting Okello to cancel out. I got home and ordered a simple dinner. Okello arrived promptly at 7 p.m. I cannot recall much of the event as I was tense with anxiety at being so ignorant of the political undercurrent at that time.

Pio and Okello spoke in Swahili and when our guest left Pio did not mention him to me again. The next day the Kenya Government quietly asked Okello to leave the country and we never heard about him again.

Pio was one of the few Goans who swam against the tide, to take on the powerful forces of colonialism and supported a colonised society in claiming its due. What propelled him in that direction? What, in your view, were the values he stood for? Tell us something about his early years in Kenya.

I cannot say what triggered Pio's call to work against colonial rule. It may have begun when he was a teenager in Goa. When Pio returned to Kenya, he decided to work as a clerk in the Magadi Salt Flats. He was befriended by Dr. and Mrs. V. De Souza. They talked about their son Fitz who at the age of 16 had gone to London to get his LLB.

Pio found time to train in track/field events and returned to Nairobi to participate in major sports events. He did so well in the middle-distance events that he was selected to represent Kenya in the 1952 Commonwealth Games in Vancouver, Canada. By this time Pio had been inextricably drawn to the inequities of land ownership and did not accept the trip to Vancouver. In 1951 Pio had enlisted the help of the Indian High Commissioner, Apa Pant for a typewriter to work on his ideas. The High Commissioner hired Pio as a secretary to the Kenya Indian Congress. Pio was given a desk at the Desai Memorial Library and he single-handily revised the Land Reform Act to allow Africans a fair share of their country.

I heard of this work many years after Pio's death from Fitz De Souza (*who went on to hold prominent posts in Kenya*). Friends informed me that later, Pio resigned from the Kenya Indian Congress and became editor of the *Daily Chronicle*, correspondent for the Press Trust of India and All India Radio.

Around this time he directed his letters to the British MP Fenner Brockway and others who had formed the Movement for Colonial Freedom. He realized that the outside world could help Kenya. Pio valued the dignity of the poor unrepresented Kenyan. He appealed to them for assistance for the release of Jomo Kenyatta (later to head the Kenyan government) and the four other leaders jailed for their involvement in the Freedom Movement. Dennis Pritt, Q.C. from London, eventually arrived to lead the case with two Indian lawyers. Fitz had just returned fresh from U.K. and joined the band. He moved into the political arena with both feet.

Since Pio was a journalist, he probably left behind his written work. How much of his writing is still available? Any thoughts of re-publishing his collected works in the form of a book?

During the years prior to Kenya's Independence, Pio used an African pseudonym in his articles to colonial and to British newspapers. He changed the name periodically for security reasons from 1960-63.

Soon after Pio's assassination, some of his friends - in good faith - burned all his office files. So that is where the matter stands in regard to Pio's articles, memos, and correspondence to (prominent African leaders like) Nkrumah, Obote, Nyerere, Kaunda and others who later became heads of state.

Only some printed material (remains) since Uhuru. The Kenya Uhuru Souvenir has an excellent article entitled "Glimpses of Kenya's Struggle" by Pio. The beautiful brochure was printed at the Pan Africa Press (which was founded by Pio). In September of 1965 the International Organization of Journalists invited me to Chile to receive a posthumous award to Pio for journalism under difficult conditions.

To shift gears to a personal subject, please tell us a little about what the family is doing now.

I wanted to leave Kenya because it was not the country Pio had dreamed of. Coming to Canada was accidental. I applied directly to the Ottawa Immigration Office and received a Landed Immigrant Permit.

Although Vice-President Joe Murumbi tried to talk me out of it and suggested the U.K. instead, I opted for Canada even though I did not know a soul in the country. My mother decided to accompany us on a tourist visa since I had three small children, the youngest not yet four years of age. Our boat from London docked in Montreal on April 28, 1967. It was Canada's Centennial Year. To my surprise the Captain already had two messages for me. One was a postcard from Pio's cousin Oscar Fonseca -- a lawyer in Toronto. The other was a message that a team of four Montreal teachers were on shore to meet me. What a relief to know that we had help.

(*Kenyan Vice-President*) Joe Murumbi had cabled Fr. Patrick Maloney of

Pio Gama Pinto, Kenya's Unsung Martyr

Loyola College and the good priest had rented us an apartment for a week. Since the business language in Quebec is French, I was advised to head for Ontario.

Oscar's postcard had opened the door to Toronto, so we took in the EXPO and then travelled to Toronto. We will be eternally grateful to Joe and Oscar and his family for helping us to get our feet wet in a new country. I felt like a duck on the edge of a vast ocean. We took up the challenge and after years of persistent hard work on the part of my mother, the children and myself, we are content.

I worked with the Scarborough Board of Education (*one of the largest in Toronto*), for 15 years and took early retirement at age 55. In the meantime, my three daughters, Linda, Malusha Marie and Tereshka received post-graduate degrees in Law, Speech, Pathology and Sports Administration respectively.

Even though Pio's friends in Kenya and abroad collected $30,000 towards the education of his children, they worked and paid their way through university for almost eight years. Finally, when the Children's Trust Fund was released, I passed the funds on to them. They have wisely invested their individual shares into the homes in which they reside. For the generosity of Pio's friends, we do not have adequate words of thanks.

Do you manage to keep links with Goa still? Do you get a chance to visit here often? Where are your family roots from? Which part of Goa?

My paternal grandfather built a large home in Borda near Margao. My maternal grandfather built a large home in Nuvem, Salsete. My early visits to Goa were to these two homes where we spent not more than two months each time. I really do not know where the family roots originated.

Pio's father or grandfather built a home in Carre, near Porvorim. I have barely any contact with relatives in Goa. Pio did not talk about his younger years in Goa with his mother, older sister and younger brother. Carre seems to be somewhat off the beaten path, and travel in those days must have been difficult. I believe he attended and enjoyed school in Dharwad with young cousin Oscar Fonseca for whom he had a deep affection.

Emma Gama Pinto in Conversation with Benegal Pereira (2012)

The interview took place in New Hampshire, USA on August 4, 2012 . The video of the full conversation is available at https://galleries.benegal. com/CandidConversations/Candid-Conversations-MrsEGP/n-FtLBG/ [Accessed: 08-05-2018]. The comments in italics in the transcript below are by the interviewer. Vita Books would like to thank Benegal Pereira for providing the transcripts of the conversation and the accompanying photos.

24. Emma Gama Pinto

Photo by Benegal Pereira, 07-06 2003 taken in North London at the home of Fritz and Romola De'Souza

You have three loving daughters...?

Yes, they are very attentive. After I finished working, Tereshka suggested that I write my autobiography. She said just spend 10 minutes a day doing it after had been to the gym. She also wanted me to write about her dad. I have written the biography and I did it in two months. I had nothing to do and wanted to write about my life story, hoping that Pio would come into it as I progressed.

Of course, it is important to record or you will start forgetting things?

…

During the first four years of my life "with" Pio, while he was in detention, I read a lot to try and understand why he was in politics for a country that was not his. It was just six months after we got married in January 1954, when Pio was sent to Nairobi Prison. Fitz de Souza took me to see him there. Soon after, Pio was moved to Fort Jesus and then to Manda Island in Lamu.

What was Pio like as a husband?

He was hardly ever there. Within the first six months, he told me "you can't stay at home". Intelligent women don't stay home, he said. Take a secretarial course and find a job, he said. And take Greggs shorthand (as opposed to the more popular Pitman's shorthand). Pio did Greggs shorthand and he said: "One day you will able to read my shorthand if I need you to read back my notes." So, I enrolled at Premier College and started learning Greggs. I had hardly finished the course and had to go to work because I realised that he wasn't earning anything.

He would come home at seven or eight in the evening. I would be quite annoyed because we had no phone and his parents were in Nairobi at the time. Pio and I lived in the servants' quarters of Fitz's house and Fitz's parents were staying in the main house. (Fitz was in England studying, hence was not able to be at the wedding). Pio had arranged a room for himself and another for Rosario [Pinto's brother], his wife, and his mother-in-law. We went on a short honeymoon to Jinja where one of Pio's uncles lived. My parents and brother who had come for the wedding had left for India. Pio's parents who had come from Nyeri (his father worked in the District Commissioner's office) also returned home. Pio and I moved into that room in which he had lived as a bachelor.

For the reception, Pio's brother had arranged everything and the whole house was involved in the preparation of food and stuff. At the time of the wedding, Joe Murumbi's first wife, Cecilia, and their son Jojo were staying with us. Cecilia was probably Somali... After finishing his schooling in India, Joe went straight to Somalia. Cecilia was the daughter of a chief but that could be just hearsay.

Joe Murumbi could not come to the wedding because Pio, fearing for Joe's safety following the detention of important elements of the Kenya African Union, sent Joe to London. Joe was the KAU vice-president.

Did you know Pio as a political activist, supporter of Mau Mau?

No. I didn't know the name, Mau Mau. (*Elsewhere she says that Pio never spoke to her about politics, it was his way of shielding her*). I knew he worked for the Indian National Congress in the Desai Memorial Building. I was not aware he was actively involved in the African political movement. He told me only that he worked at the Indian Congress office.

(*It is easy to see the courage of Emma Gama Pinto in what turned out to be a terrifying and horrific situation. As this part of the interview reveals, Emma continues to remain calm, pretty much in control until she is in complete shock when the full realisation of her loss finally hits.*)

It is now 48 years since that particular day. What do you remember about it?

On that particular day – we were living at No.6 Lower Kabete Road at the time. The house had been donated to Pio. He had bought me a little car so that I could have some independence as far as transport is concerned.

The new government was now nearly 14 months old and they had decided to get rid of all the English secretaries and Pio told me: You are going to be the secretary to Achien'g Oneko, the Minister for Information, Broadcasting and Tourism.

Pio had dropped me off at my office in Jogoo House and had returned home to collect his Parliamentary papers. About an hour later, I was in Achieng's office, around 9 o'clock when my mother called me on the phone. She had just returned from India after taking my eldest daughter Linda there for six months. My mother phoned to say that Pio had been attacked and she was hysterical, and I said: I will be home soon. I am coming home right away.
But I am a very, very calm person in any emergency. So I immediately phoned the Minister for Defence, Dr. Njoroge Mungai, and told his office that Pio had been attacked and said please send the police there (to their home). Then I picked up the phone and rang Joe Murumbi because he would not have left the office because Parliament does not start until 11 am. He was the Minister for Foreign Affairs. He and his wife Sheila lived five minutes away from us. I said to him: Joe, Pio has been attacked, please go to our house. Next, I ran into Achieng's office and said: Can I have your car. He said his car was in the garage for repairs or a service. Then I rang Oginga Odinga's office and spoke to an American girl, Caroline Odongo, Odinga's secretary and said to her: Caroline, Caroline, can I get a car to take me home? Pio has been attacked. She said she would call me back immediately. She did. She told me Odinga's spare car was being sent round to the front of Jogoo House and would be waiting for me. Odinga was the First Vice-President of the country.

All the time, I assumed that Pio had been attacked and that he had been injured and I assume … *(inaudible)*. As I got to the gate of our house, I saw our car had been parked at the gate and as I got out of Odinga's care, I saw Murumbi arriving in his car. As we walked past the car and into our home to find about Pio, my mother said: He is still in the car, he has been killed. That was the first time I had heard that Pio had been killed. So we both dashed out to the car and saw that Pio's body had been covered in a pink blanket. My mother had asked our house servant, a nice young man called Waweru, to cover Pio.

Pio usually gave our 18-month old daughter Tereshka a ride from the back of the house to the gate from where she would be collected by the maid and walked home. When the maid got to the back of the car, she heard shots and she ran back to the house to get Waweru. She really did not see too much because she was terrified. By the time Waweru got to the car, Pio had already been shot.

Were there any eye witnesses?

A woman saw two African men, one on either side of the car. At the trial of the man charged with the murder [*but released as innocent 35 years later*] they said there were two assailants.

Are you still angry?

No. Because of my reading of political matters, I am aware that politicians lead very dicey lives. They are walking a tightrope. So when Pio was assassinated I assumed it was part of the politician's life. It was shocking for me, a new immigrant to Kenya that he was shot so soon. He had already been in detention for four years. It was tragic.

Did you feel cheated?

Well, I felt disappointed that someone who had worked so hard for freedom …in my readings, I read that bitterness is like a fire in the corner of a house which will eventually consume the whole house. So I was cognisant of the fact that I should never be bitter about the whole situation. It was a fact of life. Mahatma Gandhi was murdered ….

Did you get much support from family and friends?

My twin sister, Joyce, lived just down the road from me. As for the people at the first private British company I worked for (International Aeradio Limited, engineers), I don't think they were sympathetic to Pio, but they were sympathetic to a widow.
Joe and Sheila Murumbi took me to their home for two days. My mother stayed with the girls at our house. Our friend Dr. [Yusuf] Eraj gave me a sedative because I was in a state of severe shock.

When we saw Pio's body in the car, Joe said let's get Pio inside the house. Because I was in shock I have no clear memory of the people there. Waweru and Joe's driver put Pio's body in the pink blanket and carried his body, not like a sack of potatoes, but like something, into the living room.

Fitz de Souza (MP and Deputy Speaker) arrived at one point. I had not phoned Fitz. I don't know at what point Fitz was involved. Perhaps he found out from Parliament which had been informed. *[Fitz, a barrister, heard the news while attending the Kenya High Court].*

Fitz was there when Pio's body was brought into the living room. I remember I sat down and they put the blanket down and I could see that little hole under his ribs. I was sitting with Joe and Fitz, and I said: Gosh, Pio looks so pale. And Fitz said: Get out of there, get out of the room. So that was my one and only view of Pio when he was brought into the home.

What was Pio like as a Member of Parliament?

As you may have realised, I was more or less the breadwinner and Pio and I never checked our bank balance. I did not know how much we had until he was assassinated, and I went to the bank to get the money to pay our rent which was in arrears. There was nothing. And I had to pay Cecilia's rent as well ...

I am a little confused, Joe Murumbi had two wives?
Yes. When he came back from England, he brought Sheila with
him. As I said before, just after 1954, Pio sent Joe Murumbi to the
UK to escape arrest. Pio was sending him information about the
situation in Kenya, the Mau Mau, the detainees ... so that Joe could
advise the British members of Parliament who were sympathetic
to Kenya.

**Did you know India's High Commissioner to Kenya, Apa Pant, who
said that it was Pio who introduced him to Kenyatta, Koinange and
brought him into the enclaves of the Mau Mau. Did Pio mention him
to you?**

Pio kept his political work completely secret from me.

**Several attempts have been made to write Pio's story. Most, if not all,
have fallen short. What is the hold-up in writing the complete story?**

In order to write someone's story, one has to have written facts
but when Pio was shot his two friends, Pranlal Sheth (*Pranlal, a
journalist, barrister and a businessman. He was also an outstanding
fighter of freedom both in Kenya and India. Soon after Pio's death
he was deported and went to continue his battles for people in the
UK*) and Sarjit Singh Heyer (*an economist and a confidante of Pio*)
burnt all his books, papers and other material (*Pranlal told me this
many, many years later when I visited him in England*). Pranlal had
insisted Pio's papers be burnt and I remember seeing a bonfire that
night after Pio was shot. Pio had his own office in the house and
they took Pio's books, papers and everything and they burnt them.
They didn't even ask me. They could have hidden them or taken
them somewhere.
Sheila Murumbi told me later that she would have taken the books
and papers, but they did not even ask her. I think Pranlal and Sarjit
were there, but I can't really recall because I was still in shock. All
I remember is when I looked at the back door I saw the big bonfire.

Do you think they did it to protect the family?

No. Pio did not write about the family.

So why did they burn … ?
We have to speculate because Pronlal said that Pio was not only involved in Kenyan politics but also in African politics... countries that were just emerging. I guess they were concerned that Pio might have mentioned names and they were protecting these people, the politicians, dignitaries, that Pio had come into contact with.
I had no idea who they were because Pio never told me what he was involved in or the personalities. Pio used to have people from foreign countries come to the house and have meetings in his office, but I was never involved. He never asked me to make tea or provide refreshments. I just did not want anyone living in our home, even though we had a spare room. I told Pio we should protect our family. I said we had daughters and we must protect them.

How long did you remain in Kenya after the assassination?

I remained in Kenya for two years. I was waiting for the tombstone which I was told was coming from Italy.

Pio is buried in Nairobi's City Park cemetery, is it protected?
Not really.

Was he buried in the City Park cemetery for any reason … most Goans were buried in the Langata cemetery?

All the arrangements were made by Joe Murumbi and Fitz de Souza. Fitz left Kenya soon after the assassination because he was afraid, he told me so in London not so long ago. He realised he might have been in danger. I think he was there for the funeral.

You visited Kenya twice …?

The first time Fitz invited the whole family and my mum too. We stayed with them in their Muthaiga home. The second time was when Achieng Oneko's son came to Canada and asked if he could do anything for us. He was in tourism. My daughter Linda, her husband and I took him up on the offer and he made all the arrangements for the safari.

I know you went to meet Achieng in his ancestral home …?

I went to his home and he had retired from work. In our honour he had a goat slaughtered for a barbecue. He said to me: Emma this is specially done because it our tradition. Linda and her husband stayed with his daughter 200 yards away. I stayed with Achieng and his wife Lois. We spent two nights there. One day at breakfast, Lois pointed to a room and said that was Achieng's office.

I asked Achieng what he did in his office. He said: Oh, nothing it is all locked up.
I asked: All locked up? Do you have papers in there? You must let me have some of the papers Pio wrote to you. He said: No, no, I am not opening that door. So I said: Please, Please. So he went in brought out one file folder and as I leafed through I recognised a letter in Pio's handwriting. And I said, Achieng, give me this letter.
He said: I am not going to give it to you.
I said: Make a copy for heaven's sake.
He thought about it and said: We have no photocopier here.
I said: Well I am going to Nairobi for a meeting and I will send you a copy. We left without the letter. A day or two later, I got a call from him saying come and have a coffee with him at his motel. When I got there, Pio's letter and a copy of it were there.
I said: you are not going to give me the copy? I want the original.
He said: Why?
I said: It is my husband's letter.
He took the letter and wrote: "Given to Emma" and signed his name.
I was so taken up and excited with finding one letter that I forgot to go through the rest of folder.

Pio Gama Pinto, Kenya's Unsung Martyr

After nearly 50 years, do you feel that Kenyans have served Pio's memory well?

I think they are doing quite a bit to keep his memory alive. They have named a road after him and they also included his image in a commemorative stamp 'Heroes of Kenya' (*issued in 2008*) that included Tom Mboya (who was assassinated in 1969), Ronald Ngala (a leader from the coast who died in a road accident in 1972) and Oginga Odinga. The street (*in Westlands*) in which we lived, Kabete Road, has been named after Pio. All the houses have been demolished, including ours, and the whole area has been redeveloped. A large shopping mall (*Sarit Centre*) has been erected.

25. Benegal Pereira, Emma Gama Pinto and Fritz De Souza

Photo taken in London on June 2003 at Fritz and Romola de Souza's Residence by Benegal Pereira.

Pinto was principled, purposeful and entirely without personal ambition. Whatever ambitions Pio had were for Kenya - Emma Gama Pinto.[58]

58 Quoted in: Nowrojee, Pheroze (2007): Pio Gama Pinto: Patriot for Social Justice. Nairobi: Longhorn Publishers.

The Last Word...

Mrs. Emma Pinto would like to express, on behalf of herself, her children, and the family of the late Hon. Pio Gama Pinto, her deep appreciation for the many letters of condolence and the beautiful floral tributes received.

It is regretted that, due to the very large number, it is impossible to answer all personally and it would, therefore, be appreciated if this notice could be taken as an acknowledgement to all the kind friends who wrote and sent flowers. The knowledge that so many of Pio's friends were thinking of him and his family at this tragic time was of inestimable comfort to them all.

Pio Gama Pinto: Independent Kenya's First Martyr, Socialist and Freedom Fighter (1966)

PIO
GAMA
PINTO

INDEPENDENT KENYA'S FIRST MARTYR

SOCIALIST AND FREEDOM FIGHTER

NEW KENYA PUBLISHERS
PUBLISHERS & BOOKSELLERS

LAKHANI BUILDING,
ANAR LANE,
OFF DUKE STREET.

P. O. Box 12336,
NAIROBI,
Kenya - East Africa.

3rd January, 1966.

Hon. J. Murumbi, M.P.
Minister for External Affairs,
Harambee House,
NAIROBI

Dear Sir,

As you probably know, Mr. Pio Gama Pinto was assassinated nearly a year ago. The first anniversary of his death falls on 24th February, 1966. We feel that a commemorative volume on his life in contribution to Kenya's national struggle should be published on the anniversary of his death. We envisage this publication as consisting of brief articles on various aspects of his life and work, written by those who knew him well and participated with him in the struggle. We intend this to be a fairly small pamphlet which will be sold at no more than Sh.1/- a copy, just enough to cover the cost.

We would be most grateful if you could make a brief contribution of about 800 words as "YOUR MEMOIRE". Others who knew Mr. Pinto will be writing on different aspects of his life.

Since the setting up and printing of the pamphlet will require several weeks, we would be most grateful if you could let us have your contribution by the 20th January, 966, at the latest.

We hope you will be able to find the time to write this article about a former friend and colleague whose life was devoted to so many noble causes. We are sure you would like to join others among his friends in the production of this commemorative volume.

We look forward to hearing from you at your earliest convenience and will appreciate a note indicating your willingness to make the contribution requested within the next few days.

Yours faithfully,

(A. H. PATEL)
for NEW KENYA PUBLISHERS

26. Ambu Patel to Joseph Murumbi on Pinto commemorative booklet (03-01-1966)

NEW KENYA PUBLISHERS
PUBLISHERS & BOOKSELLERS
LAKHANI BUILDING,
Anar Lane
Off Duke Street
P. O. Box 12336
Kenya - East Africa

3rd January, l966.

Hon. J. Murumbi, M.P.
Minister for External Affairs,
Harambee House,
NAIROBI

Dear Sir,

As you probably know, Mr. Pio Gama Pinto was assassinated nearly a year ago. The first anniversary of his death falls on 24th February, l966. We feel that a commemorative volume on his life in contribution to Kenya's national struggle should be published on the anniversary of his death. We envisage this publication as consisting of brief articles on various aspects of his life and work, written by those who knew him well and participated with him in the struggle. We intend this to be a fairly small pamphlet which will be sold at no more than Sh.l/- a copy, just enough to cover-the cost.

We would he most grateful if you could make a brief contribution of about 800 words as "YOUR MEMOIRE". Others who knew Mr. Pinto will be writing on different aspects of his life.

Since the setting up and printing of the pamphlet will require several weeks, we would be most grateful if you could let us have your contribution by the 20th January 1966, at the latest.

We hope you will be able to find the time to write this article about a former friend and colleague whose life was devoted to so many noble causes. We are sure you would like to join others among his friends in the production of thiscommemorative volume.

We look forward to hearing from you at your earliest convenience and will appreciate a note indicating your willingness to make the contribution requested within the next few days.

Yours faithfully
A.   H.. Patel (signed)

PIO GAMA PINTO
INDEPENDENT KENYA'S FIRST MARTYR
SOCIALIST and FREEDOM FIGHTER
Publishers: Pan African Press Ltd.

CONTENTS

Biography

PIO GAMA PINTO was born in Nairobi on 31st March 1927. At the age of eight he was sent to India for his education and spent the next nine years there. He studied Arts for two years before joining the India Air Force in 1944 for a short time. When only 17 years of age he started agitating against the system which kept so many people of Goa in poverty. When he took up a job in the posts and Telegraphs Company in Bombay, he enthusiastically took part in a general strike and got his first glimpse of mass action and organisation. He was a founder member of the Goa National Congress whose

aim was to liberate Goa from from Portuguese rule. His activities in Bombay against the Portuguese made it imperative for him to leave India in order to avoid being arrested.

In 1949 he returned to Kenya and after a succession of clerical jobs became involved in the local politics aimed at overthrowing colonialism. He turned to journalism and worked with the Colonial Times and the Daily Chronicle. In 1954, 5 months after his marriage, he was rounded up in the notorious Operation Anvil and spent the next four years in detention on Manda Island with the so called "hard-core" Mau Mau. He was kept in restriction from early 1958 until October 1959 at remote Kabarnet. On his release he once more immersed himself in the struggle for Kenya's Independence himself in the struggle for Kenya's Independence and the Release of Jomo Kenyatta. In 1960 he founded the KANU newspaper "Sauti ya KANU" and later Pan Africa Press of which he subsequently became Director and Secretary.

He worked ceaselessly in the 1961 Elections to make KANU Victorious. In 1963 Mr. Pinto was elected as Member of the Central Legislative Assembly and in July of the following year a Specially Elected Member of the House of Representatives.

In 1964 he worked late hours to establish the Lumumba Institute which was principally to train Party Officials. He was a member of the Board of Governors and took keen interest in its functions.

He kept in close touch with African Liberation movements and assisted whenever he could. He was delegate to a meeting in Delhi of nationalists from all Portuguese Colonies to plan the liberation of these colonies. A year later he was once again invited to Delhi for the celebration to mark the liberation of Goa. In 1963 he attended a conference of progressive and militant journalists in Algeria called by the International Organisation of Journalists. In September 1965, Mrs. Emma Gama Pinto was invited to Santiago, Chile, to receive a posthumous prize awarded to her husband by the International Organisation of Journalists for his contribution in journalism to the liberation of African countries from foreign domination and exploitation.

At the time of his assassination, his eldest daughter Linda was just 6 years of age, the second, Malusha was 41/2 Years and the youngest, Tereshka, only 11/2 years of age.

Oginga Odinga:[59] General Politics

No description of the history of Kenya would be complete without an assessment of Pio Gama Pinto's contribution to our struggle.

Pio was a solid Kenyan patriot. His assassination leaves a gap in our struggle for complete freedom that few men – none that I know – can fill.

I first met Pio in 1952 when we were at the height of our struggle. He was then working with the E.A Indian National Congress and in his own fashion trying to break the pattern of their narrow perspective in order for that community to participate in our bitter struggle to throw off colonial domination. Anyone who met Pio soon forgot his pigmentation because his works and deeds left no doubt that he was a Kenyan nationalist. He had immense organisation powers and ceaselessly went around bridging

59   Vice President of Kenya

all gaps in our defences as our own people were pulled away into detention camps or prison cells. He petitioned his solicitor friends to take up political cases when no money was forthcoming. When the men in the forest required support he sent money and arms secretly. He knew the consequences if he was caught in these fields of activity – detention or even death – but nothing could stop him. In 1954 the authorities

27. Pinto visits the Koinange family in restriction in Kabernet

apprehended him and he spent the next six years out of the political scene in detention camps. Immediately upon his release he threw himself into the political arena. Once more in Nairobi, he found hundreds of widows and orphans of his comrades who had perished in the struggle. Many of us surged on only with independence as our goal. Pio found time for the suffering women and children and collected money, clothing and food for them. Dr. Yusuf Eraj was swamped with sick women and children sent by Pio. Few people know that because of his immense admiration for Mr. Pinto, this medical practitioner received no fees for many years.

Pio threw himself into helping KANU win the 1961 elections, into founding our independent press, into the campaign for federation, into the struggle against imperialism, and the liberation of Portugal's colonies. He assisted refugees from South Africa, Mozambique and Angola to find their way to other countries where they could organize resistance movements.

28. Jaramogi Oginga Odinga, Vice President, at the funeral. Mrs. Emma Pinto is on his left.

As a Member of Central Legislative Assembly and Member of Parliament, Pio showed his brilliance in a quiet way. Pio was a dedicated and intelligent socialist and worked for Kenya to advance its social and economic system for the benefit of the masses.

Lumumba had been murdered in the course of his heroic activities; so was Pio. Who were his enemies if he were such a genuine patriot? It could only be the forces that knowingly or unwittingly are helping imperialism keep a grip on Kenya, those who have sacrificed the national advance to parochial or personal interests.

Joseph Murumbi:[60] An Appreciation

I write this appreciation in honour of a great and beloved brother. It is a year since an assassin's bullet cut short the life of this great patriot. I still cannot understand why the perpetrators of this crime chose Pio as the victim. It was murder without purpose. If the intention was to silence all opposition then many of us are prepared to die if in doing so we maintain liberty and democracy. These were the guiding principles of Pio's life. He was the friend of the down-trodden, the poor and above all faithful to his friends who suffered imprisonment for the cause of freedom. All over the country men still remember his generosity. He gave all he had to help the poor and no one who appealed for help was turned away from his door. He gave but asked for nothing in return. He died a pauper.

Pio was accused by his enemies of being a communist. Even if he were, surely in a democratic Kenya it is not a crime warranting death to follow any political persuasion. To me Pio was a SOCIALIST. He lived by his socialist beliefs in thought and deed. What he possessed belonged to those in need even to the extent that he deprived himself and his family of many of the simple comforts which we all enjoy. For instance, when he and I were working for the Pan-African Press our salaries were £50 each. I discovered that he was deceiving his wife by telling her that his salary was £25 per month. The other half of his salary was given to friends who suffered detention with him. Politically his views were beyond many of us in his depth of political understanding and social consciousness. To him socialism meant its true application.

Pio always felt a guilty complex with regard to poverty and he sought through his socialist principles to be of practical assistance and in his own way to help eliminate poverty and human suffering. He was quick to react to injustice. If such were the qualities of this patriot and was branded as a communist for his actions, then I must say to his accusers that their perception of political dogma is indeed distorted.

---

60   Foreign Minister.

I worked with Pio since 1952 and as a matter of fact it was through his inspiration that I entered politics. I had returned from Somalia after an absence from Kenya for almost eleven years. We met for the first time at a public meeting. I had asked the speaker a question and was persistent in getting a satisfactory reply but failed to do so. After the meeting Pio introduced himself and was interested to know who i was as he had never seen me before. This meeting developed into a sincere friendship and through him I was introduced to the Kenya Study Group, a small body of politicians and others who met regularly to study some of the pressing problems of the day. We maintained a close friendship since then. During my six months' stay in India in 1953 and that was during the height of emergency, Pio kept me posted each week with press cuttings and long commentaries of the political situations during that critical time. I was able to use the information supplied very effectively in my anti-government campaign in India and later in Cairo and London. A short while later, he was arrested and suffered six long years of detention.

Pio was a keen and popular Parliamentarian both in the House of Representatives and in the Central Legislative Assembly. His death was such a shock to members of the House of Representatives that they asked for an adjournment of the day's session. This aspect of his work was taken seriously, and he did his homework meticulously for every session, working into the early hours of the morning preparing for it. He never refused to help a friend with correspondence. He was a prolific writer. I have known him to keep appointments at 5 a.m. after working till 1 or 2 a.m. Pio never relaxed. He was always on the move. I remember a "holiday" with him in Mombasa. He spent most of his time meeting friends and talking shop –i.e., politics. Politics was his life and he devoted everything, his mind, his body and his soul to Kenya. There indeed very few who can match his patriotism.

Pio had a deep and lasting affection for his friends and this extended to a fraternal care for their health and well-being. He would never fail to visit a sick friend and would even go the extent of looking after their family while a friend was in hospital or away from home. Such was the character of the man. Decent, straight forward, fearless and honest. In all, a loyal citizen of Kenya.

29. *Oscar Kambona, Tanzania's Foreign Minister pays his last tribute at the funeral.*

Why was Pio murdered? Murder is but an evasion. Pio's name will not be forgotten because he was an honest and sincere man. Honest and sincere to his friends – these included all who were in trouble, who were poor or appealed for help. His enemies and those who engineered his death must surely feel that nothing has been gained by eliminating him from the political scene. The host of friends, European, Asian and African who attended his funeral is a testimony that Pio had many friends who loved him. We will go loving him though he is dead. His life's work and the example of clean, honest living, political integrity and patriotism will be an inspiration to us to follow his example and honour his name. Kenya has lost a great patriot and our sympathies go out to Emma and her children who have lost more than we have. God bless them and Pio.

Bildad Kaggia:[61] A Friend

I am very happy to have the honour to write a few lines about one of the best friends I have had in my life the late Pio Gama Pinto. It is with great sorrow that I relate the work of Pio when I recall the brutal murder that my

---

61   Member of Parliament.

friend met at the hands of his enemies who are also enemies of Kenya as a whole. I console myself with fact that Pio's principles cannot be killed by the assassin's bullets.

Since the day I knew Pio I have regarded him as one of the greatest man in our time. Pio was the first Asian to win and penetrate the African hearts. Within a few years of acquaintance, he won my heart and by 1952 he was the only non-African who had the confidence of the people and who knew something of what was taking place. He was the only Asian who was not afraid to identify himself with K.A.U. or militant African politics. He was not afraid to be seen with K.A.U. leaders or to visit Kiburi House, the centre of African politics and nationalism, which was looked upon by the Colonialists as the centre of sedition and rebellion.

Pio was the only Asian who helped K.AU. and African National Movements in general – more than any other non-African. I can never forget his help to me and other African politicians when we decided to run our own newspaper to fight the colonial newspaper monopoly. He did all he could to see that each and every small newspaper went forward. His advice and practical help in this work will never be forgotten.

In the early years of Kenya Trade Unionism, Pio acted as advisor and gave practical help to every union to establish sound Trade Union principles and practices. As he was not an officer of any one of them, he was free to help all of them without any rivalry – a thing that no other trade unionist could do. All early trade unionists will never forget Pio's work to establish trade unionism.

When K.A.U. leaders were arrested, Pio did not stop his communication with active K.AU. leaders and supporters. Instead he went on as actively as before and as a result was arrested and detained.

During the long and difficult years of detention Pio faced great temptation being the only Asian among the African "Mau Mau". But this did not tamper his courage and determination to continue his fight for Kenya's freedom and independence. Pio remained firm and faithful to the cause to the last minutes.

On his release Pio went straight into active service for K.A.N.U. He did a lot in the early organisation of K.A.N.U and the establishment of 'Sauti ya KANU". He played a very prominent role in the "Release Kenyatta" campaign. While he was fighting for our release he never forgot to send us at Lodwar food and a little money.

His role in KANU Election Campaign of 1961 is great and his contribution towards KANU's victory is greater than that of any other single person. In the 1963 election, Pio was in charge of the Nairobi Election Campaign and he worked for all the Nairobi and many other candidates to victory without himself looking for a position. He helped me personally in my election campaign. When the KANU Head Office turned down my nomination and denounced me, Pio was one of the many friends including Mbiu Koinange, Joe Murumbi, Fred Kubai, Achieng Aneko, J.D. Kali and others who came to my house to meet Kandara leaders to find out the truth. Pio was the only Asian among the Africans who came. After this meeting the KANU Head Office was convinced that I was in fact the right candidate and as a result the Vice- President of KANU, Mr. Oginga Odinga, was sent to Kandara to supervise a new selection meeting in which I swept all the votes and my opponent got none. Ii was accordingly declared the KANU candidate.

Pio was the only politician I know who did so much without himself holding any position – the only man I know who has done so much to get others into positions without looking for one himself. He went on to work for KANU after Self-Government and Independence as actively as before, right until his assassination. He never sought for position and it was I and other friends who persuaded him to contest the Central Legislative Assembly and Specially Elected Member seats which he won.

Pio was regarded by many Africans not as an Asian but as a real African. He was well known and trusted by many Africans of the Central Province – even more than black African.

30. Pinto at a public rally with Bildad Kaggia and Joe Murumbi in 1963.

The murderers who sat down to plan Pio Gama Pinto's death are not enemies of Asians or of Pinto's family but are enemies of all true nationalists, all true Africans, enemies of Kenya, enemies of progress and enemies of humanity. The death of Pio was not a lone Asian but the death of a great nationalist, a great freedom fighter and a true socialist who did not hesitate to share with his friends whatever little he had, in Pio's death Kenya suffered an incomparable loss because Pio was one of the very few people in the world who are prepared to do everything without expecting any reward. Since his death all of his friends and especially I have noted that the gap left by him has not been filled by anyone else. I have not been able to see anyone in our midst who is tireless, selfless and unambitious. It will take many years if at all, for this gap to be filled.

In conclusion I must console all Pio's friends, his family and myself by the fact that although Pio is dead, what he stood for, his beliefs, principles and the teachings of his actual life will live forever. Pio Gama Pinto's name will rank with that of the great leaders of our country. May we continue to follow his example.

Burudi Nabwere:[62] A Nationalist and Socialist

Joe Karanja and I arrived at Nairobi airport for the Conference of the Organisation of African Unity on Monday morning, February 22nd, 1965. Of the people who had come to meet us there was one important absentee. PIO was not there.

I wondered why. He had always seen me off and come to meet me each time I left or visited Nairobi.i learnt that he had accompanied the Vice-President, Jarsmogi Oginga Odinga, to the Coast Province. He returned to Nairobi on Tuesday and immediately came to see me. We arranged to meet again for a chat after a couple of days because I had to attend to official business at the Ministry of External Affairs. On Wednesday, February 24th at about 10.00 a.m. Odhiambo Okello ran into Joe Murumbi's office and told us that Pio had been shot dead!

And so my dear friend and brother, Pio, was no more

What manner of person was he?

I knew and worked with Pio for a period of about four years. That period started from 1961 after I had come back from England up to the time of his death last year. As I look back to that period of very close partnership three distinct characteristics stand out. First, Pio was a very hardworking person. He worked until early hours of morning and woke up very early. He was prepared to do all the donkey work for whoever had extra work to give him. During the day he did not confine himself to one job. Apart from managing the Pan African Press, he helped with party organisation, gave advice to small businessmen and farmers who came to him, and visited as many ministries as he could fit in. he usually had working luncheons whenever he had any at all.

His second quality was that he was not a text book intellectual. He relied very heavily on his native intelligence. Most of his ideas were based on common sense. Because of this altitude of mind, Pio formulated his ideas through discussions. He spent a good deal of his time discussing the various problems that face our country with whoever was prepared to discuss them.

---

62 Kenya's Delegate to the United Nations and Ambassador to the U.S.A.

As a result of these discussions he was able to modify his own ideas. By and large he preferred a pragmatic approach to solving problems.

Thirdly, Pio was one of the most generous human beings that I have ever known. In 1962/63 those of us who were engaged in party organisation did not have what is known as a steady income. We relied on whatever assistance we could get from friends. At this time, Joe Murumbi and Pio were trying to start the Pan African Press and were paid an allowance of £50 per month each. We had a practice that whoever had some money to spare must try and spread it as widely as possible to help the more "needy" in our group. And both gentlemen literally placed their allowances at our disposal. But here I am mainly discussing Pio's qualities. He tried to help anyone. If he had any money to spare he kept it for his needy friends who came from rural areas and the so-called political refugees who were frequent visitors to Nairobi.

These are some of the qualities of Pio. What makes one think of him both as a nationalist and socialist? Nationalism has to do with the love for one's own country while socialism refers to the over-all organisation of the country's economy and the way that the wealth which accrues from that economy is shared amongst its peoples. Pio loved and cared for Kenya. Above all, he loved his fellow countrymen. From my dealings with him I noticed that he had a special love for the masses of our people and particularly the ex-detainees. Although he did not boast of the sufferings that he had endured during his period of detention under British Colonial administration, in his heart, he was very proud of that period of his life.

Perhaps even more important, Pio saw Kenya's development as mainly linked with that of the rest of East Africa. He wanted and worked very hard to see that the projected East African Federation should come into being. I remember on two occasions in Dares-es-Salaam and Kampala, during the sessions of Central Legislative Assembly, when he tried to translate into practical terms the kind of cooperation which he had in mind. He urged those of us who were Representatives of Kenya to ask questions which were more to the advantage of Uganda and Tanzania and, in the short run, to the disadvantage of Kenya. These questions related to the distribution of jobs to people from the three territories. By a historical accident, in

Pio Gama Pinto, Kenya's Unsung Martyr

some sections of the East Africa Common Services Organisation Kenya had more people than the two sister States put together. Pio's aim was that those of us from Kenya should point out these anomalies and ask for a more equitable distribution of posts. He felt that in this way we shall be helping in cementing friendship amongst the East African peoples which was a pre-requisite for a successful East African Federation.

Let me now say something about Pio, the socialist. His approach to socialism was non-doctrinaire. Because of the present confusion in our country about socialism, I would like to set out consciously but clearly what Pio's brand of socialism was. He believed in and adhered to socialist principles. But he was intelligent enough to understand that what was required for Kenya was the establishment a mixed economy. He could never have advocated wholesale nationalization. He knew this would have been impossible because for another the local people with managerial know-how was woefully small. For Kenya, he wanted to see the government play a major role in economic and social reconstruction.

His concern about the lot of ordinary people was that we must try and build society where differences in wealth should not penalise the poor. He, therefore, wanted to see development under British rule. He further wanted to see the establishment of a rent control in urban areas as a way of protecting the tenants from being exploited by   landlords. He also advocated the establishment of free health service and free education as a method of assisting the less privileged people in   our community. And finally, Pio was opposed to the practice whereby a few individuals, in privileged positions were to amass excessive wealth at the expense of the masses. He believed that people in such positions should do more for the masses and that such public service would be a reward in itself.

These are some of the impressions which I formed when working and talking with Pio. The assassin's bullet abruptly put an end to his life about a year ago. The best memorial for Pio, on this first anniversary of his death should be for us to re-examine some of his ideas and see how best they could be implemented. We should also rededicate ourselves to carry on with the tasks which he and other veteran nationalist began so that our country can develop in an orderly and meaningful manner

Ramogi Achieng Oneko:[63] Detention Days

I have often been asked to what extent I knew Pio Gama Pinto and for how long we had worked together in the struggle for independence. The answer is simple. I first met Pio when he was working for the then E.A. Indian National Congress at Desai Memorial Building in 1951, but at the same time was associated with the Kenya African Union Movement. When emergency was declared in 1952 Pio was more in the background, but always active till was finally arrested in the notorious Operation Anvil leaving his newly married wife to fend for herself.

Pio was a nationalist and socialist; a man who did so many good things for others. He put himself second to the nation in everything he thought and did. He was active, able and assuming.

I had been transferred to Manda Island off Lamu after my acquittal in the notorious trial in the Supreme Court at Kitale. This unhospitable island was considered by the British administration to be the most suitable place for the "hard core" and "incorrigible" detainees. On Pio's arrest he was immediately sent to Manda to where we were not at first allowed to meet except occasionally when we went to the sea to empty the camp soil buckets. Pio confined to his own camp away from the rest of us who numbered about two hundred. Being an Asian he was given special ration of dhal, rice, wheat, edible oil, salt and meat twice a week. Whenever there was a chance Pio shared this with us.

Many people may not know that apart from politics Pio was good athlete and while in the camp he persuaded the Camp Authorities to allow him to take part in some of the sporting activities. After permission was granted from Nairobi Pio was allowed to organise football matches and other sports. Later the Prison Officers felt that isolation was harmful to Pinto, so he was given a clerical job in the office of the Officer in Charge. As a journalist and fully qualified secretary this type of work suited him well and finally he convinced the authorities beyond all doubt of his ability to work although

---

63 Minister for Information and Broadcasting

his political stand was still doubted in Nairobi. At first, we thought that Pio would obtain his release by co-operating with the authorities as so many others had. But he stuck by our beliefs and policies. When he was put in charge of the camp canteen he used this opportunity to procure food illicitly for his comrades. Pio remained with us for almost four years when he was removed to remote Karbarnet and kept in Restriction for two years.

Pio's father had worked faithfully for the colonial Government for 30 years and on his deathbed asked for one favour – to see his son Pio. But the permission was refused. Pio was terribly shocked and for the first time broke down and cried on hearing of his father's death.

After much battling with the Nairobi Authorities Pio was allowed to receive letters from his wife and reply once a month but all letters were censored. However, this method kept us generally informed on matters in the outside world as we were not allowed even newspaper in the camp. Whatever Pio received from home he shared with us. To stop him from quickly giving away everything I elected to be "treasurer" for the little amounts received. It may appear amusing and strange, but we discovered on the day Pio was told of his release that he had no shoes because he had given his away to those who were released earlier. He tried on mine but decided not to take them saying, "you see Ramogi, no one will notice my bare feet whereas you would shock so many if you were released today without shoes!"

31. Pinto speaking at a reunion of ex-detainees at the home of Achieng Oneko

To supplement our meagre diet we used to trap porcupines, wild pig and turtles and Pio took part in skinning and preparing the food. One of our comrades stitched shirts and trousers for us – entirely by hand. Pio wore these even when he was released until they fell apart! Whatever our sufferings, we were united and from this we drew strength. We studied from the few books we had and Pio also concentrated on perfecting his Swahili.

There came a time when almost everyone was giving in, and murmuring started in the camp. The Authorities had begun to engineer confusion in the camp in order to demoralize us. We realised if we did not organize counter measures and propaganda many of us would be wrecked and give up the cause. Therefore, the top group, that is, Mbiu Koinange, now member of the Senate, Muinga Chokwe, now speaker of the Senate, J.D. Kali, now Member of Parliament, Pio and myself started a counter propaganda move. Pio was one of the "editors" and played a big role in a well organised network. It was his job to dish out information to the Lower Camp by word of mouth to our own propagandists. To the astonishment and surprise of the Camp Administration the morale of the detainees was restored, and we remained hard and unpenetrable but reasonable. Towards the end the group decided to appeal to our companions to forgive as we knew release was imminent. But while we were prepared to forgive as we could not forget – history cannot just be wiped away. We felt that forgetting the past was tantamount to deny part of Kenya's history. It is true that many of our "hard-core" were not bitter and it was true that Pio was never bitter on his release. We felt proud of our activities and had great hopes for the future of our country.

We pledged to carry on the fight after our release to help create a society based on African traditions, a society in which one is his or her brother's keeper, a society of devotion and love for one another, a society of self-sacrifice and self-denial as opposed to selfishness, personal ambition and greed. I can honestly say Pio lived up to this pledge till he was assassinated.

J.D. Kali[64]: In Parliament

I can write pages and pages on Pio Gama Pinto, having been with him for so many years but I am only going to confine myself to a brief account on his Parliamentary activities.

Mr. Pinto had many friends among the present Members of Parliament, friendships which began years ago. He was appointed by them to act as their Secretary during the last General Elections' Campaign. One of his main jobs was to draft campaign slogans and print them. Pio even took it upon himself to display them all over Nairobi. Most often he stuck the posters at the dead of night. One of the most interesting of these posters was the "CONGO" poster. He printed posters and pamphlets for KANU candidates all over the country. This is why even before he became a Member of Parliament, the KANU Parliamentary Group nominated him and finally elected him as a non-African Member of to the Central Legislative Assembly. He was picked out of several African candidates. The Parliamentary Group did this in recognition of his good work for the country during and after the struggle for UHURU. When a vacancy occurred for a Specially Elected Seat in Parliament, a group of KANU Parliamentarians asked Mr. Pinto to apply. He did that, but the competition was very stiff. We were elated when he won the seat.

Apart from the KANU Parliamentary Group, the Members of Parliament had decided to form a Back-Benchers' Group – which at present is no longer in existence. He was an active Member of this and later he was elected its Publicity Secretary. As an experienced journalist and a short-hand typist, Mr. Pinto used to take accurate minutes of our Group Meetings. I remember the occasion when we had a joint Conference of the KANU-TANU Parliamentary Group on the East African Federation which lasted two days. Mr. Pinto took minutes and had them circulated before each session. He even had the Press Statements from the Conference quickly circulated.

---

64   Member of Parliament.

The Back-Benchers' Group used to be very active. It met regularly, and Mr. Pinto was never absent and he always took notes of the meetings to keep everyone informed on the up-to-date activities of the Back-Benchers. I remember the occasion when a group of French Members of Parliament visited Kenya. Here again Mr. Pinto organized us to meet and exchange parliamentary views. Once more every Member received the minutes of the French/Kenya Members of Parliament Group Meeting.

One of the things which interested Mr. Pinto most was the re-organisation of the former Back-Benchers' Group. He wanted to have three main Committees within the Group: (1) A Foreign Affairs Committee; (2) AN Economics Committee; and (3) A General Purposes Committee. He kept reminding me on the formation of these Committees until the Back-Benchers' Group was disbanded.

His idea was that through these committees Back-Benchers would contribute much which could help Ministers in their Ministries. He had an idea that instead of the Ministerial Committees which are presided by either the Minister or his Assistant, these Committees should be presided by a Back-Bencher. The appropriate Minister could attend – when invited. This, according to Mr. Pinto's opinion could make back-benchers feel that they were a part and parcel of the Government and that they also participated in nation-building.

32. Members of Parliament rejoice at Pinto's election to Parliament

I am sure that those in Parliament who knew him will agree with me that the late Mr. Pinto was one of the most active Members of Parliament. His assassination has deprived this country of a noble, generous and unselfish worker who never flinched at doing his duty.

Pio Gama Pinto, Kenya's Unsung Martyr

John K. Tettegah[65]: In Memoriam

PIO PINTO IS DEAD!

Such were the dire tiding that flashed over African and the world on February 24, 1965. An African patriot had been foully murdered in broad daylight by assassins who had sold their own conscience and their countrymen. Kenya - and all Africa – was the poorer. Yet, strangely, the world was richer, too. For this 38-year-old freedom fighter had strengthened his nation's fibre, had illumined the path ahead by his sufferings for a noble goal.

It was my privilege to have known Pio Pinto; and I say, SUCH A MAN CAN NEVER DIE! Though his body was struck down by the enemies of all Africa, by cowards who think that hired bullets can stop the people's triumph, his work, his sacrifice and his example remain to inspire others, who will rise ten-fold and take his place.

Long before I had the pleasure of meeting him personally, I knew of him. What African freedom fighter did not know the name of this talented journalist – a Kenya-born Indian of Goan parentage, educated in his parents' land, but dedicated unto his very death to the cause of African nationalism?

When, later, I actually travelled to Kenya to make contacts for our continued joint campaign against world imperialism, I had several meetings with comrade Pinto. Not only did he impress me as a dedicated fighter, heart and soul with us; he inspired me. He revitalized my energy and influenced me to even greater zeal in the arduous task of reconstructing our colonialist-burdened continent, a cause in which we have most humbly accepted to serve. In detention and banishment, his torments undergone for the freedom of Kenya remain as a living, everlasting monument to his unmatchable memory.

The last time I met him was an occasion on which he had organized a small party. There, I had opportunity of discussing and explaining the aims and objects of A.A.T.U.F. to several Kenya Parliamentarians. We assessed the difficult tasks ahead; the heavy responsibilities African workers must shoulder in the building of a continental United Africa. Late into the night,

---

65   Secretary General of the All African Trade Union Federation.

we talked on

Yet Comrade Pinto found the strength to be at the airport in the early morning hours to tell me good-bye. As we walked toward the plane, he continued to impress upon me that I should not forget the comrades in Kenya. Africa, he said, must give them all the assistance possible to ensure that Kenya take the road to socialism.

I listened and tried to reassure him, little dreaming that this was to be our last meeting.

Pio Pinto fell on the battlefield in our common war against neo-colonialism. He is not the first person to die for the cause of emancipating Africa. He will not be the last to pay the price for the path we have chosen. Along with the immortal Patrice Lumumba, Reuben Um Nyobo, and Felix Moumie, he has joined the ranks of our martyrs whose blood must be avenged. In such honourable company, his death – like – will recruit new armies of Pintos to continue the fight in which he died, the effort to create a united socialist Africa. That achievement alone can repay the honesty, the sincerity, sacrifice and love of justice that characterized the man Pio Pinto. That alone cab embodies the essence of his life, through the freeing of subject peoples.

To me, his death was noble. It was symbolic. He died a true revolutionary socialist. I for one can pledge to those comrades carrying on the good fight in Kenya, as I pledged to comrade Pinto on our last morning together: African labour will surely stand by Kenya in the building of its revolutionary will and will broaden and deepen its ideological work to which Pio Pinto devoted so much time during his last years.

Comrade Pinto! You live on in us, you live on in us, your fighting African trade union brothers! We pledge to vindicate your life and your death. Your murder has only strengthened the determination of the people – not only in Africa, but in Asia and Latin America, too. No force on earth can stem our determination to win that freedom and dignity of man for which you lived and died.

33. Pinto outside Parliament with Murumbi, Ferguson, Kenyatta, Tettegah, Oneko and Kubai

Outside Parliament with (left to right); Joe Murumbi, J. B. Ferguson (Ghanaian Labour Attache at Dar), Mzee Kenyatta, John Tettegah (Secretary-General of A.A.T.U.F.), Achieng Oneko and Fred Kubai

Mrs. Pinto at Santiago to receive the International Organization of Journalists' Award to Pio in September, 1965.

34. *Emma Pinto at Santiago receives the IOJ's Award to Pinto (Sept. 1965)*

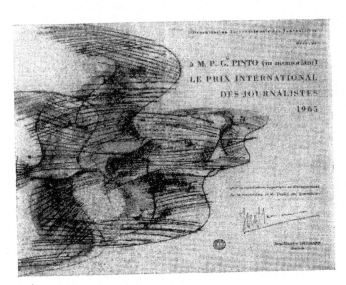

AWARD
International Organization of Journalists.

35. *The IOJ Award to Pinto, 1965*

Pio Gama Pinto, Kenya's Unsung Martyr

J. Dennis Akumu[66]: Trade Unionist

The name of Pio was known to me many years before I met him. As early as 1952-53 when I was still a student at the Medical Training School, Pio was already known to us by name as one of the few outspoken Kenya nationalists among Asians.

In his many roles as a nationalist Pio played a very key role in the formation of the Trade Union movement at a time when the movement was still illegal and enjoyed no legal status. He together with people like Makhan Singh, Chege Kibachia, Fred Kubai and Aggrey Minya can never be forgotten when the History of trade union movement is being discussed.

Pio was detained during the Emergency because of his nationalistic support for the masses and because of the role he played in the formation of the anti-imperialist East African Trade Union Congress, which was later banned.

While under detention – Pio used to give encouragement to nationalists and Trade Unionists who were continuing the fight against colonialism. When Trade Unionists and Politicians called for a boycott of buses, beer, etc. during Kenyatta Day, Pio wrote to our Union congratulating us, but added that "next time organize better and if possible, it should be a national strike demanding **Mzee Kenyatta's release".**

When Pio was released I met him for the first time in Mombasa. He met the dockworkers who admired his role in the struggle and he in turn told them that the struggle would never be over until we achieved economic liberation.

Pio made many suggestions on ways and means of reorganizing our Unions thereby making them not only stronger but effective instruments for hastening political and economic independence. We agreed with Pio that the attainment of economic independence would be impossible as long as our Trade Union remained dominated by the I.C.F.T.U. which is an agency of the same powers which dominated our country politically and economically.

We, therefore, started crusading to make our trade unions non-aligned by

---

66 Deputy Secretary General, Central Organisation of Trade Unions.

Pio Gama Pinto, Kenya's Unsung Martyr   335

pressing disaffiliation from the I.C.F.T.U. We, that is, Messrs. Ottenyo, Makanyengo, Wachira and some others boycotted stooge Trade Union rallies and conferences, and Pio went around explaining our point to Ministers, Members of Parliament and others.

When in 1964 a split became open in the Trade Union movement, we decided to form our own Federation which was to be non-aligned but Pan African in outlook. Our first Federation, the Kenya Federation of Progressive Trade Unions was not registered because the registering authority had a vested interest.

Pio was with us in the struggle and although all of us regretted the split in the Trade Union movement we maintained that out unions must become non-aligned and therefore the struggle must continue. We, therefore, formed African Workers Congress. By this time workers were supporting Congress en mass and Pio had arranged for us to renew our friendship with Brother John Tettegah of the Ghana Trade Union Congress, also the Secretary–General of the all African Trade Unions Federations. Pio also organized a number of Members of Parliament to back us when they too saw the need to have a new non-aligned Trade Union Centre committed to Africa's unity.

At the beginning of 1965 it became clear to the imperialist that we we determined. With Pio having organised the Members of Parliament and having made the issue of continental one by renewing our relationship with Brother Tettegah and knowing President Kenyatta's stand for the unity of Africa, the opposing organisation knew that our battle was half won.

In a desperate attempt to hold things back, Congress supporters were intimidated and victimized by employers and finally the cold-blooded imperialists laid their hand on Pio. We were all shocked by the brutality of the imperialists, but far from discouraging or frightening us, if anything, this only strengthened us and made us even more determined.

Pio died too soon to see the results of his efforts in Labour, but I am sure it would have pleased him to know that Kenya now has a united Trade Union movement which is non-aligned and which is waiting to affiliate to a Pan-African Trade Union movement within the frame-work of the Organisation of African Unity.

Pio fought for independence, Kenya is now free; Pio fought for a non-aligned Trade Union movement in Kenya, this has now been achieved. We who are still alive can only do what Pio would have done – continue the struggle until the country is completely free.

Imperialists and their stooges will never destroy Pio's work. Pio's determined stand for the cause, the fact that fearless, will not be forgotten. Pio remains a great inspiration to us all.

Dr. F.R.S. De Souza[67]: Goa's Liberation

My train arrived in Nairobi Railway Station at 8 a.m. one morning in February 1952, after five years as a student in the United Kingdom. There was no one to receive me; indeed I was not expecting anybody. My parents lived at Magadi, and I was hoping to give them a surprise. I left my suitcase at a shop in Government Road and walked to the office of the Kenya Indian Congress. I had never met Pio, although he had once written to me in London asking for information about some books he wanted to buy.

His welcome was very warm. I felt I had somehow known him for years. We immediately began discussing the problem of East Africa, and how we could help in the struggle for independence. We had much in common. To begin with we were both penniless and terribly dressed. We were at ease with one another, and our ideas of independence and socialism were similar. We must have talked for three or four hours. It was lunch time and he invited me to lunch with him, at a place which was then the most expensive and luxurious that non-Europeans could go to. Our meal cost us about Shs. 3/- each.

We returned to his office and continued our discussions. I read the speeches of past Presidents of the Indian Congress, of the President of the Kenya African Union. Mr. Jomo Kenyatta (as he then was) now our President. I was very impressed, and from then on, we worked closely together. At about 6.30 p.m. he asked me what I was doing about accommodation. He invited me to stay with him and I readily accepted. He shared a small room with three others in Pangani in a house run as a "mess" by a large number

---

67   Member of Parliament.

of his friends. He insisted on giving me his bed and slept on the floor for the next few days until I went to see my parents in Magadi.

His work in Kenya politics is discusses by other friends, but I know, and history will record that Pio had a hand in the preparation of most of the memoranda and statements issued by K.AU. in those days. He often used to sit up to 5 a.m. in the Congress Office drafting political papers in the nationalist cause. For all this he never expected payment. His reward was in the contribution he made to the struggle. He never looked for personal credit.

A couple of years later when he was the Editor of the "Daily Chronicle", the Royal Commission on Land asked for evidence, and there was no one to put forward the African case for all the leaders were in detention. Pio resigned his job, and through the voluminous Carter Commission Report and other documents on the land issue and took statements from Kikuyu Elders and others. He the wrote out, and personally typed and cyclostyled, always working into early hours of the morning, the 200-page Kikuyu Tribe's Memoranda for other individual Mbaris in the Central Province. Pio never told anybody about his work. I sent a copy of this Memorandum to the President at Lodwar. He was so impressed that he suggested we publish the Memorandum but for lack of funds the work was never done.

One day during our discussions. Pio suggested that we should do something in East Africa to   assist in the liberation of Goa. I was a little surprised and told him that while I was very sympathetic to the liberation of Goa, and indeed of the rest of the world, I thought that as we were East African we should confine our activities to East Africa. We might dissipate our slender resources and there was also the risk of being misunderstood, even by our friends. He explained that as a student and young man in India he had taken an active part in the struggle for the liberation of Goa. He had actively assisted in the formation of the Goa National Congress and had escaped from Goa only when police were searching for him with a warrant to arrest and deport him to an island off West Africa. It was our duty, he suggested as socialists to assist all liberation fronts. Even if we did not now consider ourselves Goans we had names such as De Souza, Pinto etc. which could be used with some effect. Portuguese colonialism was as Bad as any other. The Goan Organisation in East Africa was being used by Portuguese whose constant propaganda was that Goans overseas – even the educated ones, supported the regime and were happy with the Portuguese. Pio had already started a Goan vernacular paper in Nairobi "The Uzwod" to arouse feeling against Portugal. Pio was unfortunately arrested before we formed the East African Goan National Association in 1954. Mr. J. M. Nazareth, Q.C. was selected President, and was one of the Vice-Presidents. The Association did good work, but the Portuguese colonialists soon got to work with their fellow colonialists in Kenya and banned the organisation. The work of the organisation however, continued. We were in fact pleasantly surprised to see the great amount of support we throughout East Africa, particularly from educated Goans. It was impossible for us to stop functioning even if we wanted to. Contacts

36. Pinto and De Souza at an anti-imperialism demonstration

made with organisation and individuals in Bombay and Goa flourished. Of necessity, work had to be secret as the Portuguese Consulate and its stooges constantly sent dossiers on all of us to the Special Branch. As usual, they labelled the lot of us "Communists" as that seemed the easiest way to get us suppressed.

A few years later, in 1960, only a few months after he was released, Pio formed the East Africa Goa League. This time Portuguese Government did not succeed in persuading the Kenya Government to ban it. Nationalists were already much stronger in Kenya. He led a delegation to see Mzee Kenyatta at Maralal. The Government had persistently refused him permission to see Mzee Kenyatta but allowed an East African Goan League delegation to visit him without asking for the names of the members of the delegation, and was quite shocked when Pio arrived at Maralal as the leader!

In May, 1961, a delegation from the Goa Asleram led by Prof. Lucio Rodrigues and Dr. Laura D'Souza arrived in Kenya. Largely under the pretext of singing Goan songs and reciting Goan literature, they instilled some form of self-respect and dignity into East African Goans, many of whom had hitherto been loyal and servile servants of the British Crown. They were amazingly successful.

Hon. Tom Mboya, General Secretary of KANU and Hon. Muinga Chokwe, Coast Chairman, accepted an invitation to attend a Conference on Goa in Delhi at the Asleram. Tom Mboya was, I was later told by Goa Nationalists, extremely eloquent at the Conference. His forthright speech telling India and its Government that it hardly had a right to attempt to liberate Africa when it was afraid to liquidate Portuguese Colonies within its own country made a deep impression on Pandit Nehru and influenced his decision to liberate Goa.

37. Pinto visiting Kenyatta in detention at Lodwar

Pandit Nehru then organized an international Seminar on Portuguese Colonies. Perhaps his mind was already made up to liberate Goa – he was testing reaction among friends. Among those who attended were Mr. Kaunda from Zambia, Mr. Nsilo Swai and Pio Pinto. All the delegates urged military intervention to liberate Goa. Pio was particularly active and passionate in

Pio Gama Pinto, Kenya's Unsung Martyr

canvassing support for the liberation of Goa as a start to crack the bastion of Portuguese imperialism everywhere. He had told me he thought a few violent and passionate speeches would convince Pandit Nehru to risk the criticism this action would arouse in the West.

A few months later, Mrs. Lakshmi Menon arrived in Kenya, and it was obvious that the liberation of Goa was very much in the offing. Pio and Mr. Chokwe even offered to organize an international volunteer brigade to assist but this was not necessary. Goa was liberated by the Indian army. The cowardly Portuguese just fled. Hardly a shot was fired. The only Indian casualties were two officers who went to accept the surrender of Aguada Fort after the Portuguese had raised a white flag and were killed at almost point-blank range.

Pio, his bother Rosario, Peter Carvalho and I were invited to take part in the victory celebration. Pio met many old veterans of the campaign – whom he had not seen since he left India in 1947. Most of them begged him to return to India. They wanted him to be their leader and it was obvious that he had many friends and a good deal of support wherever he went. But he declined. He said he was born in Kenya and Kenya was his home. While he still had a soft spot for Goa and India, Kenya would be the home where he would work and die.

Pio then went to New Delhi and discussed Goa with Pandit Nehru and officials of the Indian Government. he took advantage of the opportunity to ask Pandi Nehri for assistance to start a nationalist paper in Kenya Panditji gave him funds with which Pio began the PAN AFRICAN PRESS LTD. which published "Sauti ya Mwafrika", "Pan Africa" and the "Nyanza Times". Most people in Kenya believe that the funds for the press came from China. In fact, the original funds came from India. Naturally India had to keep quiet about it then. Now that we are a free country we can tell the truth to the world.

Back in Kenya, he worked on the launching of movements for the liberation of Angola and Mozambique. With Chokwe, he formed the Mozambique African National Union in Mombasa in 1962. Many of the delegates to the inaugural meeting had travelled hundreds of miles to be present. But the British Government banned the organisation and it faded away, but Pio had formed valuable contacts with Mozambique nationalists.

Later Pio worked very closely with F.R.E.L.I.M.O. and the Committee of Nine of the O.A.U. and often visited Dar es Salaam to assist them. A few weeks before he was assassinated he told me that his ambition was to resign his seat in Parliament and retire to Lindi or Mtwara on the Mozambique border to assist the freedom fighters actively. His friends would not let him go – they argued that he was needed here. He never lived to help the struggle in Mozambique. But he died with his boots on.

Romesh Chandra[68]: Son of Africa

There is mourning in Kenya. One of the bravest of her sons is no more, one of the fighters who helped to win independence for Kenya lies buried under the soil he loved so dearly.

YES, Pio Pinto was a son of Africa. Elected to Parliament of Kenya, he was loved and respected by vasy masses of Kenya patriots. One of the staunchest leaders of the Kenya African National Union (KANU) – the party of freedom built by Jomo Kenyatta and Oginga Odinga – Pio had spent many years in British prisons for the cause of Kenya's emancipation.

He died too for Africa: he was shot dead by the agents of imperialism – the imperialism, to vanquish which Pio dedicated his entire life.

There is mourning in India too. For in Pio's veins ran Indian blood. A Goan by birth, this martyr for Africa's liberation, had his education in Bombay. Pio found no difficulty in identifying himself completely with the African cause: an anti-imperialist fighter for the same cause, wherever he may be. And the African fighters took Pio to their hearts, the real India, the staunchly anti-imperialist India, the India of our courageous workers and peasants.

Pio was a bridge between India and Africa. Pio, by his every act, demonstrated the oneness of the anti-imperialist battle, the solidarity of Asia and Africa, of India and Africa.

I am proud that I knew Pio that I had shaken his hand, hat I had sat and listened to him, talked to him, for hours at a time…

---

68   Journalist (by courtesy of *New Age*, Delhi). Available at: http://www.sahistory.org.za/archive/pio-pinto-son-of-africa [Accessed: 24-06-18].

President Kenyatta has paid Pinto the finest tributes that can be paid to ant man. And in his statement of homage to the memory of this son of Kenya, the president has referred to the years Pio suffered in prison "for his uncompromising line in politics".

It is indeed this that impressed one most about Pio. And the impression grew with every meeting.

It was in India that I met Pio first. Those were the days of the intensification of the Goan freedom struggle, and I was one of the secretaries of the National Campaign Committee for the Liberation of Goa, Daman, Diu. Pio was here twice during that period, if I remember correctly.

How impatient he was for the liberation of his beloved Goa. And I have little doubt that his inspiring words and pledges roused the Goan freedom fighters to regroup themselves, and give that last magnificent push, which compelled the Government of India to act.

The last time I met Pio was in Nairobi, in his own Kenya, in 1963. I had gone as a member of the Indian delegation to the Third Afro Asian Peoples' Solidarity Conference in Moshi (Tanganyika) and we passed through Nairobi on our way to and from Moshi.

Pio was there to greet our delegation when we arrived. He was there to see us off. And in between he was with us, to help us meet the leaders of Kenya, to understand the situation there, the problems, the hopes and aspirations.

Pio was himself part of the Kenya group which attended the Moshi conference, under the leadership of that resolute African patriot, Oginga Odinga.

Every time we talked, Pio poke of the need for solidarity against imperialists.

Yes, he would say, we are marching forward, more and more countries are becoming independent, but be vigilant, for the imperialists have not yet been liquidated – they are here, striving to come back, to divide us.

I know that it was he who was among the first in Kenya to launch a fullscale assault on the dangers of neo-colonialism. Not for him the ending of struggle with the ringing of the bells of independence. Not for him any sitting back in his chair, after he became an M.P.

Always a powerful journalist, he organised the KANU press. He bought out a militant journal titled "PAN AFRICA" and organized the progressive PAN AFRICA PUBLISHERS. As throughout his life, now too there was no compromise. The fight went on. No abandonment of principles, no weakening of resolve.

And precisely because of this tireless exposure of imperialism, this passionate crusade against neo-colonialism – the imperialists killed Pio Pinto. They shot him dead at point blank range near his home. The cowards, who killed, fired in the dark and then ran away.

But Pio's indomitable spirit lives. It lives in the work of the many brave young Africans, who had been inspired by his work, by the enthusiasm for the building of a socialist Africa which he always had.

Pio lives too in the mighty movement of Afro-Asian solidarity, which grows with every day

Muinga Chitari Chokwe[69]: Early days

I first met Pio in 1950 when he worked for an Indian organisation called the East African Indian National Congress which had its offices in Desai Memorial Hal, Victoria Street. He was employed there as a part - time secretary. During those times the Trade Unions were gaining momentum and Mr. Makhan Singh was prominent. However, Markhan Singh was quickly disposed off by the regime for allegedly having admitted being a communist. The Printers Union had been associated with Mr. Makhan Singh and therefore became a little frightened, but the Nairobi Taxi Drivers' Union was very active.

Pio was youthful and energetic. He darted like an antelope between his office in Victoria Street and the Union Offices in Grogan Road to keep up the morale of the people. His ability to make friends was immeasurable and many were surprised and asked why this young Indian should concern himself with affairs of the under-dog. We were considered sub-citizens at a

---

69 Speaker of the Senate.

Pio Gama Pinto, Kenya's Unsung Martyr

time when the Settler community kept up a hue and cry over "black

38. Pinto with Kali, Karumba, Ngei and Chokwe

With ex-Detainee Colleagues: J. D. Kali, Kungu Karumba, Paul Ngei and Muinga Chokwe.

nationalism". To them this was synonymous with communism! Pio joined the staff of a small newspaper organization and started whipping up public opinion in favour of thee African. Pio enlisted the help of Mr. D. K. Sharda who had a small Lino-press and got him to print various vernacular papers. Bildad Kaggia with his "Inoro ria Gikuyu" strengthened the armada of vernacular opinions the "Kenya Weekly News".

That was not enough for Pio. He gathered some young Asians from colleges, like Fitz De Souza, a few European progressives and some civil servants like Peter Wright to form a caucus. The main aim was to have our political party re-organised with people like J. D. Kali, Fred Kubai, Paul Ngei and others. Through the caucus we sent memoranda to the Colonial Secretary in Britain, and whipped us support through the Indian High Commissioner, Apa Pant. Indeed, the situation was tense, but Pio appeared at every session and invariably everywhere. He never hesitated to go into the Reserves to meet old men like the late George Ndegwa Kirongothi on Kiambu, John Adala of Kakamega and Gideon Riber of Rabai. In short, his drive was such that it acted like an intoxicant on those exposed to it. The Special Branch was busy tracking him and all trade unionists were black-listed.

People in Mombasa used to say that but for his colour they would have thought him to be my brother. Such was Pio's nationalist fervor. The pendulum of momentum swung from Desai Memorial Hall to Kiburi House through-out the time Pio was in action. In 1952 when the emergency was declared, Pio was left like an orphan but within two years he joined us in detention on Manda Island. He was detained because he was popular with the terrorists in the forest even though his role was to try and bring the dissidant factions to a conference with the Settler Group.

To my knowledge, Pio remained a true nationalist throughout and therefore his assassination will never be understood. If the murder was to avenge the zeal against the imperialist forces, then there are many more of us willing to meet death.

———————— * ————————

PRINTED
IN EAST AFRICA
BY
PRINTCRAFT
P.O. BOX 355
NAIROBI
February, 1966

Pio Gama Pinto: Report of the Truth, Justice & Reconciliation Commission (2013)

Truth, Justice & Reconciliation Commission, The Final Report of the Truth, Justice & Reconciliation Commission of Kenya (2013),

TJRC Final Report - Volume IV. Chapter 1

https://www.jfjustice.net/downloads/1460970274.pdf. [Accessed: 23-06-2018].

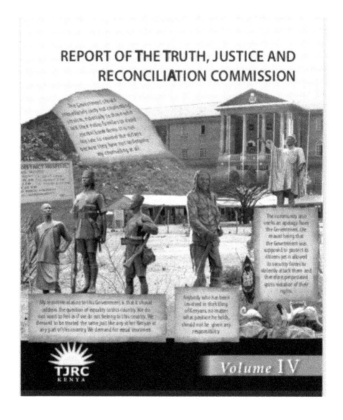

Primary Findings

22. The Commission finds that between 1895 and 1963, the British Colonial administration in Kenya was responsible for unspeakable and horrific gross violations of human rights. In order to establish its authority in Kenya, the colonial government employed violence on the local population on an unprecedented scale. Such violence included massacres, torture and ill-treatment and various forms of sexual violence.

1. The Commission also finds that the British Colonial administration adopted a divide and rule approach to the local population that created a negative dynamic of ethnicity, the consequences of which are still being felt today. At the same time the Colonial administration alienated large amounts of highly productive land from the local population, and removed communities from their ancestral lands.

2. The Commission finds that between 1963 and 1978, President Jomo Kenyatta presided over a government that was responsible for numerous gross violations of human rights. These violations included:

    • in the context of the Shifta War, killings, torture, collective punishment, and denial of basic needs (food, water and health care);

    • political assassinations of Pio Gama Pinto, Tom Mboya and J.M. Kariuki;

    • arbitrary detention of political opponents and activists; and

    • illegal and irregular acquisition of land by the highest government officials and their political allies
    —

Political Assassinations

General findings

104. The Commission finds that during the mandate period, political assassination was one of the tactics used by the state and the political elite to repress dissent or eliminate political competition.

3. The Commission finds that political assassinations have exacerbated ethnic divisions and tensions. The assassination of Tom Mboya is a prime example of how assassinations can further divide communities and increase ethnic tensions.

4. The Commission finds that investigations into specific assassinations, when undertaken, were usually deliberately shut down before conclusion. Even in instances where such investigations had been concluded, their reports of findings and recommendations were never publicized. The multiple investigations into the assassination of Robert Ouko are an extreme example of this phenomenon, but it is not the only example. The Commission finds that there is a lack of critical political goodwill to conduct thorough and objective investigations into cases where the victims are suspected to have been assassinated for political reasons.

5. The Commission finds that the lack of a credible legal and institutional mechanism for witness protection continues to hamper any objective inquiry into cases of suspected political assassination. Witness intimidation and murder continue to pose fundamental challenges to such inquiries. While there have been attempts at fortifying legal and policy structures for witness protection, much more is needed before credible and thorough investigations in such sensitive issues can be undertaken.

Specific findings

Pio Gama Pinto

6. The Commission finds that the assassination of Pio Gama Pinto was motivated by ideological differences that were at the heart of the global Cold War but also mirrored in domestic Kenyan politics.

7. The Commission finds the conviction of Kisilu Mutua did little to clarify the circumstances and motives behind Pinto's assassination. The Commission agrees with the finding of Justice Ainley that "the case wears an unfinished aspect and that we may not have all who were involved in the crime before us."

8. The Commission finds that Kisilu, Chege Thuo and a third unidentified man who disappeared, were used as scapegoats to divert attention away from the true motive and the more responsible perpetrators of Pinto's assassination.

9. The Commission finds that there is sufficient circumstantial evidence, including the failure by the government to uncover the truth of who was responsible, to conclude that the government was involved in the killing of Pio Gama Pinto.

Recommendations

■ The Commission recommends that the government establish public memorials commemorating the lives Pio Gama Pinto, JM Kariuki, Robert Ouko, Father Antony Kaiser, and Crispin Odhiambo-Mabi and that such memorials include an educational component detailing the contributions such individuals made to the nation. Such memorials may include statues, museums, or educational institutions and shall be completed within 2 years of the issuance of this Report.

REPORT OF THE TRUTH, JUSTICE AND RECONCILIATION COMMISSION

Volume IIA *Chapter* FOUR

Available at: https://digitalcommons.law.seattleu.edu/tjrc/2/ [Accessed: 10-04-18]

https://digitalcommons.law.seattleu.edu/tjrc/

pp. 364 - 440

23. A little over a year since independence, on 25 [sic] February 1965, Kenya suffered its first major political assassination. The Pinto assassination demonstrates all of the complexities and tragedy of political assassinations in post-independence Kenya. Its context included: a global cold war that was mirrored in domestic political debates; a domestic struggle to consolidate power and narrow dissent; and a resort to violence to address political differences.

Political context

24. The newly independent Kenyatta Administration had to grapple with myriad challenges after independence in 1963. Besides fighting illiteracy, lack of education, poverty and disease, the country was the target of ideological and strategic interests of the capitalist West and communist East during the Cold War. Both parties to the Cold War thus nurtured and cultivated ideological and political allies within Kenya. At the same time President Kenyatta's government used many of the laws and institutions of the colonial government to minimize and even suppress dissent. Those in President's Kenyatta's inner circle who had ambitions to succeed him utilized numerous mechanisms to neutralize political opponents. One of the tools used in these early days, and ever since, was political assassination. The first victim of political assassination to be weeded out through the barrel of a gun was Pio Gama Pinto.

25. Pinto was a nominated member of parliament in Kenya's first government, and was among the few Kenyan Asians to face detention in colonial Kenya. While Kenyatta leaned towards the west and capitalism, his Vice President, Oginga Odinga, was more sympathetic to the east and socialism. Goldsworthy describes Pinto as 'Odinga's foremost tactical adviser and link-man with Eastern embassies" that bankrolled his socialist ideas'. Indeed, it is reported that Pinto had organized a meeting between Odinga and a Chinese delegation that discussed Kenya adopting a more socialist path, entering into a defence pact with Kenya, and the possibility of using Kenya as a conduit for Chinese arms to liberation movements in Africa.[70]

26. It was later alleged by the press that The Lumumba Institute, which Pinto headed, was teaching scientific socialism to party members (selected largely for their receptivity to such ideas). President Kenyatta did not take kindly to such activities, and in a series of speeches and statements attacked, among others,'alien' ideologies and activities of traitors of KANU. President Kenyatta asked Mboya to draft a policy on African socialism to counter Odinga's socialism. It was to be tabled in

---

70   Kamau Ngotho, *Daily Nation,* June 20, 2000, p.8.

Pio Gama Pinto, Kenya's Unsung Martyr

Parliament in April 1975. When the Odinga group got wind of this move, they asked Pinto to write a counter draft to be tabled on the same day as Mboya's and mobilized parliamentarians to vote against the government.[71] Had this plan come to fruition, it could have made Pinto the architect of the first parliamentary coup and thus the man closest to organizing a real political revolution in Kenya.[72]

27. It was during the heat of these early debates about the direction of Kenyan economic and political policy that Pinto was assassinated. He was shot outside his home in Westlands in front of his 18 month-old daughter, Tereshka. Kenyans were shocked, and the possibility that this was a political assassination was immediately raised. Vice President Joseph Murumbi sobbed openly. Information Minister Achieng Oneko reacted to the news with: 'No, no, no! Kenyatta must explain! He must explain!'[73] President Kenyatta, who retorted *"Bwana Waziri* do you think it is Kenyatta who has killed Pinto?"* lamented that the country had lost 'one of the conscientious workers for freedom who suffered many years in detention for his uncompromising stand in politics'. Kenyatta asserted that his government 'will exert every effort to hunt down and bring to justice the perpetrators of this outrage'. Underscoring the widespread suspicion of a political murder, Oneko termed it a 'deliberate and cowardly move in what I believe to be a planned assassination'. Joseph Murumbi resigned as Vice President to 'protest Pinto's murder and subsequent intrigue in Kenyatta's inner circle'.

Arrest and trial of alleged assassins

28. Following the assassination of Pinto, the Kenya Police mounted a massive manhunt for the three gunmen who it was alleged ambushed and murdered Pinto. Two teenage suspects were arrested: Kisilu Mutua, who was 18 years old, and Chege Thuo, who was then 19. During their arraignment before Supreme Court Justice, Sir John Ainley, they pleaded 'not guilty' to the murder. Kisilu admitted he was near the scene when the shooting took place, having been paid to scare Pinto after his recent opposition activities in Parliament. He testified that as he approached

---

71   Kamau Ngotho, *Daily Nation*, June 21, 2000, p. 8.
72   *Kamau Ngotho, Daily Nation, June 21, 2000, P.9.*
73   *Kamau Ngotho, Daily Nation, June 18, 2000 p.4*

Pinto's house, shots rang out and he saw Pinto collapse in his car. He testified that he was unable to see who had fired the shots.

29. During the preliminary hearing, it was found that none of the ten fingers and palm prints found on Pinto's Saab car belonged to the two teenagers who were charged with what wbeing described as a 'well planned and efficiently executed' killing.[74] It was also revealed that thirteen hours before his murder, Pinto had told his house servant, Waweru Ng'ang'a, that a man had been offered money to kill him. A CID corporal told the court that the two had been sent to frighten Pinto by Ochola Mak'Anyengo 'because he had been interfering with his union'.[75] When the trial ended, the three assessors found Kisilu and Thuo 'not guilty'.[76]

30. Although Chief Justice Ainley conceded that 'the case wears an unfinished aspect and that we may not have all who were involved in the crime before us', and while he was satisfied that Kisilu had not pulled the trigger, he nevertheless said that the young man could not have gone to Pinto's place without an idea of what was to happen. He found him guilty and sentenced him to hang. This sentence was later changed to a life sentence. Thuo was however freed on grounds of insufficient evidence.

Theories

31. The trial and conviction of Kisilu did not put the matter of Pinto's assassination to rest. Over the years, a number of theories have been put forward to explain the assassination. Some have suggested that Pinto was killed by members of President Kenyatta's inner circle, while others speculated that Pinto was assassinated by neo- colonialist forces because he was viewed as an avowed Communist with links to the Mozambican liberation movement.[77] A declassified cable from the

---

74 *Daily Nation, April 10, 1965, p.4*
75 *Daily Nation, April 10, 1965, p.4.*
76 *Ibid*
77 "RIGHTS-KENYA: Tasting New Life after 36 Years in Jail. *Inter Press Service News Agency.* July 11, 2001

US Department of State captures the breadth of the conspiracy theories that were being circulated in the period following Pinto's assassination: Other rumours centre around resentment against Pinto as an Asian and speculate that he was killed because he was a major recipient of communist largesse who may have been holding out on money received, or tried to blackmail a high official, or was killed by the Chicoms [Chinese Communists] because he was moving closer to the Soviets or by Kikuyu who feared he was a threat to Kikuyu dominance.[78]

32. Thirty five years after the Pinto trial, an investigation by the Daily Nation concluded that Kisilu, Thuo and a third man who disappeared, were peripheral players in the murder. The Daily Nation asserted that Kisilu in fact did not kill Pinto, but was instead set up by the Directorate of Security Intelligence.[79] According to the Daily Nation, the plan to assassinate Pinto began three years earlier. A memo by the Kenya Intelligence Committee dated 13 December 1962 had labelled Pinto as a "man to be watched very closely." By 1965, Kenyatta felt threatened by Pinto's strong trade union base.[80] Pinto's positioning as a substantial threat to the existing Government ultimately led to his elimination. The subsequent cover up, according to the Daily Nation, included keeping Kisilu behind bars against numerous recommendations by the Prisons Review Board for fear of the dossier that he might spill on the Pinto murder.[81] The Commission was unable to verify or disprove the allegations made in the Daily Nation report. Indeed, although the Commission heard testimony on the assassination of Pinto, it was unable to discover any additional evidence that would shed light on any of the theories concerning Pinto's death. As noted elsewhere in this Report, the Commission was not allowed access to many of the documents held by the Government that would have assisted in investigations such as this, including the archives of the National Security Intelligence Service.

---

78   Daniel Branch ,Kenya Between Hope and Despair 1963-2011 (2011) 46
79   Kamau Ngotho, Daily Nation, June 18, 2000, p.4
80   David Goldsworthy, Tom Mboya: The Man Kenya Wanted to Forget, 1982.
81   Kamau Ngotho, Daily Nation, June 18, 2000, p.4.

Aftermath

33. Pinto was the first of what was to prove to be many Kenyan politicians assassinated after independence. At the time of his assassination, Pinto was 38 years old. He was survived by his wife, Emma and his three daughters Linda, Malusha and Tereshka, the last of whom witnessed her father's killing when she was only eighteen months old. Two years after the assassination, Emma and her daughters moved to Canada.[82]

34. While Pinto's death continues to be shrouded in mystery, the Pinto Trust Fund was established after his death to benefit Emma and the children. In September 1965 the International Organisation of Journalists invited Mrs. Emma Gama Pinto to Santiago, Chile, to receive a posthumous trophy awarded to her husband for his contribution to journalism that furthered the liberation of African countries from foreign domination and exploitation.[83] Many years later in 2008, the Postal Corporation of Kenya released a series of four stamps titled Heroes of Kenya, one of which featured Pinto.[84]

39. Lumumba Institute

82 Meusburger, Peter (2011). Knowledge and Space: Cultural Memories: the Geographical Point of View. Heidelberg: Springer. pp. 318.
83 Vaz, J. Clement (1997). Profiles of Eminent Goans, Past and Present.New Delhi: Concept Publishing Company. p. 243.
84 Pio Gama Pinto (1927–1965)". Safari Africa Radio.

Pio Gama Pinto, The Patriotic Journalist (IOJ, 1965)

A speech delivered by an official of the International Organisation of Journalists (IOJ) in Chile which Emma Pinto attended to receive Pinto's posthumous award.

The Patriotic Journalist

The mass media has played a very important role in our struggle against imperialism and was used as an organizing and uniting force by the patriotic forces fighting for liberation. Pio Gama Pinto was at the centre of the publishing activities of the freedom fighters. This publishing role did not limit his contribution to the struggle for land and freedom in Kenya. He stood foremost as an activist who clearly saw the danger posed to the young Kenyan nation from imperialism and their local allies. He devoted his whole life to the fight for true independence for Kenya, in all spheres, economic, political, social and cultural. No sacrifice was too great for achieving this aim. He suffered economic hardships, detentions, and finally gave his life. His example can only fill our youth with a greater sense of dedication to the service of the people. Pio Gama Pinto was a prominent person in publishing activities of the period (1948-65). As he was deeply involved in every aspect of the struggle for independence, Pinto was in a better position to serve national interests through his publishing activities.

The Pan Africa Press Ltd, which Pinto had established, published a short biography entitled 'Independent Kenya's First Martyr' in February 1966, the first anniversary of Pinto's death. It records that, 'In 1949, after a succession of clerical jobs, [Pio Gama Pinto] became involved in the local politics aimed at overthrowing colonialism. He turned to journalism and worked with the *Colonial Times* and the *Daily Chronicle*. In 1954, five months after his marriage to Emma, he was rounded up in the notorious Operation Anvil and spent the next four years in detention on Manda Island with the so called "hard core" Mau Mau. He was kept in restriction from early 1958 until October 1959 at remote Kabarnet . . . In 1960, together with Odinga and Gichuru, he founded the KANU newspaper *Sauti ya Kanu.*

In 1961, Oginga Odinga, Joseph Murumbi and Pio Gama Pinto founded the Pan African Press. Pinto became the director and secretary and started the publication of three newspapers, namely *Sauti ya Mwafrika, Pan Africa* and *Nyanza Times.*

'In September 1965, Mrs Emma Gama Pinto was invited to Santiago, Chile, to receive a posthumous prize awarded to her husband by the International Organisation of Journalists for his contribution in journalism to the liberation of African countries from foreign domination and exploitation.'

The editors of the *Democratic Journalist,* organ of International Organisation of Journalists, Prague wrote thus:

On February 24 we received a report which upset us very profoundly and left us extremely dismayed. P G Pinto, the national deputy, member of the leadership of the periodical *Panafrica,* the great African revolutionary and nationalist, a great man, had been murdered by hired assassins. A man had been killed who meant much to the international movement of progressive, democratic people, both to the trade union or journalist movement, and to the movement for the international co-operation of members of parliaments, and so on.

In P G Pinto we lose a man of great qualities, of great revolutionary enthusiasm, of great personal courage. His name is linked with the struggle against British colonialism. Pinto was several times held in colonial concentration camps together with thousands of other Kenyan patriots, together with those who

The mass media has played a very important role in our struggle against imperialism and was used as an organizing and uniting force by the patriotic forces fighting for liberation. Pio Gama Pinto was at the centre of the publishing activities of the freedom fighters. This publishing role did not limit his contribution to the struggle for land and freedom in Kenya. He stood foremost as an activist who clearly saw the danger posed to the young Kenyan nation from imperialism and their local allies. He devoted his whole life to the fight for true independence for Kenya, in all spheres, economic, political, social and cultural. No sacrifice was too great for achieving this aim. He suffered economic hardships, detentions, and finally gave his life. His example can only fill our youth with a greater sense of dedication to the service of the people. Pio Gama Pinto was a prominent person in publishing activities of the period (1948-65). As he was deeply involved in every aspect of the struggle for independence, Pinto was in a better position to serve national interests through his publishing activities.

Aware of the importance of information and communication in a liberation struggle, he became editor of the *Daily Chronicle*. Over the years he produced a plethora of newspaper articles, campaign slogans, posters, memoranda, press statements, pamphlets, leaflets and general correspondence. He would draft, write, print and distribute them.

The Pan Africa Press Ltd, which Pinto had established, published a short biography entitled *Independent Kenya's First Martyr* in February 1966, the first anniversary of Pinto's death. It records that, 'In 1949, after a succession of clerical jobs, [Pio Gama Pinto] became involved in the local politics aimed at over throwing colonialism. He turned to journalism and worked with the *Colonial Times* and the *Daily Chronicle*. In 1954, five months after his marriage to Emma, he was rounded up in the notorious Operation Anvil and spent the next four years in detention on Manda Island with the so called "hard core" Mau Mau. He was kept in restriction from early 1958 until October 1959 at remote Kabarnet.

In 1960, together with Odinga and Gichuru, he founded the KANU newspaper *Sauti ya Kanu*. Later he established the Pan African press of which he subsequently became director and secretary. In 1961, with finances donated by Pandit Jawaharlal Nehru of India, Oginga Odinga, Joseph Murumbi and Pio Gama Pinto founded the Pan African Press Ltd. Pinto became its director and secretary and started the publication of three newspapers, namely *Sauti ya Mwafrica, Pan Africa* and *Nyanza Times*. The newspapers and printing press gave Pinto the tools to do what he always loved most – sensitizing the masses through underground pamphlets and propaganda.

So self-effacing was Pio that he never wrote about himself or collected any of his own writings. It is difficult to trace his authorship as he often wrote using pseudonyms. And the documents which survived him were burnt by his friends in a bonfire at the back of his house following his murder.

'In September 1965, Mrs Emma Gama Pinto was invited to Santiago, Chile, to receive a posthumous prize awarded to her husband by the International Organisation of Journalists for his contribution in journalism to the liberation of African countries from foreign domination and exploitation.'

The Editors of the Democratic Journalist, organ of International Organisation of Journalists, Prague wrote thus:

On February 24 we received a report which upset us very profoundly and left us extremely dismayed. P G Pinto, the national deputy, member of the leadership of the periodical Panafrica, the great African revolutionary and nationalist, a great man, had been murdered by hired assassins. A man had been killed who meant much to the international movement of progressive, democratic people, both to the trade union or journalist movement, and to the movement for the international co-operation of members of parliaments, and so on.

In P G Pinto we lose a man of great qualities, of great revolutionary enthusiasm, of great personal courage. His name is linked with the struggle against British colonialism. Pinto was several times held in colonial concentration camps together with thousands of other Kenyan patriots, together with those who today stand at the head of a free country. Since the winning of freedom Pinto has played an important role in the trade union and journalist movement, the periodical in which he had a leading position has become the spokesman of democratic, freedom-loving ideas, an energetic fighter against colonialism, neo-colonialism and imperialism. His name will always be linked with the Lumumba Institute in Nairobi, which he helped to create, to which he gave much of his energies and part of his heart. The Lumumba Institute became the spokesman of all the new world that today is fighting in Africa for humanism, progress, the dignity of man, man freed of imperialism, freed of racial discrimination, freed from hunger and poverty. Every African patriot who passes through this school, either from the east, the north, the south or the west of Africa, takes with him part of P G Pinto's heart, his enthusiasm, his wisdom, his determination and courage.

And neither will our organization ever forget P G Pinto. He was with us at our last executive committee meeting held in Algiers in April 1964. He was a modest man, knowledgeable in many matters, knowledgeable on African and world problems, wise and well-balanced. Many of us knew him from personal contacts either in Kenya or elsewhere in Africa, Asia or Europe. P G Pinto was murdered because he stood in the way of neo-colonialism; he was undoubtedly removed by those who wish to go on exploiting, misusing and oppressing Africa and the Africans. Pinto fought and fell in battle.

But he did not lose. This crude murder is merely proof of the weakness of these reactionary circles which hired the murderers. Pinto will go on fighting: in every African patriot, in every democrat throughout the world. And our organization will also honour the memory of this great journalist by fighting even more effectively for the materialization of the ideals of freedom, equality, democracy for which Pinto was working. We shall never forget our heroic colleague.

Pio Gama Pinto, Kenya's Unsung Martyr

Pinto seen by others - Selected Quotes

Chinese Ambassador Yu-tien (1965)[85]

To Joseph Murumbi: "Mr. Pinto stood steadfastly with the Kenyan people in the early days of their struggle for independence. My colleagues and I grieve together with the Kenyan people at his unfortunate death".

♦

Russian Ambassador Lavrov (1965)[86]

In his message of condolences dispatched directly to Pinto's widow, Russian Ambassador Lavrov did not mince his words - as expected of diplomats - and termed Pinto's killing a politically-motivated assassination. He wrote, on behalf of his government:

We are deeply shocked to learn of the tragic death of the Hon Mr. Pio Gama Pinto by villainous assassination. The death of Hon Mr. Pio Gama Pinto is a great loss not only to those who knew him personally as a tireless fighter for freedom, democracy and social progress but to all who believe in these noble ideals.

*

John Tettegah, All-Africa Trade Union Federation (1965)[87]

The secretary-general of the Leftist All-Africa Trade Union Federation, Mr. John Tettegah, delivered the punchline salute to the fallen comrade-in-arms when he said:

Comrade Pinto! You live on in us, your fighting African trade union brothers. We pledge to vindicate your life and your death. Your murder has only strengthened the determination of people - not only in Africa, but in Asia and Latin America, too. No force on earth can stem our determination to win that freedom and dignity of Man for which you lived and died.

*

---

85   Quoted in: Kamau Ngotho The Nation (Nairobi) 23-06-2000: His friends stayed loyal even in death. Available at: https://www.nation.co.ke/news/1056-366092-l8iffjz/index.html. [Accessed: 24-06-2018].
86   *ibid.*
87   *ibid*

Romesh Chandra (1965)[88]

I know that it was he who was among the first in Kenya to launch a fullscale assault on the dangers of neo-colonialism. Not for him the ending of struggle with the ringing of the bells of independence. Not for him any sitting back in his chair, after he became an M.P.

Always a powerful journalist, he organised the KANU press. He bought out a militant journal titled "PAN AFRICA" and organized the progressive PAN AFRICA PUBLISHERS. As throughout his life, now too there was no compromise. The fight went on. No abandonment of principles, no weakening of resolve.

And precisely because of this tireless exposure of imperialism, this passionate crusade against neo-colonialism – the imperialists killed Pio Pinto. They shot him dead at point blank range near his home. The cowards who killed, fired in the dark and then ran away.

But Pio's indomitable spirit lives. It lives in the work of the many brave young Africans, who had been inspired by his work, by the enthusiasm for the building of a socialist Africa which he always had.

Pio lives too in the mighty movement of Afro-Asian solidarity, which grows with every day. - Romesh Chandra: Son of Africa. *in: Pio Gama Pinto, Independent Kenya's First Martyr: Socialist and Freedom Fighter.* (1966). Nairobi: Pan African Press. [Edited by Ambu Patel]. Reproduced in this book.

*

Drum magazine (1965)[89]

Pinto made no secret of his politics. He believed in freedom and socialism because he could not see complete freedom being attained by any other road… Like other non-Africana leaders, such as Makhan Singh, he was considered expendable by some after Uhuru. But in 1964 he was elected to Parliament

---

88   Romesh Chandra: Son of Africa. *in: Pio Gama Pinto, Independent Kenya's First Martyr: Socialist and Freedom Fighter.* (1966). Nairobi: Pan African Press. [Edited by Ambu Patel]. Reproduced in this book.

89   *Drum* May 1965. Quoted in Bailey, Jim (1993): Kenya, the National Epic: From the Pages of *Drum* Magazine. Nairobi: Kenya Publications.

Pio Gama Pinto, Kenya's Unsung Martyr

and carried shoulder high by jubilant Cabinet Ministers when the results were known.

-

[Pinto's] forthright views on trade unionism made him unpopular in some quarters. He openly supported the splinter trade union group led by Dennis Akumu which broke away from KFL [Kenya Federation of Labour] in 1964.

-

Spurned and often ostracised by his fellow Goans for throwing in his lot with with the Africans, only absolute conviction in the rightness of his cause carried Pio Pinto through difficult years.

*

Oginga Odinga (1967)[90]

April 1953: In Nairobi, Pinto was an invaluable supply man, working with the Nairobi War Council that siphoned food, money, arms, and intelligence information through to the forests, and smuggling out of Kenya and into the world's press reports and photographs of atrocities by the security forces, until his activities were discovered and he, too, was detained.

-

Large sums were used to build our independent press (1961?). Pinto had been released from detention on Manda Island and from restriction and he immediately plunged into work for the release and return to political life of the Kenyatta generation of leaders and was the moving force in the acquisition of a small press and the publishing of our weekly KANU paper *Sauti ya Kanu* and later, *Sauti ya Mwafrika*.

-

I could complete no description on my political life and our struggle in Kenya without writing about Pio Pinto who was assassinated outside his house early in the morning of 24 February 1965. Pio Gama Pinto was a great Kenyan patriot. He leaves a gap in our political struggle for full freedom that few men – none that I know – can fill. I first met Pinto in 1952 when he worked as an official of the Kenyan Indian Congress to try to break

---

90   Odinga, Oginga (1967): Not Yet Uhuru, An Autobiography of Oginga Odinga. Nairobi: Heinemann Educational Books.

the pattern of its conservative policies and get the Asians of Kenya to throw themselves fully into the African liberation struggle. Pinto might have been a Goan, but he was African as the truest Kenyan nationalist. There is no phase of our struggle in which he did not play an invaluable part. When the repression was launched against KAU, Pinto organized political defences. When fighting started from the forests Pinto maintained political liaison and supplied arms and money to the fighters from supply lines in Nairobi. When the authorities caught up with his activities, he served his term in detention. When he was released and free from restriction he devoted himself to the campaign for the release of the other detainees and the support of their dependents. He was brilliant orgainiser and resourceful political leader. He threw himself into helping KANU win the 1961 elections, into founding our independent press, into the campaign for East African Federation, into the struggle against imperialism, especially in a cause dear to his heart, the liberation of Portugal's colonies. He was conscientious member of the Central Legislative Assembly and one of Kenya's delegates to the Afro-Asian Solidarity Conference at Moshi in 1963. Elected to our parliament in July 1964, he had but a few months of work there, but he set to it with the vigour and devotion that made Pinto a special man. He was a dedicated and intelligent socialist, prepared to sacrifice to the limit for our people, but determined that we should not lose the battle to build real Kenya independence and a social and economic system that would lead to real advance for our population. At his funeral, when the country was shocked and angry at his killing, I said that just as Lumumba had been murdered during the course of his heroic activities, so did Pio Pinto die. It may be some years before Kenyans see the full worth of Pinto and the part he played in our struggle before and after independence but there must come the time when this is well understood. Who were his enemies, if he were such a genuine patriot? The forces that knowingly or unwittingly are helping imperialism keep a grip on Kenya, those who have sacrificed the national advance to sectional or personal interests.

*

Donald Barnett (1972)[91]

Kenya has unmistakably entered the path of neocolonial accommodation. The Kenyatta regime, even before the flag-waving independence ceremony of 12 December 1963, had embarked on a course of self—aggrandizing opportunism and blatant disregard for the peasant and worker masses of Kenya. Virtually every warning contained in this article, every "pitfall of national consciousness" Fanon cautioned against in his Wretched of the Earth has been succumbed to in a Kenya which today is the very antithesis of that creative and developing socialist nation hoped for by radical Kenyans in 1961. Leaders of integrity and dedicated to serving the interests of the masses, men such as Pio Gama Pinto, Bildad Kaggia and Oginga Odinga, have been assassinated, deported, imprisoned or harassed and intimidated into silence and accommodation. Kenya is today a police state run by a mafia-like clique of self-serving politicians-cum-businessmen. Jomo Kenyatta; two-time betrayer of the Kenya masses (in 1953-4 at Kapenguria and 1962-3), largest African landowner in Kenya, leader of the new Black bourgeoisie and of the corrupt bureaucratic bourgeoisie which comprises the government was described to me in 1962 by Pio Pinto - then editor of Sauti ya Mwafrica and a top Kenyatta adviser - as simply an "amoral man". Pinto was assassinated by the regime on 24 February 1965 and Kenya has yet to replace him. - Barnett, Donald (1972): Kenya: Two Paths Ahead. Introduction to Muchai, Karigo (1973): The Hardcore: The Story of Karigo Muchai/ taped and illustrated by Don Barnett. Richmond, B.C.: LSM Information Centre.

*

Munyua Waiyaki (2000?)

Dr. Munyua Waiyaki recounts that, on the whole, Pinto was very instrumental in delivering victory for Kanu in the 1963 elections. For maximum efficiency, Pinto chose not to contest any seat. Recalls Waiyaki (one-time Foreign Minister): "Pinto preferred quiet operations. When most of us were shouting ourselves hoarse in the field, he remained in the office to think and plot". As Kanu's top campaign strategist, Pinto set up late in the office drawing up and printing campaign materials for the party candidates. He

---

91 Kamau Ngotho. *Daily Nation* 19-06-2000.

also doubled as Kanu's top propagandist via the party newspaper he founded, *Sauti ya Kanu.*

*

Daniel Branch (2011)[92]

Kenya turned next to harassment of the radical faction and began efforts aimed at undermining the institutions from which his rival derived support.

The first move was made against Odinga's most important supporter, Pio Gama Pinto. Pinto was, so the US embassy thought, Odinga's "brilliant political tactician". The British agreed. MacDonald described Pinto as "a dedicated communist, and the principal brain behind the whole secret organisation of Mr. Odinga's movement". The high commissioner credited Pinto with having mobilised backbench opposition in Parliament to Kenyatta and with leading "other anti-government movements". But Pinto was an important figure in his own right.

*

Anne Thurston (2015)[93]

The guiding principal of Pio's life was to maintain liberty and democracy and a fair chance for all, particularly those he loved and respected - the elders who bore the brunt of the struggle for independence, the old men of the KCA, who also joined him in detention. He met them, he lived with them, he was detained with them, and therefore he felt he knew them sincerely, and he never let them down - Thurston, Anne (2015): Joseph Murumbi: A Path not taken, the story of Joseph Murumbi. Nairobi" -The Murumbi Trust.
-

Politically, his views were beyond many of us in his depth of political understanding and social consciousness. To him socialism meant its true application. Pinto lived his socialism. He lived by his principles, and he died by his principles. He was quick to react to any injustice, and he spent long

92   Branch, Daniel (2011): Kenya: Between Hope and Despair, 1963-2011. London: Yale University Press.
93   Thurston, Anne (2015): Joseph Murumbi: A Path not taken, the story of Joseph Murumbi. Nairobi". The Murumbi Trust.

hours helping other people, but he never helped himself.

*

Kamau Ngotho (2000)

Pio Gama Pinto's colleagues and friends in the socialist movement defied diplomatic protocol and, in the face of the Kenya Government's indifference, even made secret donations to the family trust fund started after his death.

Pheroze Nowrojee (2007)[94]

The persons who had organised the killing had hoped that by getting rid of Pinto, others would become afraid to question the way these persons were selfishly taking the wealth of our country for themselves. These persons hoped that Kenyans would forget the history of the freedom struggle and forget the noble goals of our fight for *uhuru*. However, even though they removed Pinto from the scene, the questioning has still not stopped. Kenyans understand clearly that Pio Gama Pinto was right: that his demands were for the benefit of others and not for himself, and that he died the death of a martyr. He laid down his life for his principles.

-

Pinto is remembered to this day, and his ideals, ideas, beliefs and actions are those that have helped Kenyans to withstand oppression and injustice whenever these have returned to Kenya in the years since his assassination in 1965.

-

Pinto was active in Mau Mau, the movement fighting for independence. He collected and transported money, food and other supplies that the freedom fighters needed all the time. He also made sure that the fighters remained in touch with other leaders and with their supporters while they fought their battles in the forests and towns.

*

---

94   Nowrojee, Pheroze (2007): Pio Gama Pinto: Patriot for Social Justice. Nairobi: Longhorn Publishers.

Wangari Maathai[95]

We are extremely proud to share his {Pinto's] legacy. He is part of our history, part of what we are. We see in his work the love that this man had for his country. We must honour those on whose shoulders we stand.

Joseph Murumbi[96]

Pio always worked for other people, he never worked for himself. He was always writing petitions, memoranda for Members of Parliament, helping people out of their problems, trying to find money to assist them, going to see the families of people who were away from Kenya on some job or the other. I remember when as Foreign Minister I was ot of the country, he used to visit my wife Sheila and ask her whether she needed money, or he would take her out for a meal and make her feel comfortable whilst I was away. He did this for many people and when people were sick in hospitals, he would visit them.

...the police officer told me, "Don't say anything to him, he is dead" … The whole day we had people coming to the house. They were poor people, friends of Pio, people he had helped, people who had been with him in detention, and the place was jammed the whole day. The next day we buried Pio...They all came to the funeral. It was really pathetic to see elderly Kikuyu weeping their hearts out for a man they loved and respected, for a man who helped them in need, a man who was their colleague in detention and a man who had never forgotten them.

---

95 Nowrojee (2007) *ibid.*
96 Rothmyer, Karen (2018): Joseph Murumbi: A Legacy of Integrity. Nairobi: Zand Graphics.

Pio Gama Pinto: A Timeline

1927, 31 March: Antonio Rudolf Jose Pio Gama Pinto born in Nairobi.

1938: To India for education.

1944:

- Worked as a clerk in the. Indian Air Force.

- While in India, Pinto took an active part in the Goa National Congress and was one of its founder members and a member of its National Executive.

1949: Returned to Kenya following warrant for arrest by Colonial Goan government.

Worked in Magadi as a clerk.

1950:

- Left service at Magadi, came to Nairobi, obtained his certificate of permanent residence and "took the plunge in the freedom struggle" (Makhan Singh, Patel, 2006, p.450).

- Pinto helped in reorganising the E.A. Labour Trade Union after the arrest of Makhan Singh and Fred Kubai. (Patel, Ambu, 1963, p.155).

1951: Started working as paid secretary for East African Indian Congress at Desai Memorial Building.

1952: Editor of the Daily Chronicle.

1954 Jan.: Pio and Emma got married.

1954, 19 June: Arrested from his office in Desai Memorial Hall as part of the notorious Operation Anvil and imprisoned in the Takwa Detention Camp on Manda Island with the so-called "hard-core" Mau Mau. Others in detention there included Aching Oneko and Muinga Choke - and nearly a thousand other leaders (Nowrojee, p.24).

1954-1957: Prison, Manda

1958-1959: Restricted at Kabernet.

1958 Dec: First child, Linda, born in restriction at Kabernet.

1959, Dec.: Released from restriction.

1960: Started the weekly newsletter in Kiswahili *Sauti ya Kanu* with Odinga Odinga and James Gichuru. Later *Sauti ya Mwafrika*.

1960(?): Founded the Kenya Freedom Party with Chanan Singh, K.P.Shah and others as a "way of giving oral support of Kenyan Asians to the African people and their leaders in the struggle for freedom" (Durrani, N. 1985).

1960:

- Pinto, with Odinga Odinga and Joseph Morumbi founded the Pan African Press. Pinto became the Director and Secretary and started publishing three newspapers: Sauti ya Mwafrika, Pan African, and Nyanza Times

- Emma and Pio's second child, Malusha Marie born.

1961 Nov.: Bildad Kaggia released from detention; he and his wife first returned to Nairobi where they stayed with Pio and Emma in Nairobi. (Nowrojee, 2007).

1962, Feb.: Pinto was part of the KANU team to the Lancaster House Conference which led to independence for Kenya.

1963:

- Dec. 12: Kenya achieved independence
- June: Emma and Pio's third child, Tereshka, born.

- Elected Member of the Central Legislative Assembly of the East African Community.

1964,

- July: Elected as a Specially Elected Member of the House of Representatives.

- Selected as Publicity Secretary of the Back Benchers' Group.

- Pio chosen as Specially Elected Member of Kenya Parliament

- Established the Lumumba Institute to train Party Officials. He was a member of the Board of Governors.

1965

- 24 February: Pinto assassinated.

- April: Lumumba Institute closed down by the Government.

- Awarded posthumously the International Prize by the International Organisation of Journalists

1987, April

- The Green Belt Movement celebrated its tenth anniversary. Activities included planting seven trees in honour of Kenyans who contributed much to the country. Pio Gama Pinto was one of the seven so honoured.

2005

- Pinto awarded the first Uhuru Award for the Jaramogi Oginga Odinga Foundation.

2007

- Pinto awarded the Milele (Lifetime Achievement) Award by the Kenya National Commission on Human Rights (KNCHR)

Pio Gama Pinto: A Photo Story

40. Pinto with parents and siblings

L to R: Pio's father, Anton Filipe; mother, Emma; Rosario, Sevigne and Pio.
Photo: Audrey Da Gama Pinto.

41. Pio Gama Pinto – 3 images

42. Pinto, Jan. 1965

43. Pinto in 1951 with sports(field & track,, tennis etc,) trophies.

44. *Pinto with two daughters, Linda and*   45. *Pinto and Friend, 1962*

   Malusha in India (1962)

46. *Dr. Yusuf Eraj with Pinto daughters (l to r): Linda, Malusha Tereshka (sitting) Nairobi (1966)*

Pio Gama Pinto, Kenya's Unsung Martyr

Pinto with children sitting at the front door of his house not far from the gate where he was later shot. These are Joyce de Mendonca's (Emma's twin sister's) children and his two daughters. Boys: Rudolf (biggest), Preston, Morel and Andre (smallest).

47. Pinto with children

Girls: Malusha and Tereshka (smallest). Linda not in the picture as she was in India at the time.

Note: Pio was busy reading a newspaper as well as listening to the radio (ever the news addict!) - [Awaaz].

Right to left: Leo Gama (a second cousin from his father's maternal grandparents side i.e the old Gama wing) and J.M Nazareth (later QC and MP)

48. Pinto speaking at his wedding (Jan. 1954)

49. Tereshka Pinto, 1966 *50. Emma and Pio engagement (Oct. 1953)*

51. Kabernet restriction house, 1958

52. Pinto in his Parliament office.

53. *Members of Parliament rejoice at Pinto's election to Parliament*

54. *Pinto outside Parliament with others*

55. *Pinto at a public rally with Bildad Kaggia and Joe Murumbi (1963)*

56. Pinto speaking at a reunion of ex-detainees at the home of Achieng Oneko

57. Pinto visiting the Koinange family in restriction at Kabernet

Pio Gama Pinto, Kenya's Unsung Martyr

58. Pinto visiting Kenyatta when he was in detention in Lodwar

59. Pio Gama Pinto and Fitz de Souza at an "anti-imperialist" demonstration

60.. Pinto outside Parliament with Murumbi, Ferguson, Kenyatta, Tettegah, Oneko and Kubai

Left to right: Joe Murumbi, J B Ferguson (Ghanian Labour Attache in Dar), Jomo Kenyatta, John Tettegah (Secretary-General of AATUF), Achieng Oneko, Fred Kubai, Pio Gama-Pinto

61. Pinto's coffin in the family living room: Linda (left), Malusha (right), Emma

62. Linda and Malusha Pinto lead the cortege. Emma in black sari, her mother, Linda Dias, behind her

Pio Gama Pinto, Kenya's Unsung Martyr

63. Oscar Kambona pays his last tribute at the funeral

Left to right: Bildad Kaggia, Tome de Mendonca, Emma's brother in law, Oscar Kambona, Joseph Murumbi

64. Odinga consoles Emma at the funeral

Left to right: Makhan Singh, Jaramogi Oginga Odinga, Rosario Da Gama Pinto, Emma Pinto, K P Shah

65   Oginga Odinga at the funeral

Pio Gama Pinto, Kenya's Unsung Martyr

66. *Outside Pinto's house, a few moments after his assassination*

67. *Drum Magazine: Africa mourns a brother (May 1965)*

68. *Drum Magazine Article on Pinto*

69. *Pinto Postal Stamp*

Pio Gama Pinto, Kenya's Unsung Martyr

70. *Special issue of Awaaz on Pinto (2005)*

Nowrojee, Pheroze (2007): Pio Gama Pinto: Patriot for Social Justice. Nairobi: Longhorn.

71. *Nowrojee (2007): Pio Gama Pinto*

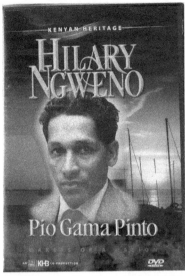

Hilary
Ngweno: Pio
Gama Pinto.
Makers of a
Nation Series.
DVD. NTV-
KHB.

72. Ngweno: Pio Gama Pinto (DVD)

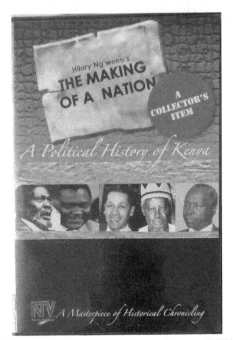

Hilary Ngweno:
A Political
History of
Kenya. Making
a Nation. DVD
NTV

73. Ngweno: A Political History of Kenya (DVD)

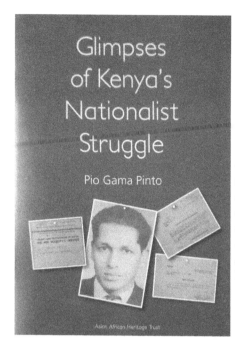

*Pinto, Pio Gama
(1963) Glimpses of
Kenya's Nationalist
Struggle
Republished in
2014 by Asian
African Heritage
Trust (Nairobi)*

74. *Pio Gama Pinto: Glimpses of Kenya's Nationalist Struggle (1963)*

Vita Books
Publications List
2018

PIO GAMA PINTO Kenya's Unsung Martyr 1927 - 1965	Durrani, Shiraz (Ed.): Pio Gama Pinto, Kenya's Unsung Martyr, 1927-1965. 2018. ISBN 978-9966-1890-0-4 (paper); 978-9966-1890-4-2 (eBook) "This book provides information on Pio Game Pinto from different sources: his personal writings, original material as well as published and archival sources. It is of immense historical and political significance" - Prof. Kimani Njogu, Nairobi.
KENYA'S WAR OF INDEPENDENCE	Durrani, Shiraz: Kenya's war of independence: Mau Mau and its legacy of resistance to colonialism and Imperialism, 1948-1990. 2018. ISBN 978-9966-1890-1-1 (paper); 978-9966-1890-2-8 (eBook) This book restores Kenya's stolen history to its rightful place, stripped of colonial interpretations. It covers Mau Mau's resistance to colonialism and neo-colonialism and reflects on its ideology, organisation and achievements. It looks at the influence of organised, radical trade unions as the engine of resistance.
	Durrani, Shiraz: Mau Mau, the Revolutionary, anti-imperialist force from Kenya, 1948-1963. 2018. ISBN 978-9966-1890-7-3 (paper); 978-9966-1890-8-0. (eBook) Kenya Resists No. 1. This book provides essential facts about Mau Mau. It seeks to give voice to the Mau Mau resistance fighters. It is a tribute to those who played a part in the war of independence and in Mau Mau without whose contribution independence would have remained a dream.
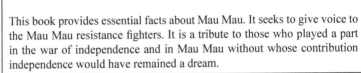	Durrani, Shiraz: Trade unions in Kenya's war of independence. 2018. ISBN: 978-9966-1890-9-7 (paper); 978-9966-114-53-2 (eBook) Kenya Resists No.2 This book recalls relevant events in the history of the militant trade union movement in Kenya and records the contribution that the trade union movement made to Mau Mau and to Kenya's war of independence.

	Durrani, Shiraz: People's resistance to colonialism and imperialism in Kenya. 2018. ISBN: 978-9966-114-52-5 (paper); 978-9966-114-51-8 (eBook). Kenya Resists No.3. This book looks at the third pillar of resistance to British colonialism – people's resistance. It brings together several aspects of people's resistance to colonialism and imperialism – before and after independence and includes resistance by nationalities, women, students, peasants and workers in what can only be described as people's resistance.
	Durrani, Nazmi: Liberating minds, restoring Kenyan history. 2017. ISBN: 978-9966-097-41-5 (paper); 978-9966-1890-3-5 (eBook). Liberating Minds consists of biographies of progressive South Asian Kenyans. Originally published in Gujarati in the 1980s, they are available here in English for the first time. Also included is Naila Durrani's "Kenya Asian Participation in People's Resistance", while Benegal Pereira introduces Eddie H. Pereira (1915-1995).
	Durrani, Shiraz (Ed.): Makhan Singh, a revolutionary Kenyan trade unionist. 2014 ISBN: 978-1-869886-22-6 Examines the life and work of a remarkable trade unionist and revolutionary. Makhan Singh laid the foundation for radical trade unionism and influenced the liberation struggle in Kenya.
	Shiraz Durrani: Progressive Librarianship: Perspectives from Kenya and Britain, 1979-2010. 2014. ISBN: 978-1-869886-20-2 (print); 978-2-869886-21-9 (eBook) "Durrani challenges us to look at the concept and practice of library differently, while also providing invaluable information on the alternatives in both Kenya and Britain. He thus continues the critical tradition he has already established." Ngugi wa Thiong'o.

Durrani, Shiraz: Never Be Silent: Publishing and imperialism in Kenya, 1884-1963. 2006.

ISBN: 978-1-869886-05-09 (Paper).

The book examines the struggle for independence in Kenya in the communications field. It looks at the publishing activities of the main contending forces and documents the part played by the communications activities of the organised working class and Mau Mau in the achievement of independence.

Shiraz Durrani: Information and Liberation: Writings on the politics of information and librarianship. 2008.

ISBN: 978-9966-1890-7-3 (print)

The book is a retrospective collection of Durrani's writings on the politics of information. It documents the struggle for progressive and relevant information policies and practices over a period of 25 years in Kenya and Britain.

Karimi Nduthu: A life in the struggle. 1998.

ISBN: 1-869886-12-7 (paper). Vita Books and Mau Mau Research Centre.

The book records the achievements of Karimi Nduthu, a Mwakenya activist, a political prisoner and a human rights advocate who was brutally assassinated by agents of the Moi dictatorship in 1996. The book is a celebration of the immortality of Karimi Nduthu's selfless dedication

P.O Box 62501-00200
Nairobi. Kenya
http://vitabooks.co.uk info.vitabkske@gmail.com
info@vitabooks.co.uk
Distributed Worldwide by: African Books Collective
PO BOX 721 Oxford, OX1 9EN
orders@africanbookscollective.com